NEWMAN'S UNQUIET GRAVE

By the same Author

Newman's Unquiet Grave

THE RELUCTANT SAINT

By

JOHN CORNWELL

continuum

Continuum International Publishing Group

The Tower Building	80 Maiden Lane
11 York Road	Suite 704
London	New York
SE1 7NX	NY 10038

www.continuumbooks.com

First published 2010
Reprinted 2010

British Library Cataloguing-in-Publication Data
A catalogue record for this book is available from the British Library.

ISBN 978-1441-15084-4

Designed and typeset in Adobe Minion by Tony Lansbury, Tonbridge, Kent.
Printed and bound by the MPG Books Group, Bodmin, Cornwall.

In memory of
Henry Francis 'Ikey' Davis
(1902–1986)

O unforgotten voice, thy accents come,
Like wanderers from the world's extremity,
Unto their ancient home.

MATTHEW ARNOLD, 'THE VOICE', 1849

Contents

Preface

Anyone writing about Newman's life and character faces the problem – where to begin? He believed his story would be revealed in his letters. 'It has ever been a hobby of mine (unless it be a truism, not a hobby) that a man's life lies in his letters.'[1] Newman's correspondence allows him at every juncture – he died in 1890 aged 89 – to speak for himself, although selectivity and extensive familiarity are crucial. He had a remarkable, dialectical capacity to hold in tension two sides of an argument. To read through the 32 published volumes (to date) of his letters and diaries is a daunting yet rewarding task: tenderness, waspish wit, feline sensitivity, irony; literary brilliance, theological and philosophical profundity; intriguing mixed messages and maddening paradoxes – amidst a mass of diurnal business, like so many diamonds set in lead. The voluminous records of his dealings over money, property, litigation, ecclesiastical squabbles, locate him in a busy, often fretful life. He could read a balance sheet and negotiate a property deal with the best of them. There is nothing about him of the reclusive scholar-monk (*le grand reclus*, as the Abbé Bremond put it grandiloquently but inappropriately); still less the plaster saint.

No one attempting a portrait of Newman can fail to pay tribute to the editorial labours involved in the publication of his letters and diaries under the auspices of the Birmingham Oratory across a span of fifty years. There has been, besides, an ever growing proliferation of Newman scholarship – commentary, monographs, proceedings of conferences – taking soundings across the wide seas of his thought. He has been the subject, moreover, of no fewer than four major biographies in the twentieth century, and many minor portraits. His principal living scholar-biographers, Dr Ian Ker, of the University of Oxford, and Professor Sheridan Gilley, of Durham University, are essential reading for the student of Newman. I am substantially in their debt. The biographies of Wilfrid Ward (1906) and the late Meriol Trevor (1962) remain crucial for the student too. I have derived considerable profit, moreover, from commentaries on Newman in essays and books by the late Stephen Dessain and Henry Tristram, Nicholas Lash, Owen Chadwick, Avery Dulles, Stephen Prickett, the late John Coulson, Roderick Strange, Frank M. Turner, to name but a few.

So why yet another portrait of Newman?

In the light of Newman's beatification, and other circumstances that have thrust him into the media limelight, it seemed timely to offer a shorter, less academic account of his life, accessible not only to Catholics, but non-Catholics and non-Christians as well. While being yet another version of his life, my interest focuses more on his character and importance as a writer than on his holiness. If my account touches on his foibles and human failings it is not intended to detract from the current celebration of his undoubted piety and saintly charisma.

Finally this book is the fruit, but by no means the culmination, of a personal quest which began in my late teens under the guidance of a friend and teacher, the late Doctor Henry Francis 'Ikey' Davis. Davis was for a quarter of a century Professor of Theology and Vice Rector at Oscott College, the Catholic seminary for the archdiocese of Birmingham. It was Davis who first proposed the cause for Newman's canonisation in the late 1950s. His deep knowledge of the Early Fathers, Thomas Aquinas, Newman, and Karl Barth, formed the basis of his lectures and class notes on systematic theology. Davis sacrificed a life of writing for teaching. His students, at Oscott and later at Birmingham University, were the beneficiaries; the legacy is his personal influence on generations of theologians and philosophers of religion in Britain and in Europe.

Of the many stories told of him, this must suffice. During the Second World War he cycled every weekend 167 miles, each way (he was a champion cyclist), from Birmingham to a prisoner of war camp outside Colchester, Essex. There he spent Saturdays and Sundays teaching theology with a Newman bias, and in fluent German, to imprisoned seminarists who had been forcibly recruited into Hitler's armed forces (he had studied for his doctorate in theology at the University of Freiburg in German-speaking Switzerland). Some eighty of those students became priests after the war; four of them bishops. It can be justly claimed that Davis contributed to the impetus of Newman studies in post-war Germany and beyond in Europe.

John Cornwell
Jesus College, Cambridge

Prologue

On 5 October 2008 the following item was posted on the *TimesOnline* website:

The grave of the Venerable John Henry Cardinal Newman (1801–1890) was excavated with utmost care on Thursday 2 October 2008 … During the excavation the brass inscription plate which had been on the wooden coffin in which Cardinal Newman had rested was recovered from his grave. It reads (in English translation): 'The Most Eminent and Most Reverend John Henry Newman Cardinal Deacon of St George in Velabro Died 11 August 1890 RIP.' Brass, wooden and cloth artefacts from Cardinal Newman's coffin were found. However, there were no remains of the body of John Henry Newman.

It was later explained by the Fathers of the Birmingham Oratory that on Newman's express orders his grave in a burial ground in the Lickey Hills, Worcestershire, was filled with a rich mulch to hasten decomposition. When one takes into account reports that the graveyard was sited on saturated clay, the mystery of the vanished remains is more or less resolved. It is arguable that his instruction was tantamount to a final sermon, although Newman would have been amused at the attendant irony of his vanishing. On the day of the exhumation, those acquainted with Newman's last published sermon might have remembered his homily 'On the Fitness of the Glories of Mary': 'Who can conceive', he preached, 'that that virginal frame, which never sinned, was to undergo the death of a sinner? Why should she share the curse of Adam, who had no share in his fall? "Dust thou art, and into dust thou shalt return", was the sentence upon sin; she then, who was not a sinner, fitly never saw corruption.'[1] Newman's orders to mulch his coffin was evidently an acknowledgment of his own sinfulness, deserving of final physical corruption. How could he have known that his burial instructions would result, paradoxically, in a circumstance parallel with the fate of Mary's assumed body. The sermon continues: 'Pilgrims went to and fro; they sought for her relics, but they found them not.'[2]

But a more crucial, if mundane, fact is missing in the *TimesOnline* report: Newman, according to his own repeated wishes, shared his last resting place with a close friend, Father Ambrose St John. Nothing was found of St John's remains either, although the mechanical digger employed for the exhumation removed the soil down to eight feet. That the joint burial involved two celibate priests, one destined for sainthood, prompted media curiosity about Newman, now long neglected except by Catholics and those with a taste for nineteenth century Church history. A wide constituency of people, unacquainted perhaps with the Catholic cult of sainthood and relics, complained that Newman's wishes had not been respected. Gay rights activist Mr Peter Tatchell proclaimed on the BBC current affairs programme, *Tonight*, that Newman was 'gay', and charged that the exhumation was a gesture of Vatican homophobia. The presenter Jeremy Paxman called on Father Ian Ker, the Newman scholar, to respond. Father Ker stated emphatically that, on the basis of all the evidence with which he was acquainted, Newman was 'heterosexual'. On the day of the exhumation the graveyard was guarded by members of the local constabulary lest Gay Rights demonstrators should intrude upon the scene to cause an affray. No such insult occurred.

My interest in John Henry Newman began, as it happens, at that same graveside in the Lickey Hills in the Spring of 1960. On a cold, wet morning I set forth on foot to cross the city of Birmingham from the north to the south. I was nineteen years of age and a student for the Catholic priesthood at Oscott College. My companion was John Winterton (who later changed his Christian name to Gregory), a convert from Anglicanism. Wearing black suits, black raincoats and deep plastic clerical collars (as was the custom for Roman Catholic seminarians in those days), we were on 'exeat', a rare holiday from our cloistered confines. Winterton, a wraith-like man, stooped and intense, had fought during the Second World War in North Africa and Italy. We his younger fellow students assumed that since he was the son of a knighted Major General he was 'in funds'. He had taken a shine to me, and promised 'a rewarding mystery tour' on our day out. I had visions of a traditional exeat treat: beef-steak lunch and a bottle of wine in the cosy bosom of a West Midlands hotel restaurant.

We marched in the freezing rain, Winterton, the military veteran, always a yard or two ahead; we took a bus, then walked some more as morning wore into afternoon. Eventually we arrived at the gate of a secluded rural cemetery. Striding ahead of me, Winterton went down on his knees. We had arrived at our mystery destination, Cardinal Newman's last resting place, and I learned for the first time of his cohabitation in death with Ambrose St John who had predeceased him by fifteen years. Sodden and footsore. I could not bring myself to kneel in the mud; my thoughts were mainly on the missed lunch. Winterton entered a prayerful trance which lasted for a very long time.

I did not give the fact of the joint burial much thought; nor had anyone else, as far as I know now. On the return journey to the seminary, hungry as well as wet through, I sulked as Winterton enthused about our visit. But drying out my clothes on one of Oscott's lukewarm radiators, it struck me that my interest in Newman, from boyhood in the junior seminary, had been confirmed by the dead Cardinal himself. That's how we seminarists thought in those days.

PART ONE

CHAPTER 1

Who is John Henry Newman?

'… here below to live is to change, and to be perfect is to have changed often.'
J. H. NEWMAN, *ESSAY ON DEVELOPMENT*

Not so long ago a senior Anglican priest remarked to me, 'John Henry Newman is just a Catholic pin-up boy: isn't he?' That characterisation, which has more than a grain of truth, is one of many: from the Newman of whom his fellow English Cardinal, Henry Manning, said, 'He was a great hater!', to Newman deemed by the Catholic Church a holy exemplar destined for sainthood. In Victorian England, depending on whether you were a Catholic or a Protestant, he was Newman who had seen the light and gone over to Rome; or Newman the apostate, who had betrayed friends, family, Church, to enter the idolatrous and superstitious embrace of the Whore of Babylon. He has been characterised as Newman the friend of liberalism, Newman the enemy of liberalism; Newman champion of conscience over dogma, Newman the champion of dogma over conscience. Lytton Strachey's famous characterisation in *Eminent Victorians* depicted Newman as a dove to Cardinal Manning's eagle. On reflection, Strachey wondered whether Newman was more like a hawk.

From his thirties Newman appeared in a variety of guises in portraits and caricatures: the austere, pinched-looking, bespectacled vicar dressed in surplice and black stole, preaching from St Mary's pulpit, Oxford; G. Richmond's flatteringly handsome head, without spectacles, which, according to James Anthony Froude, was 'remarkably like that of Julius Caesar'; the Vatican's poodle in *Punch* magazine holding up the train of Cardinal Wiseman ('Newboy' to his Eminence's 'Wiseboy'); the early photographs of Newman the ageing 'Father' among his clerical 'family' in Birmingham's Hagley Road. Then there is the portrait in the keeping of the National Portrait Gallery in London: Sir John Everett Millais' Cardinal Newman, Prince of the Church. There he sits, swathed in scarlet shot silk and lace cuffs, the worn ascetic face gazing out at us apologetically: His Reluctant Eminence. The spectacular iconography would have signalled corrupt associations for a Victorian Protestant: Henry VIII's Cardinal Wolsey; devious Papal Emissaries.

Accused by the writer Charles Kingsley of promoting lying on a system, while pretending to be an Anglican when secretly a Catholic, Newman made a remarkable bid to explore and confirm the integrity of his personality and beliefs through a period of change:

> I must, I said, give the true key to my whole life; I must show what I am, that it may be seen what I am not, and that the phantom may be extinguished which gibbers instead of me ... I will draw out, as far as may be, the history of my mind.[1]

In 1864 he published his autobiography *Apologia Pro Vita Sua*, a history of his opinions through the course of more than half a century. The *Apologia*, widely deemed a great spiritual classic in Newman's day as in ours, is yet another version of the life, amply citing letters, drafts of letters, memoranda, journal entries, texts of sermons, to create a tightly crafted narrative. While the book has had enduring influence it hardly constitutes the final word even on the question of his honesty. His biographer of the early 1960s, Meriol Trevor, declared: 'Dishonest Newman was laid for ever; not a critic, however hostile, but conceded that he was the last man on earth to be called a liar and deceiver.'[2] But Newman's honesty, after the publication of the *Apologia*, was impugned by a constituency of well-known Victorian and Edwardian figures, including Benjamin Jowett, Leslie Stephen, T. H. Huxley, and F. D. Maurice,[3] of which, take Huxley: 'That man is the slipperiest sophist I have ever met with. Kingsley was entirely right about him.'[4] Cardinal Manning, his fellow Catholic convert and confrere in religion, would later say: 'He bamboozles you with his carefully selected words, and plays so subtly with his logic that your simplicity is taken in.'[5]

THE WRITER

Yet whatever the versions, the mythologies and iconographies, ecclesiastical and secular, his most compelling, and perhaps most neglected, reputation is as Newman the writer. The *virtuosity*, the energy, was prodigious: polemic, essays, poetry, hymns, tracts, satires, histories, scholarly monographs, discourses, lectures, meditations, novels, sermons, letters – scores of them daily. His prose, described by James Joyce's character Stephen Dedalus as 'cloistral silverveined',[6] is commonly characterised as luminous, melodic, marked by *politesse*. Such characterisations fail to acknowledge the sheer dogged, driven, multi-drafted, self-disciplined industry. The impression is of a night and day foundry, an indefatigable, pressurised, letting-off-of-steam. One is reminded of his friend John Keble's notion of literary energy as a 'vent for over-charged feelings, or a full imagination, ... which are apt to fill and overpower the mind so as to require a sort of relief'.[7] To borrow from Newman's own industrial metaphor for Catholic Christendom, his output was like 'some moral factory, for the melting, refining, and moulding, by an incessant, noisy process, of the raw material of human nature, so excellent, so dangerous, so capable of divine purposes'.[8] He was, in short, a superabundant literary workaholic, a tutor in Christendom's vast 'training school', as copiously productive in his genre as Carlyle, Arnold, Dickens, Gladstone, in theirs. Newman's role as a writer defines his character and relationships. His companion and minder in old age, Father William Neville, remarked that Newman even prayed with a 'pen in his hand'.[9]

Newman's literary gifts were those of a prose writer rather than a poet. His script, in black ink, written with modest pens, barely altered from youth into old age. It was spare, forward tilting, keeping to a straight line, the loops in the small letters hardly noticeable (especially on the f's and the h's); no loops on the g's, but with a tendency to flourish the d's and the capitals. The manuscript of his hymn 'Lead Kindly Light', written at sea, shows the same evenness as at his desk on land.

In a letter to W. G. Ward,[10] looking back over a lifetime's writing, he employed an image he claimed he had often used: 'It is one of my *sayings* (so continually do I feel it) that the composition of a volume is like gestation and childbirth. I do not think that I ever thought out a question or wrote my thoughts, without great pain, pain reaching to the body as well as the mind.'

As early as 1838 he was complaining of the toil that went into the editing of his published *Lectures on Justification*, his major offensive on the Evangelical wing of the Church of England. Few writers have ever described the labour of drafting, and redrafting, in such vivid and specific detail:

I write – I write again – I write a third time, in the course of six months – then I take the third – I literally fill the paper with corrections, so that another person could not read it – I then write it out fair for the printer – I put it by – I take it up – I begin to correct again – it will not do – alterations multiply – pages are re-written – little lines sneak in and crawl about – the whole page is disfigured – I write again. I cannot count how many times this process goes on.[11]

He was convinced, quoting Shakespeare ('The poet's eye, in a fine frenzy rolling'), that writers of genius laboured over their work. He would write of the need to 'pause, write, erase, re-write, amend, complete …' Whereas the mere 'dealer in words cares little or nothing for the subject', the true artist 'has his great or rich visions before him'.[12]

Why all this labour, these corrections on corrections, those lines sneaking and crawling? When he became a Cardinal he chose as his motto the words '*Cor ad cor loquitur*' (Heart speaks to heart). He strived and toiled to reach out through the medium of cold print to achieve a heartfelt luminosity and personal contact and feeling. He worked hard for it, all the while conscious of the power of mass publishing that dominated the reading public.[13] Not long after becoming a Catholic he would give a talk on the overwhelming power of the press to alter public consciousness:

Never could notoriety exist as it does now, in any former age of the world; … private news as well as public, is brought day by day to every individual … by processes so uniform, so unvarying, so spontaneous, that they almost bear the semblance of a natural law. And hence notoriety, or the making a noise in the world, has come to be considered a great good in itself, and a ground of veneration …[14]

In his own view, his literary vocation would disqualify him from sainthood. 'I have no tendency to be a saint – it is a sad thing to say so. Saints are not literary men.…'[15] Whatever the case, his claim to eminence consists not in his status as a prelate, nor in claims for conventional piety, but his genius for creating new ways of imagining and writing about religion.

⚜

John Henry Newman was born in 1801 and died in 1890. When he was four years of age he saw candles burning in the window in celebration of Nelson's victory at Trafalgar. He was a young Oxford scholar when dreams of the Romantic egotistical sublime were at odds with the scepticism of Hume and the growing utilitarianism of Bentham. He was born in the late age of horse power and sail, and lived to see the awesome expansion of the modern age of Victoria: the rapid growth of Britain's cities, mass market books, newspapers, photography; proliferating discoveries in the natural sciences; the mighty juggernaut of industry, trade, and capitalist wealth; widespread poverty, insecurity, and oppression of working people. He came into his prime during a period that spanned the electoral liberalisation of Britain's Reform Act, the flourishing of the Chartists, the publication of the *Communist Manifesto* (the first English edition, 1850), and the challenge to Christian belief of Darwin's *On the Origin of Species*. He harnessed the modern age of travel, communications, and publishing in the service of his pastoral and polemical aims.

He departed home aged sixteen for Oxford in a horse-drawn carriage; by his mid-fifties we find him hurrying around England, to Ireland and across Europe, by rail and steamship. He spent the first half of his adult life in an Oxford college, and the second in one of Europe's largest industrial cities. In his sixties, twenty years after leaving the university, he wrote: 'I have never seen Oxford since, excepting its spires, as they are seen from the railway.'[16] It was as if he marked the distance he had travelled in the second half of his life from the perspective of the age of steam locomotion and production. Had he remained in Oxford he might well have become cloistered, self-incensing, sterile.

Until old age, Newman was constantly developing, constantly converting, in

10

the hope of becoming ever more true to himself: 'We can only set right one error of expression by another.'[17] His writing is multilayered, metaphorical, free, tactile, concrete. He was engaged in growth, development. He was not attempting a lapidary magisterium. He wrote as he thought, endlessly drafting, revising and expanding – generating polarities, contradictions, reconciliations, and connections. One of his most influential books, *Essay on Development*, explored how the Catholic Church had remained ever the same and true to itself while undergoing remarkable change.

Newman realised that the loss of faith would, in time, become publicly manifest in the 'educated intellect of England, France, and Germany',[18] spreading to every dimension of culture and society, driving faith into the recess and final refuge of individual privacy. He spent thirty years drafting a book on the justification of belief, the *Grammar of Assent*.

Newman, as we shall see, was by no means anti-science, nor did he see in Charles Darwin's ideas a repudiation of religious faith. Attending geology lectures in Oxford as an undergraduate and young don, he was prepared for the impact of the huge age of the world, and in consequence the theory of evolution. As he wrote to a correspondent in 1868, nine years after the publication of Darwin's great work:

It does not seem to me to follow that creation is denied because the Creator, millions of years ago, gave laws to matter. He first created matter and then he created laws for it – laws which should *construct* it into its present wonderful beauty, and accurate adjustment and harmony of parts *gradually* ...[19]

If there is one outstanding written achievement, beyond his theological legacy, it is his *Idea of a University*. Asked by Rome, and an Irish archbishop, to found a Catholic university in Dublin, he laid down the notion of 'a University, viewed in itself, and apart from the Catholic Church, or from the State, or from any other power which may use it'.[20] It would become the basis of the ideal academic institution, free of the constraints of mere professional training, with independence, time and freedom to bear its fruits – without insistence on usefulness, and allowing each comprising discipline to reach its own perfection. The ideal university, he wrote, is a place

in which the intellect may safely range and speculate, sure to find its equal in some antagonist activity, and its judge in the tribunal of truth...where the professor becomes eloquent, and a missionary and a preacher of science, displaying it in its most complete and most winning form, pouring it forth with the zeal of enthusiasm, and lighting up his own love of it in the breasts of his hearers.[21]

What follows is a portrait of man who continues to speak to us from beyond the grave; a man much larger in desire, imagination and literary genius, than the simplistic mythologies that have clustered around his reputation. I set out to write a book that would answer the question – why should Newman be of interest to a readership beyond Catholics or nineteenth-century Church historians? My overarching purpose is to show that Newman's unrelenting literary obsession was the story of his own life: he was the ultimate, self-absorbed autobiographer. He was increasingly absorbed in textual, literary self-referential preoccupation. Yet this was no narcissistic endeavour. Every detail of his story, his relationships, his feelings and insights, at every stage in his life, were noted, identified, and contemplated in the light of the mystery of God's Creation, Revelation, and Redemption. Newman's undying, 'unforgotten' voice, is nothing less than an insistent search for ultimate meaning, through the telling of the story of his own life.

CHAPTER 2

Meeting Doctor Newman

'I do not believe there has been anything like his influence in Oxford,
when it was at its height, since Abelard lectured in Paris.'
WILLIAM GLADSTONE OF J. H. NEWMAN

What was it like to encounter John Henry Newman in his mid to late-thirties at the height of his influence as a university don and popular preacher at Oxford? W. G. Ward, an enthusiastic member of Newman's close group:

In Oriel Lane light-hearted undergraduates would drop their voices and whisper, 'There's Newman', as with head thrust forward and gaze fixed as though at some vision seen only by himself, with swift, noiseless step he glided by. Awe fell on them for a moment almost as if it had been some apparition that had passed.[1]

Every Sunday young and old, men and women, gathered in the university church of Saint Mary the Virgin as if drawn by a mystic Pied Piper. One young woman in the congregation 'wept with emotion' at his very appearance – 'impressive, powerful and a little forbidding'.[2] Newman's charisma was described as 'mesmeric', a 'magnetic stream'. Gladstone wrote that he felt like shouting out loud on encountering Newman.[3] That his influence was mysterious is confirmed by the church historian and contemporary, A. P. Stanley: 'there was no contact with the hidden springs of action which controlled the movements of this inscrutable personage.'[4] Was it a hunger that he satisfied? Rain for famished lands? 'He rooted in their hearts and minds', said one, 'a personal conviction of the living God.'[5] Here he was, preaching on the Passion:

For a few moments there was a breathless silence. Then, in a low, clear voice, of which the faintest vibration was audible in the farthest corner of St Mary's, he said, 'Now I bid you recollect that He to whom these things were done was Almighty God'. It was as if an electric stroke had gone through the church, as if every person present understood for the first time the meaning of what he had all his life been saying.[6]

Yet his charisma had not always been so. For some it never was. Thomas Arnold Junior wrote of Newman's preaching: 'the delicacy and refinement of his style were less cognisable by me than by my brother [Matthew], and the multiplied quotations from Scripture, introduced by "And again" – "And again", the intention of which I only half divined, confused and bewildered me.'[7] For others, like the writer Charles Kingsley, the charisma was felt – and later regretted, and despised. He charged Newman with magus-like duplicity and an insidious form of seduction of the young:

I know that men used to suspect Dr. Newman, – I have been inclined to do so myself, – of writing a whole Sermon, not for the sake of the text or of the matter, but for the sake of one single passing hint – one phrase, one epithet, one little barbed arrow, which, as he swept magnificently past on the stream of his calm eloquence, seemingly unconscious of all presences, save those unseen, he delivered unheeded, as with his finger-tip, to the very heart of an initiated hearer, never to be withdrawn again.[8]

Others appeared not only immune, but decidedly repulsed. Sir Charles Murray, one of Newman's students at Oxford, remembered Newman like this:

He never inspired me, or my fellow-undergraduates, with any interest, much less respect: on the contrary, we disliked, or rather distrusted, him. He walked with his head bent, abstracted, but every now and then looking out of the corners of his eyes quickly, as though suspicious.[9]

The awe felt by several generations of students developed only gradually, over a decade, from the late 1820s into the 1830s. As a disciplinarian he became a 'master', as his contemporary Frederick Rogers put it, 'of formidable and speaking silence calculated to quell any ordinary impertinence'.[10] Another pupil left this recollection: ' "What did he say to you?" was asked of one who had been called up by Newman for some more or less serious matter. "I don't know", said the other, "but he looked at me".'[11]

Newman likened spiritual charisma to a heady fragrance, symptomatic of metanoia – a deep, spiritual and intellectual alteration in a person's life; religious conversion, or reconversion; an ineffable scent that would strike some and not others. In his first novel, *Loss and Gain*, written in the year following his reception into the Roman Catholic Church, he wrote of the character Charles Reding, his alter ego:

And even before that blessed hour, as an opening flower scatters sweets, so the strange unknown odour, pleasing to some, odious to others, went abroad from him upon the winds, and made them marvel what could be near them, and made them look curiously and anxiously at him, while he was unconscious of his own condition.[12]

But what did they *see*? He was not a man of impressive stature: five feet nine in height, slightly built, with a scholar's stoop from youth. In one self-description he wrote: 'my eyesight is short; my voice is weak, my whole frame is very nervous; my constitution is very susceptible of cold.'[13] He was so quietly spoken that people often strained to hear him. He spoke with emphatic enunciation. He had a prominent hooked nose out of proportion with his face, a high forehead;

his dark hair lank and unruly; but he was fastidious about personal cleanliness. He took daily cold baths.

Newman's friend Charles Casartelli spoke of his 'aristocratic mien'; yet he was not of the English nobility. His father was a member of the commercial middle-classes, a banker; his mother second generation Huguenot stock. Yet, as his spiritual influence developed in his thirties, he came to appear not quite of this earth: hence Matthew Arnold's famous adulatory description of a 'spiritual apparition, gliding in the dim afternoon light'; his words 'a religious music, – subtle, sweet, mournful'.[14] That preaching voice, which Arnold had described in an early poem, 'The Voice', as 'unforgotten ... so sweet and still' seems to have echoed in space and time to the susceptible, even to those who had not heard it, and never would. Matthew Arnold met Newman, but never actually attended his sermons as a student; only later in life. Newman's manner of speaking was perhaps emulated, passed on, as sometimes happens with charismatic teachers. The critic, the late David J. DeLaura, speculated that Newman's singular voice represented 'an enduring myth of a lost generation, permanently caught between an irrecoverable past and the unspeakable future'.[15] The comment lends significance to Evelyn Waugh's description of Oxford in the immediate post-First World War era: 'In her spacious and quiet streets men walked and spoke as they had done in Newman's day.' How would Waugh have known?

While Newman could appear spectral, numinous, to his congregations, he could be physical and convivial. A visitor to Pusey's house recorded how after dinner a child 'climbed Newman's knee and hugged him. Newman put his spectacles on him, and next on his sister, and great was the merriment of the Puseyan progeny.'[16] His sudden alteration from clerical *spirituel* to avuncular mortal could be disconcerting. Emily Bowles, a family friend, was overwhelmed by his 'exquisite' voice and demeanour at a Sunday service; when lunch was served after the 'exalted experience' she fell suddenly to earth when Newman uttered the words: 'Will you have some cold chicken?'

THE VEILED LADY

Aubrey Thomas de Vere, the Irish poet and essayist, had an impression of delicate health and gender ambivalence.

Early in the evening a singularly graceful figure in cap and gown glided into the room. The slight form and gracious address might have belonged either to a youthful ascetic of the middle ages or to a graceful high-bred lady of our own days. He was pale and thin almost to emaciation, swift of pace, but when not walking intensely still, with a voice sweet and pathetic, and so distinct that you could count each vowel and consonant in every word. When touching on subjects which interested him, he used gestures rapid and decisive, though not vehement.[17]

15

So Newman gives the impression of being chaste as an eternal monastic novice, yet refined as a 'high-bred lady': as if aristocracy were a guarantee of acceptable effeminacy. W. G. Ward told his son, Wilfrid Ward, that Newman's 'keen humour, his winning sweetness, his occasional wilfulness, his resentments and anger, all showed him intensely alive, and his friends loved his very faults as one may love those of a fascinating woman ...'[18] The suggestion, so subtly raised, is of fickleness; a batsqueak of coquettishness. Ward tells how he dreamt that 'he found himself at a dinner party next to a veiled lady, who charmed him more and more as they talked. At last he explained, "I have never felt such charm in any conversation since I used to talk with John Henry Newman, at Oxford". "I am John Henry Newman", the lady replied, and raising her veil showed the well-known face.'[19] This impression of capricious, unstable gender identity – at least, in the eyes of certain of his contemporaries – revealed itself in striking fashion after Newman's intimate student friend, John Bowden, married. While staying with the couple, Newman noted that Bowden would constantly 'call me Elizabeth and her Newman'.[20] Charles Kingsley would reveal in retrospect a keen anxiety, and hence resentment, nursed against his perception of Newman's effeminacy. Thirty years on from the Pied Piper Oxford days, Kingsley famously would assert that Newman had taught that 'cunning is the weapon which Heaven has given the saints wherewith to withstand the brute male force of the wicked world which marries and is given in marriage'.[21] He saw in Newman a species of 'perversion', when that word meant both religious apostasy and a violation of the laws of nature, that might include gender transgression and sexual repression, or excess. When the *British Quarterly* reviewed the *Apologia*, its critic observed that 'the instances of perversion to the Romish faith which have come within our knowledge have been nearly all such as may be traced to a womanly weakness in the women, and to the want of manly courage in the men'. Kingsley, it seemed, could never forgive Newman for having once made him conscious of anxieties about his own gender status. Kingsley's consequent rage was directed not only at Newman but at his entire Oxford circle. Writing in 1851, Kingsley opined: 'In ... all that school, there is an element of foppery – even in dress and manner; a fastidious, maundering, die-away effeminacy, which is mistaken for purity and refinement; and I confess myself unable to cope with it, so alluring is it to the minds of an effeminate and luxurious aristocracy.'[22]

Yet for Newman a measure of effeminacy did indeed define, with a hint of irony perhaps, the reserve and self discipline of the Oxford scholar and gentleman:

[The gentleman] is a friend of religious toleration, and that, not only because his philosophy has taught him to look on all forms of faith with an impartial eye, but also from the gentleness and effeminacy of feeling, which is the attendant on civilization.[23]

16

It was, however, the impression of Newman's charismatic mix of vulnerability and strength, his singular grace, and subtle, capacious intelligence, his evident piety, earnestness and eloquence, that would lend pathos, tragedy even, to his eventual fate: conversion, or 'perversion', aged 44, from Anglicanism to Roman Catholicism.

How can one convey, in our own day, when one religion is deemed as good or as bad as any other, the Victorian reaction to Newman's apostasy? To Newman's Protestant contemporaries his 'going over' to Rome with all its perceived superstitions and corruptions was an act of treachery, sending shock waves through the nation and beyond. It was, to the scandalised, an act of moral and social turpitude. For those who never forgave him, it showed visibly in his face.

Newman was aware of the impression made by his altered physiognomy. 'How am I changed even in look!' he wrote. 'I [once] had my mouth half open, and commonly a smile on my face – & from that time onwards my mouth has been closed and contracted, and the muscles are so set now, that I cannot but look grave and forbidding.'[24] In that era he became, according to one acquaintance, 'pale, careworn, and meditative … with … sunken cheeks … experience of ages imprinted on his thoughtful brow'.[25] For those openly disgusted by his conversion, his worn features were outward signs of inward disgrace. One remarked of 'the terrible lines deeply ploughed all over his face, and the craft that sat upon his retreating forehead and sunken eyes'.[26] Craft. Cunning. Equivocation. But what might he have gained in the view of his critics? 'How his eye glistened and his whole face glowed, as he turned round to the Altar …', prompting a 'thrill through the congregation',[27] wrote one with a Faustian flourish. There is a strange irony in this comparison of his own face over time, for he would contrast in his *Essay on Development* persistence and change in a person's unique facial identity with the persistence and change in the living development of the Catholic Church down the ages.

He earned of course the respect, indeed adulation, of many Catholics, although by no means all, as we shall see. His personality among admirers was said to be 'intense', 'wondrous' even. 'With those who enjoyed his intimacy', wrote a friend, 'his great attraction lay in what belonged to his personal being – the strange force of which often made itself felt almost at once, so entirely free was he from conventionality.'[28] He continued to walk 'with a swift, light step'. People still spoke of the 'strange, sweet music of his voice'. Yet a younger generation of Catholic, with the licence perhaps of aristocratic privilege, could focus on his foibles with fond irreverence. Sir John Acton, for example, on bringing unwelcome news to 'Old Noggs' (as he referred to Newman) describes him moaning and rocking himself backwards and forwards over a fire, 'like an old woman with a toothache'.[29]

Yet well into his seventies his beguiling voice (*douce et belle*, according to Maria Giberne), the gender ambivalence, the impression of tough frailty, still had the power to entrance. Scott Holland visited Newman when he was well into his seventies:

I turned at the sound of the soft quick speech, and there he was – white, frail and wistful, for all the ruggedness of the actual features. I remembered at once the words of Furse about him, 'delicate as an old lady washed in milk'… So the urgent enquiries went on, in silvery whispers, keen and quick…. I had to fly for my train, and sped home tingling with the magic of a presence that seemed to me like the frail embodiment of a living voice. His soul was in his voice, as a bird is in its song.[30]

Throughout Newman's long life there were abiding traits. He had learned to play the violin aged ten, and played into old age. He preferred Mozart and Beethoven to Brahms and Mendelssohn. 'I never wrote more', he told Richard Church, an Oriel friend; 'I always sleep better after music. There must be some electric current passing from the strings through the fingers into the brain and down the spinal marrow. Perhaps thought is music.'[31] He was quick to tears; but he would laugh out loud, especially at puns and malapropisms. He had the 'gentlest apologetic smile'.[32] He worried about his health to the point of hypochondria; he was plagued by bad teeth. He was anxiously curious about the ailments of others. He could be catty. 'A most simple-minded conscientious fellow', he commented of a young Oratorian, 'but as little possessed of tact and commonsense as he is great in other departments.'[33] Self-disciplined, ascetic, he beat himself weekly with a discipline until age forbade; the discipline was always in his luggage. He was prone to fasting, yet he enjoyed his food and wine. On a holiday in Ramsgate we find him whinging over the small size of a single lamb cutlet served up to him in a hotel dining room: a portion of 'cutlets' in the plural, he pointed out, had been listed on the menu.

He had depended emotionally and practically on several intimate male friendships, in particular Ambrose St John. He had a wide circle of female correspondents, despite what one woman described as his 'singular chivalrous courtesy mingled with an indescribable reserve' towards the gentle sex.[34] He was capable of endearments bordering on the extravagant, yet he was conscious of being limited in his 'affections'. In middle age he wrote an examination of conscience in which he admitted: 'I have this peculiarity, that in the matter of the affections, whether sacred or human, my natural powers cannot exceed certain limits.'[35] He was not inclined to make small talk with those he did not love. Another of his younger Oratorian brethren received this letter from him: 'Such is my fate just now and for some time, that, since I have nothing to say to you, I must either be silent or unseasonable … Many is the time I have stood over the fire at breakfast and looked at you at Recreation, hunting for something to talk about.'[36] Newman's brother Frank noted Newman's reserve when they met after a long separation in their early thirties: 'On first confronting my brother on our joint return from abroad, his dignity seemed as remarkable as his stiffness.'[37]

Newman's charisma continued to exert its magic within the religious all-male community of his own creation, the Oratorians – whom Pugin unkindly described, even during their early days, as 'old women of both sexes'.[38] In some respects this Oratorian circle resembled the close friendships of his Oxford days. Only in a post-Freudian culture would questions, well beyond Pugin's and indeed Kingsley's species of innuendo, be raised. It was Geoffrey Faber, in his *Oxford Apostles,* published in 1933, who first attempted to explore the alleged homoerotic ambiance of Newman's s Oxford circle in the 1820s and 1830s – how it related to the 'homosexual' practices of Ancient Greece; how it coincided with Newman and his friends' conversion to Catholicism. Geoffrey Faber's lengthy study of the group is fraught with innuendo and prejudice, combined with category confusions. Comparing Newman with his close friend Pusey at the time of the former's becoming a Catholic, Geoffrey Faber states that Pusey 'was, in fact, what Newman never was – a man'. Newman, Faber goes on, could succumb with his 'escort of hermaphrodites', to those 'alien, imperious fascinations' of Roman Catholicism, but, '[Pusey] would not believe it, until it had actually happened'.[39]

The attempt to disinter Newman from his grave has prompted more popular and explicit interest in his relationship with Ambrose St John as evidence of their homosexuality, prompting yet another version of his life and character, as unsubtle as the saccharine characterisations that threaten to cluster around the cult of his beatification. The former Oratorian Press Officer, Peter Jennings, wrote of his hope that on exhumation the coffin would be opened and that the onlookers (led by the Provost of the Birmingham Oratory) might be able to gaze on the face of Newman just as it was on the day that he was buried. The aspiration echoes Carlyle's story of Abbot Samson of St Edmundsbury who gazed on the incorrupt body of the holy martyr Edmund seven hundred years after his death. The exhumation of Edmund had anticipated the translation and enshrining of his relics to a grander location in the Abbey. Newman, who almost certainly would have read Carlyle's account, was determined to thwart any such exposure of his own remains by hastening their dissolution.

But now, Newman's beatification raises questions about the fate of his reputation. His importance is long established, and the huge range of his works, correspondence and diaries are now available in print; but will the process of beatifying and canonizing him, trap and petrify his protean genius into a straightjacket of 'approved' Catholic orthodoxy? Or will the Catholic Church find itself energised and liberated by his wide-ranging literary and religious imagination? Newman, by his own admission, was reluctant to be regarded a saint: perhaps because of his modesty; more likely because he feared the ossifying travesty it would make of his life and contribution.

CHAPTER 3

Dreams and imagination

'There is no telling what is in a boy's heart … The heart is a secret
with its Maker; no one on earth can hope to get at it or to touch it.'
CHARLES REDING'S CLERGYMAN FATHER: *LOSS AND GAIN* BY J. H. NEWMAN

'I used to wish the Arabian Tales were true', Newman wrote when he was sixty-three years of age. 'My imagination ran on unknown influences, on magical powers, and talismans.'[1] In his portrait of Cardinal Manning (*Eminent Victorians*), Lytton Strachey exploits this admission to create one of the more spiteful and best-known epigrams ever penned about Newman: 'When Newman was a child he "wished that he could believe the Arabian Nights were true". When he came to be a man, his wish seems to have been granted.'[2]

Newman would relate, however, that he owed to these tales an early and abiding encounter with God.

By the first decade of the nineteenth century the *Arabian Nights Tales* had reached a peak of popularity among the children of England's literate classes. Eastern mystery, genies, magic, invisible worlds, tyranny, cruelty to women, thrilled and disturbed the imaginations of many generations of the young. The tales were staple childhood reading of future poets – Blake, Wordsworth, Coleridge, Southey, Keats, all conceded the debt they owed to the Arabian stories for the growth of their imaginative talent. The predicament of Scheherazade was recognized as a crucial catalyst: her life was suspended on a thread, saved only by her talent for story-telling. But if the tales unblocked the hidden well springs of imagination, releasing strange urges and unbidden fantasies, they also drove young readers inwards – raising doubts about the world of mere appearances.

Samuel Taylor Coleridge, a typical young reader, recalling his copy of *Arabian Nights* in middle-age, wrote how 'with what a strange mixture of obscure dread and intense desire I used to look at the volume and watch it, till the morning sunshine had reached and nearly covered it, when, and not before, I felt the courage given me to seize the precious treasure …'[3] His father, a pious Devon parson, threw the book on the fire. In consequence of those tales, Coleridge tells us, he became a 'dreamer', with an understanding 'forced into almost an unnatural ripeness'. His 'whole being was with eyes closed to every object of present sense'.

John Henry Newman, the eldest of five siblings – two brothers and three sisters, was similarly drawn into imaginative interiority by the Arabian stories. He wrote in his *Apologia*: 'I thought life might be a dream, or I an Angel, and all this world a deception, my fellow-angels by a playful device concealing themselves from me, and deceiving me with the semblance of a material world.'[4] Newman would write that his early sense of isolation from surrounding objects confirmed his mistrust of the 'reality of material phenomena', thus enabling him to 'rest in the thought of two and two only absolute and luminously self-evident beings, myself and my Creator'.[5] He is not precise as to when this conviction of the 'two and two only' self-evident beings dawned on him, but he gives the impression that it was gradual, early, and defined a consistent quality of his imagination into adulthood. For Newman's French biographer, the Abbé Henri Brémond, the conviction reveals Newman's profound *autocentrisme*, locating him within an ambit of benign Romantic egotism – what Keats would call 'the egotistical sublime'.

Newman's central preoccupation in life, by his own admission, was from the outset his inner life. No figure in the nineteenth century, save Wordsworth perhaps, would spend so much time, energy and emotion, absorbed in every aspect of the story of his own development as Newman. Living to a great age, he would spend long hours reflecting, re-reading, re-writing, correcting and destroying, those papers that had a bearing on his history, while recalling from correspondents materials that had gone out of his hands. Every stage, every relationship, every controversy, argument, insight, feeling, and idea, would be checked, double-checked, mulled over, tweaked. The interest of Newman's life is the story of his voracious, unrelenting fascination with the quest to locate his story within the meaning of that second 'luminously self-evident being', his Creator.

While Newman had an early 'feeling of separation from the visible world',[6] 'what a dream life is', and his sister accused him, when he was still a boy, of a Berkeleian idealistic solipsism, his domestic years of childhood, his education at school, and later at Oxford, reveal that he was no introvert. There was from the beginning a remarkable interplay between his inward-directed dreaminess and his outward sensitivity to people, relationships, and the tangible world about him. The fascination with the exterior was characteristically self-referential. And it was religious. He could look back on his childhood remembering the suggestiveness of 'little details … some relic or token of that early time, some spot, or some book, or a word, or a scent, or a sound …'.[7] To one of his women correspondents he would write:

I think nothing more interesting, and it is strange to think how evanescent, how apparently barren and result-less, are the ten thousand little details and complications of daily life and family history … are they themselves some reflexion, as in an earthly mirror, or some great truths above? So I think of musical sounds and their combinations – they are momentary – but is it not some momentary opening and closing of the Veil which hangs between the worlds of spirit and sense?[8]

CONVERSION

His family was prosperous; there were servants, a house in town, a second home in the country; a sense of privilege, entitlement to affluence and the good things of life. He had memories of languid days at their family rural retreat: lying in bed on a summer's morning, hearing the sound of the scythe in the grass outside; picking wildflowers, gazing at magnolia blossoms. Aged 44, he went back to the rural cottage of his Aunt Elizabeth where the sight of a room where he once had breakfast prompted a memory: 'coming down in the morning and seeing the breakfast things looking bright and still – and I have some vague reminiscence of dry toast. And I have a sort of dream of my father and mother coming one day to call, and the room being crowded.'[9] The stillness of the breakfast things eternalizes the enchantment of the moment through the eye of childhood. The written recollection reveals a benign self-absorption spanning childhood to adulthood.

The details of his childhood speak of a doting mother, a protective father, highly intelligent loving sisters Jemima, Harriett, and Mary, and gifted, if increasingly neurotic younger brothers Charles and Francis. Newman's brothers would mean less to him (and he to them) than the eight female members of his extended family: his lively sisters, his mother, his devout grandmother Elizabeth Newman, and his Aunt Elizabeth Good, known as Betsy. It was Betsy who encouraged him as a child to read the Bible. The influence of so many intelligent, voluble women in his younger life might well have affected his speech and mannerisms.

His father was an assiduous working partner of a bank in Lombard Street. Mr John Newman appears a detached figure, but vigilant for his children's welfare; prompt on one occasion to advise his son against religious enthusiasm. 'Take care … you are encouraging a nervousness and morbid sensibility, and irritability, which may be very serious', he warned the earnest teenager.[10] The father sent him, aged seven, to a private boarding school in Ealing, where he was happy and academically successful. It appears that he was clever, curious, precocious. He struck his sister Harriet as a 'very philosophical young gentleman, always full of thought and never at a loss for an answer, very observant and considerate.'[11]

When he was fourteen years he went through a period of smart scepticism. He read 'Paine's *Tracts against the Old Testament* …' also 'some of Hume's Essays; and perhaps that on Miracles'.[12] Hume wrote famously against miracles: 'When anyone tells me that he saw a dead man restored to life, I immediately consider with myself, whether it be more probable, that this person should either deceive or be deceived, or that the fact, which he relates, should really have happened.'[13] Newman remembers copying out verses 'perhaps Voltaire's, in denial of the immortality of the soul'.[14] During this period he recollects saying to himself 'something like, "How dreadful, but how plausible!"'[15]

Then his father's business failed in the 1816 banking crisis that followed the end of the Napoleonic war. Inflation was rampant, thousands of secure fortunes sank as in a dream. Newman fell ill and remained at school through that summer while the family was obliged to leave the London home. They eventually took up residence at a house in Alton, Hampshire, where Mr Newman embarked on a new career as manager of a brewery. It was the beginning of several years of sliding fortunes, humiliation, and, in time, a succession of temporary and increasingly down-at-heel abodes – Kentish Town, Holborn, Covent Garden. Watchful over the family's middle-class respectability and his father's reputation (another Mr Newman of the City of London had notoriously committed suicide during the financial crisis), John Henry would attempt to expunge details of his father's financial difficulties. Mr John Newman was eventually declared bankrupt and would die in his prime of what they used to call a broken heart.

The anxiety drove the boy in on himself; unwell, depressed, and solitary, he became receptive, and perhaps a target, of the religious enthusiasm of one of his young school teachers. Mr Walter Mayers, a classicist, had recently converted from mainstream Anglicanism to fervent Evangelicalism. It was a familiar shift in the early nineteenth century. The previous fifty years had seen a decline in fervor within the Church of England, partly owed to its Establishment torpor and fragmentation, partly owed to a widespread appeal to 'rationalism' in support of religious belief. Evangelicalism and Methodism offered an antidote to spiritual indifference through powerful preaching and emphasis on Bible reading.

Newman has left no clear impression of the dramatic impact on his feelings that summer. Looking back from late middle age, he focused on the literature that influenced him rather than his emotions. The fervent Mr Mayers placed in the young Newman's hands *The Force of Truth* by Thomas Scott, who had himself undergone an Evangelical conversion. But Scott, as Newman would write later, enabled him to avoid the 'detestable' Evangelical doctrine, expounded by the Calvinists, which held that many were predestined to Hell. Scott 'made a deeper impression on my mind than any other, and to whom (humanly speaking) I almost owe my soul'.[16] Scott convinced Newman that acceptance of Christianity brings the 'living truth' in all its 'unfolding riches'. Newman would write that he now, for the first time, consciously accepted revealed religion. 'I fell under the influences of a definite Creed', he would write in the *Apologia*, 'and received into my intellect impressions of dogma, which, through God's mercy, have never been effaced or obscured.' [17] A conviction of the truth of the Holy Trinity was accompanied by a sense of his 'inward conversion of which I was conscious (and of which I still am more certain than that I have hands and feet) would last into the next life, and that I was elected to eternal glory.' [18] According to Henri Bouyer, the young Newman received confirmation of, and assented to, the truth of the indwelling God, already sensed in childhood as the presence of that second luminous being in the depths of his consciousness. 'If it be true', writes Bouyer, 'as he was now beginning to feel that it was, that all complete consciousness of self is moral consciousness, he realised that moral consciousness is the con-sciousness, the awareness, of Someone, of God.' [19]

Yet, aged fifteen, he was already taking a position on the conflicts and squab-bles of institutionalized Christianity. He would admit, in retrospect, 'the seeds of an intellectual inconsistency'. [20] He believed in the Church founded by Christ's apostles, and yet he was convinced that the Pope, Peter's successor, was a tool of Satan. The problem was, he wrote later, that he had been reading *The History of the Church of Christ* by Joseph Milner, with its extracts from Augustine, Ambrose and other great writers of the early Church, the 'Early Fathers'. At the same time he was plunging into Thomas Newton's *Dissertations on the Prophecies*, which argued that the Pope was the Antichrist foretold in Scripture. Newman would later comment, 'I speak of the process of conversion with great diffidence, being obliged to adopt the language of books. For my own feelings, as far as I re-member, were so different from any account I have ever read, that I dare not go by what *may* be an individual case.' [21] He also tells us in the *Apologia* that he be-came convinced that he would never marry.

I am obliged to mention, though I do it with great reluctance, another deep imagination, which at this time, the autumn of 1816, took possession of me, – that there can be no mistake about the fact; viz. that it would be the will of God that I should lead a single life. [22]

Why he should mention this with 'great reluctance', he does not tell; although at the time of writing (in his sixty-third year) he had been involved in the contentious issue of clerical celibacy. The 'deep imagination' indicates that this was an emotional impulse based on his notion of what it would be like to be married, rather than a moral imperative deriving from a belief that celibacy was a holier state.

UNDERGRADUATE

Trinity College, Oxford, stands back from Oxford's spacious street, known appropriately as the Broad. High railings and massive ornate gates, beyond which lie lawns and flower beds, lead up the impressive neoclassical chapel, giving the impression of the vista of a grand English house rather than a college. In the second quad is a medieval building facing the panelled dining hall; then one enters a three-sided classical building, reinforcing the neoclassical impression, built in honey-coloured stone. This four-storey building looks out towards Wadham College.

In 1817 Newman, aged 16, went up to Trinity; his father had left it to the last moment before directing the carriage towards the city of dreaming spires rather than to the Fens. He was lodged on staircase VII, with a view on one side over Balliol and an inner court with climbing snapdragon, and on the other towards Wadham. He fell in love with Oxford from the first and was soon dreaming of settling there for the rest of his life. Referring to himself in the third person, he wrote in his journal: 'He recollected with what awe and transport he had at first come to the University, as to some sacred shrine; and how from time to time hopes had come over him that some day or other he should have gained a title to residence on one of its old foundations.' He goes on:

One night, in particular, came across his memory, how a friend and he had ascended to the top of one of its many towers with the purpose of making observations on the stars; and how, while his friend was busily engaged with the pointers, he, earthly-minded youth, had been looking down into the deep, gas-lit, dark-shadowed quadrangles, and wondering if he should ever be a Fellow of this or that College, which he singled out from the mass of academical buildings.[23]

While his friend prepares to lose himself in wonders of the night-sky, there is Newman lost, by his own admission, in thoughts about himself and the seductions of Oxford. It was Matthew Arnold who would write of Oxford's allure during this period in the preface to his *Essays in Criticism*: 'Beautiful city! So venerable, so lovely … so serene…. Steeped in sentiment as she lies, spreading her gardens to the moonlight, and whispering from her towers the last enchantments of the Middle Age …'[24]

Newman showed immediate promise as a mathematician, but he was behind in Latin and Greek; although not for long. He won a much needed scholarship the following year. Academically ambitious, confident of his intellectual ability, he embarked on a severe regime of study in preparation for 'Schools', the Oxford BA honours examination. If he read for only nine hours on any one day, he would make up for it by reading fourteen hours the next. There is an impression of high seriousness, agonizing scrupulosity over whether to pray for academic success. He wrote to his brother Francis in Evangelical vein:

I read very much certainly, but I may say (I trust), without deceiving myself or losing sight of my unnumbered transgressions, that God sanctifies my studies by breathing into me all the while thoughts of Him, and enables me to praise Him with joyful lips, when I rise and when I lie down, and when I wake in the night.[25]

Newman was not athletic; indeed he had not 'a grain', he wrote, 'in [my] composition of that temper … so natural to young men'. [26] Yet, while shy, sensitive, devout, and occasionally priggish, he reveals himself in his vivid correspondence as high-spirited. He had in his boyhood attended dancing lessons (with reluctance), swam, and rode ponies and horses. We see him making kites, being a spectator at sailing competitions, going to plays and concerts, feasting himself on almond cakes and barley sugar (small wonder his teeth decayed early); practicing the violin for half hour intervals between reading stints, and occasionally performing. 'I was asked by a man yesterday to go to his room for a *little* Music at 7 o'clock', he wrote as an undergraduate. 'I went. An old Don, a very good natured man, but too fond of music – played Bass: and through his enthusiasm I was kept playing quartets on a heavy tenor from seven to twelve! Oh my poor arm and eyes and head and back.' [27]

Despite a later tendency to fast, especially during Lent, he had a hearty interest in food and drink. He describes with relish a typical meal served in Trinity hall: '… beautiful salmon, haunches of mutton, lamb etc and fine, very fine (to my taste) strong beer, served up on old pewter plates, and mis-shapen earthenware jugs … gooseberry, raspberry, and apricot pies … such a profusion that scarcely two ate of the same joint.' [28] Then: '… the other day I had a nice dinner set before me of veal cutlets and peas, so much to myself that I could hear the noise I made in chewing through the empty hall.' [29]

Acutely self-conscious in his early days at Oxford, he was convinced that he dressed oddly and stood out from his fellows: 'Whenever I go out I am stared at; and the other day there was a party of people laughing at my dress.' [30] Then he complains in priggish vein to his father: 'I am not noticed at all, except by being silently stared at. I am glad they do not wish to be acquainted with me, not because I wish to appear apart from them and illnatured, but because I really do not think I should gain the least advantage from their company.' [31]

On one occasion a group of students attempted to make him drink heavily while begging him to play his violin. He stood his ground and refused. On another occasion he was the butt of bullying. He records the episode with terse narrative skill. There is a hint, by his own admission, that he was suspected of effeminacy; Newman, however, is more interested in what it means to be a gentleman:

Is it gentlemanly conduct to rush into my room, and to strut up to the further end of it, and ask me in a laughing tone how I do; and then, after my remaining some time in silent wonder, to run and bolt the door, and say they are hiding from some one?

Then, to tell me they have come to invite me to wine, and, when I answer in the negative, to ask me why, pressing and pressing me to come, and asking me in a gay manner if I do not mean to take a first class, telling me I read too much, and overdo it, and then to turn from me suddenly and to hollow out 'Let him alone, come along', and to throw open the door?

I said such conduct was not the conduct of gentlemen – and ordered them to leave the room. One then said he would knock me down, if I were not too contemptible a fellow. (He was 6 feet 3 or 4 inches high, and stout in proportion.)[32]

The following day Newman confided to his journal: 'The One has been here just now, and said he was very sorry for his conduct, that a sudden gust of passion had overset him – that I had acted very well, that he had seldom or never seen any one act more firmly.' Newman told the young man 'not to think more about it'. They shook hands.[33]

Dignified, courageous, he was nevertheless nervous, highly strung, and fastidious. He reports his queasiness on being assailed by a strong smell: 'While I was out today, some men who are painting throughout the College have painted my windows, and I am nearly sick with the smell. I do not know how I shall sleep tonight for it.'[34] In St Mary's church during a service he had a sudden fainting fit: 'A dizziness came over my eyes, I could see nothing, and, to my surprise, I found my head was on the shoulder of the gownsman who sat next to me.'[35] The man took Newman out into the fresh air and brought him to his college rooms.

He complains of toothache, headaches, eye problems. He writes to his mother, setting out in detail advice he has been given: 'Strain not your sight at distant objects; rather use a glass. When you read, have your neckcloth loose, your head erect, avoid every thing like a stooping posture. In bed, your head very high, your feet low … In your diet avoid any thing which may cause a sudden rush of blood to the head …'[36] He was preoccupied with his own ailments and with news of indispositions in the family: his sister Jemima's cough, Mary's chilblains, his brother Charles's softening gums.

He was fascinated by his dreams, and noted his dream life, especially when it featured religious themes. One night he dreamt of a spirit coming to him to talk of religious mysteries:

Among other things [the spirit] said that it was absolutely impossible for the reason of man to understand the mystery (I think) of the Holy Trinity, and in vain to argue about it; but that every thing in another world was so *very, very plain*, that there was not the slightest difficulty about it. I cannot put into any sufficiently strong form of words the ideas which were conveyed to me. I thought I instantly fell on my knees, overcome with gratitude to God for so kind a message … out of dreams often much good can be extracted.[37]

And all the while Oxford, the surrounding country and villages, and the atmosphere of the place was entering his soul. He describes his rooms for Jemima with a mix of pride and parody ('though my feeble pen can ill describe the endless beauties with which it is adorned'):

The room is lofty, and lighted by two windows, from which are seen, the gardens of the college and the turrets of Wadham. Scarlet Morine curtains shed a rich glow over the apartment – On turning to the right a massy chimney-piece of marble discovers itself …[38]

Despite the daunting regime of study he could bask in the enchantment of Oxford's bells on a Sunday evening. 'Bells pealing. The pleasure of hearing them. It leads the mind to a longing after some thing I know not what. It does not bring past years to remembrance. It does not bring anything. What does it do? We have a kind of longing after something dear to us and well known to us … Such is my feeling at this minute, as I hear them.'[39]

THE APPRENTICE WRITER

He soon made friends with a fellow undergraduate, John William Bowden, and they became inseparable. Together they embarked on the writing of a romance based on the St Bartholomew's Day Massacre, and started a magazine called *The Undergraduate*; although Newman withdrew the moment he was identified as editor. In 1819 we find him devising a debating society, eleven years ahead of the founding of the Oxford Union. 'The subjects of disputation should include the whole range of history, poetry and the fine arts.' He was against the inclusion of 'politics of the last 100 years', showing a degree of guardedness against party political polemic. But 'the members should be all undergraduates elected by the undergraduates'.[40]

He was reading, translating, composing in the styles of Homer, Aeschylus, Plato, Sophocles, Virgil, Cicero, Herodotus, among others. His modern reading included Shakespeare, Milton, Johnson, Gibbon, Crabbe, Southey, Scott. He shared his enthusiasms with his mother. Here he is, having read the new novel *Ivanhoe*:

The last chapter in it is horribly sublime. O what a poet! his words are not like a novelist – O certainly a poet. I never really recollect reading any thing which so took away my breath with admiration as the last half of the second volume.[41]

Writing to his sisters, he enjoys showing off his parodies – from Johnsonian pomposity, to Addisonian urbanity, to mock-heroics in the style of Gibbon, then letting rip in energetic demotic. You can hear him speak:

Bishop Hobart of New York is in Oxford – I dined with him … he is an intelligent man … he is however I fear dirty – so at least were his hands and neckcloth…. [Bowden's] sister's music master, brought Rossini to dine in Grosv. Place … Labouring indeed under a severe cold, he did not sing; but he accompanied two or three of his own songs etc in the most brilliant manner, giving the Piano the effect of an Orchestra – no, *three* Orchestras ... surrounded in a low dark room by 8 or 9 Italians, all talking as fast as possible, who, with the assistance of a great screaming *macaw* (o.th! [only think] and of Mad[ame] Colbran Rossini in a dirty gown and her hair in curl papers, made such a clamour ...[42]

Yet writing to Walter Mayers, he echoes his Evangelical mentor's moralizing animadversions:

It is sickening to see what I might call the apostasies of many. This year it was supposed there would have been no such merry making. A quarrel existed among us; the College was divided into two sets, and no proposition for the usual subscription for wine was set on foot. Unhappily a day or two before the time a reconciliation takes place, the wine party is agreed upon, and this wicked union to be sealed by drunkenness is profanely joked upon with allusions to one of the expressions in the Athanasian Creed.[43]

He writes to Mayers: 'I sincerely trust that my conscience, enlightened by the Bible, through the influence of the Holy Spirit, may prove a faithful and vigilant guardian of the principles of religion.'[44] In his journal he records in similar vein his struggles with belief and consciousness of sin:

... I have had anguish in my mind. Yes, and all owing to my former sins. My soul would have been light and cheerful, I could have rested in the lovingkindness of the lord, I should have been of good courage, but He seems to be threatening retribution, and my enemy takes occasion to exult over his prey.[45]

In years to come he would write of style as 'the faithful expression of [a literary genius's] intense personality, attending on his own inward world of thought as its very shadow ... It follows him about *as* his shadow'.[46] As an undergraduate he was revelling in his ability to write in a range of styles, and wrote to his sister Jemima showing off the secrets of stylistic mastery: 'I dare say you find great entertainment from Pope's Homer', he writes. 'You would find it a good exercise, after you have read so much as to accustom your ear to the modulation of the metre, to *translate* a paragraph into French prose, and, in a few days when you have forgotten the verses, to turn them back again.'[47]

He admires the gothic conceits in Aeschylus. He is 'lost in astonishment', 'stupefied', 'out of breath'. 'You may feed on metaphors in it for days together.'[48] He found Sophocles 'stiff and yet ... majestic'. Then he is off on a literary perambulation: 'A peculiarity of the styles of Johnson and Gibbon came into my head the other day while walking ... two peculiarities one of Johnson, one of Gibbon which may be contrasted with each other.'

Newman the undergraduate had the instincts and disciplines of a writer-in-the-making by emulation.

EXAMINATION FAILURE AND SUCCESS

In the event, he suffered a breakdown during the examinations, and only managed a lower second class honours in classics, failing altogether in mathematics. He would write of his failure in the third person: 'He had overread himself … he lost his head, utterly broke down, and after vain attempts for several days had to retire.'[49] He wrote home reporting that he felt composed, less disappointed for himself than for his parents. He wrote to his father:

What I feel on my own account is indeed nothing at all, compared with the idea that I have disappointed you; and most willingly would I consent to a hundred times the sadness that now overshadows me if so doing would save my Mother and you from feeling vexation.[50]

His sensible mother replied:

Your Father and I write in the warmest affection to you, and beg you not to think we are disappointed or vexed at the contents of your letter. We are more than satisfied with your laudable endeavours; and, as I have said to you before in anticipation of what has occurred, you must wait patiently and cheerfully the time appointed for … your merit; and your very failure will increase the interest they feel for you.[51]

Supported by his scholarship, he remained at Trinity, and decided to attempt to reverse the disaster of his BA finals by entering for a college fellowship at Oriel, the Oxford college with the most prestigious reputation for scholarship and intellect in the university. It was a bold and responsible bid. The family fortunes were calamitous and he had two younger brothers to help support. He took on pupils, including his own brother Francis, to add to his scholarship bursary. His friend Bowden rented Newman and his brother a house he had occupied in Oxford with a restaurant attached. To pay debts, there was a house sale of virtually everything the Newmans owned, including John Henry's music. He felt that his boyhood was over. He wrote to his mother: 'I felt much affected, and quite shed tears to think I could not longer call myself a boy.'[52]

Despite the financial pressures and the anxiety of preparing for another gruelling set of academic examinations, Newman embarked on a treatise on astronomy, a light and airy concerto for piano, and a huge circuit of reading in law, geology, philosophy, Hebrew. For a second time he went to the entertaining geology lectures of the Reverend William Buckland, who speculated that the 'beginning' in Genesis was an undefined period, and that there had been great extinctions in natural history. Buckland was one of the earliest Christian scientists to attempt a reconciliation between the evidence of fossils and Genesis. He would challenge, for example, the popular notion that the bones of hyenas found in a cave in Yorkshire, and evidently gnawed on by tigers, had been washed there after Noah's flood. The young Newman, however, was not prepared to swallow Buckland whole, as he felt that geology was so in its infancy and that 'that no regular system is formed'. [53]

In April 1822 Newman sat the Oriel fellowship examination in competition with ten rivals. He was required at the outset to translate into Latin part of a *Spectator* essay on Milton's *Paradise Lost*, and to write an essay in English on the difference between self-confidence and arrogance. The Provost and several Fellows of Oriel were so impressed by Newman's early efforts that three of them went over to Trinity to make discreet inquiries about his background. Newman, however, was so depressed about his performance that he told his tutor, Thomas Short, that he was thinking of retiring. Short wisely filled him with lamb cutlets and cheered him on. Papers followed papers: philosophy, more Latin, mathematics, logic. One day he sat for eight hours on the hard examination bench in Oriel's dining hall and thought that his spine would burst. He was consoled by the motto in the stained glass above him (there to this day): '*Pie repone te*' ('repose with pious confidence': the version of Oriel's current chaplain, as of October 2009, is: 'Chill out!').

Newman was playing the violin in his rooms at Trinity, when a man arrived requesting him to report to the Provost of Oriel. He allowed the messenger to depart before throwing down the instrument and running all the way to his new college. The route would be no different today. He would have hared across the Broad and into the Turl, passing Jesus College on his right, Exeter and Lincoln on his left. Crossing the High Street he would have dashed along the two lanes that take you into Oriel Square to be greeted by the noble façade of Oriel. As he hurried along, the whole of Oxford appeared to be rejoicing. He was congratulated, he wrote, by strangers. Among his overjoyed and hilarious accounts of the day was this:

The news spread through Trinity with great rapidity. I had hardly been in Kinsey's room a minute, when in rushed Ogle like one mad. I then proceeded to the President's and in rushed Ogle again. I find that T. rushed to E's room, and nearly kicked down the door to communicate the news. E. in turn ran down stairs. Th. heard a noise and my name mentioned, and rushed out also, and in the room opposed found E.W. and Ogle leaping up and down, backwards and forwards. Men rushed in all directions to Trinity to men they knew, to congratulate them of the success of their College. The Bells were set ringing from three different towers (I had to pay for it). [54]

A life of scholarship, teaching, Holy Orders, and pastoral activities both within the university and city of Oxford, lay ahead.

CHAPTER 4

Fellow of Oriel

'… I am more than ever imprest too with the importance of
staying in Oxford many years – "I am rooted …"'
J. H. NEWMAN LETTER TO JEMIMA NEWMAN, 17 MARCH 1829

The main gate and façade of Oriel College, with its distinctive Flemish style curved gables, faces out across a square to the classical back entrance of Christ Church and the Peckwater building. Founded in 1324, it is the fifth oldest college in the university, and steeped in royal history: its Visitor is the British monarch. On a recent visit, I was assured that Newman's rooms, on the second floor of the third staircase in the first quadrangle, remain much as they were in the early nineteenth century. A perfectly proportioned sitting room, about fourteen by sixteen feet, with a fireplace (now boarded up), adjoins a smaller bedroom area which leads to a lobby, next to the chapel's organ, which Newman used as an oratory. One set of windows looks out across a busy lane to the side of Corpus Christi College, the other looks into the front quadrangle of Oriel in the direction of the building that houses the Senior Common Room and Library.

In this relatively small college, Newman found an ideal home for his talents and tendencies. The routine of Oxford college life suited him: regular meals, servants, financial security; a serious and scholarly peer group; the round of religious services and opportunities for pastoral duties; the stimulation of student contact. It was a perfect balance between the structured life of the bachelor scholar and community life. He had now decided to take Holy Orders, and since Oxford colleges of those days were peopled with ordained men he would be surrounded by priests and fellow candidates for the priesthood.

An Oriel fellowship had acquired extraordinary status in the early decades of the nineteenth century. The Provost, Edward Copleston, and his predecessor, John Eveleigh, had broken with Oxford college tradition by inviting all-comers to compete for fellowships. It was a 'trial', according to Copleston, 'not of how much men knew, but of how they knew'.[1] Whereas fellowships and other university appointments were invariably based on patronage, backed by success in the BA honours examinations ('the quackery of the Schools', as Copleston referred to them), the Oriel fellowship examination was open to all. 'Every election to a fellowship which tends to discourage the narrow and almost the technical *routine* of public examinations', wrote Copleston, 'I consider as an important triumph.'[2] He was prepared to take risks even with candidates who had actually done badly in their BA examination. Although there had been one at least who had failed to live up to his confidence. That was Coleridge's eldest son, Hartley, who had done badly in his finals, yet impressed the Oriel fellows only to disgrace himself as a drunkard. But they were prepared to take a risk again with young Newman, who also had done disastrously in his finals. 'He was not even a good classical scholar', commented Copleston, 'yet in mind and powers of composition, and in taste and knowledge, he was decidedly superior to some competitors who were a class above him in the Schools.'[3] Copleston believed that it was more important to exercise a student's mind 'than to pour in knowledge'.[4]

Newman was joining a circle of remarkable Oxford figures. The Oriel senior common room was noted for its love of intellectual conversation; and in consequence the fellows were known as the 'Noetics'. Oriel dons preferred to drink tea rather than port after high table dinner, prompting ribaldry from hearty students who would call out, inquiring whether the kettle was on, when passing the porter's lodge.

At dinner on his first evening Newman sat next to John Keble, regarded in those days as one of the pre-eminent minds in the university. Keble, who was nine years older than Newman, looked so young, and was 'so perfectly unassuming and unaffected in his manner', noted Newman, that he seemed more like an undergraduate than Oxford's 'first man'.[5] Arriving in 1807 as an undergraduate at Corpus Christi College, aged only 14, Keble had taken a double first in Mathematics and Classics, and later won the university prizes for English and Latin essays. When Newman was elected, Keble was a college tutor and a university examiner; more importantly he was a poet, already turning out the sacred verse that would make a best-seller of his book *The Christian Year*, published in 1827.

Another notable Oriel character was a tall flamboyant man called Richard Whately, recently married and so no longer a resident fellow. He took Newman under his wing, encouraging him to assume greater self-confidence. An Oriel Fellow wrote: 'The first time I saw Whately, he wore a pea-green coat, white waistcoat, stone-coloured shorts, flesh-coloured silk stockings. His hair was powdered.'[6] Newman remembered: 'If there was a man easy for a raw bashful youth to get on with it was Whately … a great talker, who endured very readily the silence of his company.'[7] Whately was known for his uncouth manners. One contemporary reported: 'I myself have seen him expectorate over his shoulder in the Corpus Common Room, wipe his mouth with his fingers, and then plunge them into a dish of almonds and raisins.'[8] Whately admired the young fellow Newman, judging that Oriel had appointed 'the clearest-headed man he knew'.[9]

Another Oriel figure soon to become an intimate of Newman's was Edward Bouverie Pusey. Pusey, a year older than Newman, was tense and pious; he suffered from migraines. They walked together frequently, conversing on religious themes and in particular the question of the Evangelical spirit. Newman noted prayerfully in his journal: 'that Pusey is Thine, O Lord, how can I doubt? … yet I fear he is prejudiced against Thy children.'[10] Newman gives us a vivid description of his first encounter with this future kindred spirit, demonstrating, with the lightest of observational touches, his developing literary skills:

> His light curly head of hair was damp with the cold water which his headaches made necessary for comfort; he walked fast with a young manner of carrying himself, and stood rather bowed, looking up from under his eye-brows, his shoulders rounded, and his bachelor's gown not buttoned at the elbow, but hanging loose over his wrists. His countenance was very sweet, and he spoke little.[11]

On one of their many walks Pusey made a form of religious confession to Newman, who consequently wrote in his journal: 'O, what words shall I use? My heart is full. How should I be humbled to the dust! What importance I think myself of! my deeds, my abilities, my writings! whereas he is humility itself, and gentleness, and love, and zeal, and self devotion. Bless him with Thy fullest gifts, and grant me to imitate him.'[12]

Newman had found absorbing intellectual and emotional companionship, but he still treasured his solitude, a circumstance noted by the Provost. Meeting Newman one afternoon as the young don walked alone wrapped in thought, Copleston accosted him with the Ciceronian phrase: '*Nunquam minus solus, quam cum solus,*' – 'Never less alone than when alone.'

HOLY ORDERS

In May of 1824 Newman was appointed curate to the ageing rector of St Clement's Church, Oxford, and the following month received the diaconate, penultimate stage to the priesthood, in the cathedral of Christ Church. 'The words "for ever"', he reflected, 'are so terrible … I feel as a man thrown suddenly into deep water.'[13] St Clement's was situated at the east end of the city of Oxford where the roads from London, Iffley and Cowley converge before the traveller crosses Magdalen Bridge and enters the High. With 1,500 working class parishioners, and an ailing rector, he was soon hard at work, teaching catechism, raising money for a new church building, and visiting the sick. He would raise £2,000 for the new building, including a gallery for ninety children.

Newman's mentor during this early pastoral period was Edward Hawkins, fellow of Oriel, and Vicar of St Mary's, the University Church. Hawkins was one of those acute hypochondriacs who lived to be ninety-three. Newman benefited, however, from his tendency to precision and clarity in thought and expression. He would write that Hawkins taught him to 'weigh my words, and to be cautious in my statements'.

He led me to that mode of limiting and clearing my sense in discussion and in controversy, and of distinguishing between cognate ideas, and of obviating mistakes by anticipation, which to my surprise has been since considered, even in quarters friendly to me, to savour of the polemics of Rome.[14]

Newman's reputation, among his future enemies, for slippery casuistry, was, according to his own view many years later, Oxonian intellectual precision rather than Roman equivocation. Hawkins criticized the draft of Newman's first sermon in which he separated, in Evangelical mode, the sheep from goats, saints from sinners, converts from unconverted. Hawkins insisted that religious and moral excellence is matter of degree, rather than black and white.[15] Newman was soon to find in his pastoral work that this was indeed the case, although he continued, much to the dismay of his parishioners, to preach the doctrine of eternal damnation.

At the heart of Hawkins's criticism, however, was Newman's apparent attachment to the doctrine of Baptismal Regeneration. The widely accepted Anglican view, based on the *Book of Common Prayer*, was that baptism conferred rebirth in the spirit by the act of washing with water whether of infants or adults. The Evangelical view was that regeneration, rebirth in Christ, was a result of actual, conscious will to convert rather than the ritual itself: hence infant baptism was deemed to be inadequate by many Evangelical preachers. Newman remained in a quandary on the question for many months; but Hawkins's influence marked the beginning of the end of his Evangelical convictions.

That year he read Bishop Joseph Butler's influential *Analogy of Religion: Natural and Revealed*. Butler, who had been a fellow of Oriel as a young man, argued that there are two ways to religion and knowledge of God: through nature and through revelation, and that both paths are complementary and analogous. In Butler, Newman found confirmation of his conviction, since boyhood, that God was to be found in the depths of conscience. Butler taught that human beings are guided by two principles: the impetus of self-interest, and a desire to assist others. Human beings are not determined towards either self-interest or altruism, he argued; we are moral agents with a capacity to choose between the two. Newman had taken Butler's notion of conscience, the supreme authority in one's life, as a way of finding God in nature and thence to finding Him in Revelation.[16] In a sermon Newman would preach before the university in 1830, 'The Influence of Natural and Revealed Religion Respectively', he would expand on the idea:

... it is obvious that Conscience is the essential principle and sanction of Religion in the mind. Conscience implies a relation between the soul and something exterior, and that, moreover, superior to itself; a relation to an excellence which it does not possess, and to a tribunal over which it has no power. And since the more closely this inward monitor is respected and followed, the clearer, the more exalted, and the more varied its dictates become, and the standard of excellence is ever outstripping, while it guides, our obedience, a moral conviction is thus at length obtained of the unapproachable nature as well as the supreme authority of That, whatever it is, which is the object of the mind's contemplation.[17]

Newman received full Holy Orders at Christ Church in May 1825. He would write of baptismal regeneration a year into his first pastoral job: 'Then, I thought there were many in the visible Church of Christ, who have never been visited by the Holy Ghost; now, I think there are none but probably, nay almost certainly, have been visited by Him … Then, I thought the *onus probandi* lay with those who asserted an individual to be a real Christian; and now I think it lies with those who deny it.'[18]

Meanwhile on a walk around Christ Church Meadow, another fellow of Oriel, the Reverend William James, expounded the doctrine of apostolic succession: that the continuity of the Church back to its original foundation depended on the unbroken line of bishops who owed their Holy Orders to the first apostles. Such a historical contention could only raise a number of uncomfortable questions: not least the discontinuity of the English Reformation. Newman would write in the *Apologia* that he was not entirely sure that he came round to accepting the doctrine at that time; that he was somewhat impatient of it in the course of their conversation. But the seed had been planted.

BROTHERLY LOVE

Newman's father lay dying in London during September 1824, broken by his business failures. John Henry was at his side: 'He knew me, tried to put out his hand and said "God Bless you".' His last words were 'God bless you, thank my God, thank my God … my dear'. Newman wrote: 'Can a man be a materialist who sees a dead body?'[19]

Newman thus became the head of the family, assuming both emotional and financial responsibilities for his mother and siblings, while attempting to exert moral responsibility over at least one of his brothers. At the same time he was busy in Oxford. He was already junior treasurer of Oriel College when he was invited by Richard Whately, now the new Principal of St Alban's Hall (a private residential hall for scholars adjoining Oriel) to become effectively 'Dean, Tutor, Bursar and all'. Newman would acknowledge that the pressures had an effect on him. He wrote of those early days that he had a 'contemptuous manner' and was 'hasty and authoritative', 'proud, ill tempered, insincere, implacable'.[20] It was this harsh side of his character perhaps that got the better of him when dealing at this time with the religious scepticism of his brother Charles. And yet, on another level, the quarrel anticipated a crucial insight into the question of justification of religious belief. For Newman, the justification of belief had far more to do with a person's disposition than specific arguments for and against Christianity.

Charles, who had none of Newman's self-discipline, and probably suffered from being in his elder brother's shadow, had written: 'I am glad to say I have come to a satisfactory conclusion with regard to religion …' He found himself, he went on, 'entirely against Christianity; which I expected to find synonymous with wisdom and knowledge, but which is far otherwise. I think Mr Owen for practical motives to action … beats St Paul hollow.' The philosophy of Robert Owen, one of the British founders of nineteenth century socialism, taught that human action was determined by environment and education, and that religion weakened the mind. Charles's preference for determinism, utilitarianism, pragmatism, and socialism, so shocked Newman that he suspected that his younger brother might be insane.[21] Instead of offering counter-arguments he accused his brother of not being 'in a state of mind to listen to argument of any kind …', of giving vent to feelings 'in wild combinations of thought and expression'. He told Charles that he was '*in every thing* … self-willed'; and 'too excited to decide fairly". He excoriated the younger brother for the 'hurry and confusion' of his thoughts, and 'now having so hastily cast off what I verily believe you never fully understood, your mind swells and boils'. Then came a sermon: 'In spirit of the allsufficiency of knowledge, you will find it a cold and bleak state of things to be left carelessly and as it were unkindly by the God who made you, uncertain why you are placed here, and what is to become of you after death.' After more in this vein, Newman concluded: 'Pray excuse me if I appear to have said any thing hastily or severely: I have not wished to do so.'

Apart from the arguments that went to and fro between them, Newman was clearly angry at Charles's apparent lack of respect for his status as clergyman, don, and elder brother. 'You may think me weak and narrow minded; and some about you may reckon every one of my profession necessarily bigoted …' His parting shot was: 'but I am your affectionate brother; I am a natural adviser and friend.'

When Mrs Newman got wind of the spat between her sons, she wrote to John Henry: 'Poor dear Charles is sadly harassed at present, various ways, in religion. He is anxious to find the truth; in time, I pray and trust he will seek it in the right way, and delightful will it be, if you should be the kind and gentle guide …' She added that Charles would come round, if he ever would, as a result of 'a superior power'.[22]

If Newman's correspondence reveals self-righteousness and a lack of kindness and gentleness, the passing of the years would not soften his judgmental attitude towards his younger brother. Some fifty years later he would write a harsh memorandum on Charles's character. He had evidently resented his brother's requests for financial support, 'just as if he were a cripple or bedridden. Hence his attraction from the age of 21 or 22 to the teaching and views of the Socialists.' While granting that Charles had a good mind and was a scholar in French and German literature, he judged him to have led a 'forlorn and aimless life' on account of his 'preposterous pride and want of common sense'. [23]

In a second letter written in the Spring of 1825, Newman suspended his attacks on his brother's character in order to quiz him catechetically, 'that I may get at your opinions on the whole subject'. [24] They would constitute a difficult exegetical quiz for any scriptural scholar, let alone an excitable younger brother with a head full of socialism. 'Were any of [Christ's] miracles believed by the Pharisees etc to have been really wrought?', asked Newman. 'Is it true that the great men among the Jews constantly opposed his pretentions?' And, 'did the people in general, and among them the apostles themselves, expect (before his death) a temporal Messiah?' On and on went the Q and A: thirty-five hectoring questions in all.

Then the letter shifts to an insightful and characteristic perspective that he would develop in years to come as he pondered the widespread growth of atheism and agnosticism. What was is it about the attitude of an individual that makes a person a believer or an unbeliever? He starts: 'I consider the rejection of Christianity to arise from a fault of the heart, not of the intellect; that unbelief arises, not from mere error of reasoning, but either from pride or from sensuality.' He goes on:

The most powerful arguments for Christianity do not *convince*, only *silence*; for there is at the bottom that secret antipathy for the doctrines of Christianity, which is quite out of reach of argument. I do not then assert that the Christian evidences are *overpowering*, but that they are *unanswerable*. [25]

He ends by reflecting that 'to be entering into a defence of Christianity against a brother, is, I will not merely say, a novel and astonishing, it is a most painful, a most heart-rending event'.

Ten years on, addressing not his troubled younger brother but his entranced congregation in the university church, Newman would advocate a more positive approach to encounters with unbelief:

When a person for the first time hears the arguments and speculations of unbelievers, and feels what a very novel light they cast upon what he has hitherto accounted most sacred, it cannot be denied that, unless he is shocked and closes his ears and heart to them, he will have a sense of expansion and elevation. [26]

The justification of religious belief would become central to his life's work.

'YEARNING HEART'

While preoccupied with his role as a tutor at Oriel, his pastoral work had taken a new direction. Edward Hawkins, who had been his early guide at St Clement's, became Provost of Oriel, and Newman was appointed Vicar of St Mary's, the university church, in his place. St Mary's would become the main venue for his preaching for two decades. The appointment involved responsibility for a handful of non-university parishioners in Oxford as well as for an entire parish at the village of Littlemore, a fairly poor community some two and a half miles south of the city. In time he would attract large numbers of junior and senior members to the University Church.

Meanwhile, there had come into his life one Hurrell Froude, a man destined to have a profound effect on his spiritual and emotional life. Son of a prosperous archdeacon in Dartington, Devon, Froude was two years Newman's junior, and was elected to an Oriel fellowship in 1826. He was described as 'tall, erect, thin'[27]; bold and volubly high-spirited, he was given to slang and irreverence. He had no time for affectation. He was attractive to men. One close friend spoke of his 'delicate features, and penetrating grey eyes, not exactly piercing, but bright with internal conceptions, and ready to assume an expression of amusement, careful attention, inquiry, or stern disgust, but with a basis of softness'.[28] Newman's description of him a quarter of a century later, in the *Apologia*, breathes undying adulation. He would write of Froude's 'gentleness and tenderness of nature, the playfulness, the free elastic force and graceful versatility of mind, and the patient winning considerateness in discussion, which endeared him to those to whom he opened his heart'.[29] More than this, went on Newman, he had 'high genius, brimful and overflowing with ideas and views, in him original'. But there was a fragility. The ideas 'were too many and strong even for his bodily strength'.[30] Froude was stricken with tuberculosis.

Ebullient and outspoken, Froude was in many ways opposite to Newman in temperament; they nevertheless became fast friends in the senior common room, and began spending time together outside of the college. Newman had been ordered by his doctor to take exercise, and they often rode out together and competed in daring equestrian jumps. Newman wrote that the attachment developed into 'the closest and most affectionate friendship'.[31]

Froude had been an undergraduate at Oriel from the age of eighteen and an intimate of John Keble, a friendship that had been forged at Keble's parsonage where Froude had spent a long vacation being tutored. Keble, it seemed, saw in Froude, despite his outward going character, a remarkable capacity for spiritual growth and set about encouraging it. After being elected to his fellowship, moreover, Froude's piety deepened after reading his dead mother's journal. It was a document of intense moral self-examination which he began to emulate. His practice of self-mortification and minute self-examination of conscience can be read in the *Remains of the Late Reverend Richard Hurrell Froude*, edited and published by Keble and Newman after his death. Reminiscent of the spirituality of seventeenth-century French Roman Catholic ascetics, the journal exemplifies the growing spiritual mores of the Newman-Keble-Pusey circle.

Froude's journal, anticipating the anorexic anxieties of twentieth century youth, records his fasting regimes in minute detail, his self-congratulation on achieving them, and abject self-castigation for occasional failures.

Looked with greediness to see if there was a goose on the table for dinner: and though what I eat was of the plainest sort, and I took no variety, yet even this was partly the effect of accident, and I certainly rather exceeded in quantity, as I was muzzy and sleepy after dinner … As to my meals, I can say that I was always careful to see that no one else would take a thing before I served myself; and I believe as to the kind of my food, a bit of cold endings of a dab at breakfast, and a scrap of mackerel at dinner, are the only things that diverged from the strict rule of simplicity.[32]

He connects fasting with the need to expunge feelings of pollution and self-disgust. A sense of sexual anxiety is suggested in at least one sermon several years later in which he spoke of the need for 'external purification' and the need to avoid all 'sinful pleasures'. It was necessary, he preached, to acquire the innocence of little children, and 'to regard as filth what they now set their affections on, and to vomit from their minds every pleasant recollection connected with sin'.[33] Froude's obsession with food, fasting, excessive exercise, the desire to feel himself ever a child, low self-esteem, remarkable thinness, and preoccupation with vomiting, suggest a form of bulimia.

There are passages in the journal that contain hints of sexual guilt: 'O Lord', he writes, 'the thoughts which sometimes come into my head are too shocking even to name.'[34] Late in 1826 he confesses to his journal an interior conflict over one of his pupils: 'It seems the fates have thrown us together. I must repress all enthusiastic notions about the event … and above all watch and pray against being led out of the way by the fascination of his society; but rather the steady perseverance in the right course.'[35] Early the following year, his anxieties deepen: 'I stand in my naked filthiness before Thee, whose eyes are purer than to behold iniquity.'[36] A few days later he can write: 'O may the recollection of these dreadful things so fill my soul with deep humility…. Strengthen me … that I may dare to look in the face the hideous filthiness of those ways, in which, for the sins that with open eyes I have acted, Thou has permitted me blindly to stray.'[37] Then again, 'My soul is a troubled and restless thing, haunted by the recollection of past wickedness'.[38]

Froude was at one with Newman not only on the importance of fasting but the necessity of virginity and celibacy. Newman's decision, for a second time, never to marry, as he tells us in the *Apologia*, dates from the period when his intimacy with Froude deepened. There can be no doubt that of all Newman's male friendships, his attachment to Froude found him more loving than loved. With Froude, who nevertheless routinely addressed Newman as 'Dulcissime' (sweetest), it was the other way about. Newman, with Froude's illness in mind, would pen these lines:

And when thine eye surveys,
With fond adoring gaze,
And yearning heart, thy friend –
Love to its grave doth tend.[39]

Meanwhile Froude's intellectual and spiritual influence proved profound. He expounded High Church convictions which encouraged Newman to re-examine his disdain for Rome and the Pope as Anti-Christ. He urged Newman, moreover, to consider the importance of early Church tradition as opposed to the primacy of scripture. Froude's earliest doctrinal influence involved apostolic succession – the unbroken link of Church authority, through the succession of its bishops, from the apostles.

Apart from the Evangelicals, the enemies of Froude's vision of the apostolic Church in England were the 'liberals' – a term with many connotations. There was the liberalism prompted by the French Revolution, which encouraged rationalism, utilitarianism, democracy; there was the liberalism of a loose interpretation of Scripture; and the liberalism that welcomed Catholics and Dissenters into the public life and the universities. But liberalism in Newman's time in Oxford, especially among Oriel's senior dons, involved a tendency to treat the supernatural and God's direct intervention in the world, as in miracles, with a degree of mild scepticism. Oxford's liberalism took a prosaic view of sacred symbolism, with implications for the reverence due to the sacraments, and the Eucharist in particular. For a time Newman saw in this form of liberalism an attractive alternative to Evangelicalism. The influence of Froude, and his reading of the Early Fathers, the writers, saints and theologians of early Christian antiquity, were to provide an antidote.

We have seen how Newman made his first acquaintance with the Early Fathers when he read Joseph Milner's *Church History* as a boy. Newman now found himself drawn increasingly to these texts. When Pusey set off on a trip to Germany, Newman asked would he buy copies for him. Through the early nineteenth century many abandoned editions had been made available following the break up of libraries after the French Revolution. Newman's huge collection of the Fathers, he used to boast, cost him no more than a shilling a volume. He started with Ignatius and Justin, reading them from a Protestant perspective to begin with; which led him, he later admitted, to misconstrue their true significance. But the inevitable and crucial question forming in his mind was this: could one cite the Fathers and the early Christian Councils in support of the claim that the Church of England was solidly within the Church, as described in the Creeds as 'Catholic', or did they not?

By the autumn of 1827 his regime of reading had become so hard and lengthy that his health was suffering. He took a brief break to accompany Robert Wilberforce on a visit to friends in Kent. While there he wrote the poem 'Snapdragon. A Riddle', comparing his bachelor life to the climbing flower on the walls of Trinity:

Nature's vast and varied field
Braver flowers than me will yield,
Bold in form and rich in hue,
Children of a purer dew;
Smiling lips and winning eyes
Meet for earthly paradise …
May it be! Then well might I
In College cloister live and die.[40]

As the weeks passed he found himself in a 'low fever', not helped by his exertions to rescue his aunt Elizabeth from financial ruin. While conducting interviews and invigilating at Oxford's examination schools, he suffered a mild nervous breakdown. His own disastrous final examinations combined with the news that Copleston was to depart from Oriel to become Bishop of Llandaff, resulted in a sequence of nightmares. One Sunday in November he 'drooped' and felt 'the blood collect in my head'. The next day, he wrote, '[I] found my memory and mind gone, when examining a candidate for the first class … and was obliged to leave the Schools in the middle of the day.' Leeches were placed on his temples . He had a 'twisting of the brain, of the eyes. I felt my head inside was made up of parts. I could write verses pretty well, but I could not *count*'.[41] He did not return to the examination rooms, but his trials were far from over.

DEATH OF SISTER MARY

In the New Year of 1828 Newman's youngest sister, Mary, aged nineteen, died suddenly, probably of appendicitis. Pious, yet vivacious, she had been learning by heart the poems in Keble's *The Christian Year*. Newman wrote in his journal: 'O my dearest sister Mary, O my sister, my sister, I do feel from the bottom of my heart that it is all right – I see, I know it to be, in God's good Providence, the best thing for all of us; I do not, I have not, in the least repined – I would not have it otherwise – but I feel sick, I must cease writing.' [42]

As the weeks passed he wrote to Jemima that it would 'be desirable to write down some memoranda generally concerning [Mary] … Alas, memory does not remain vivid.' He adds: 'To talk of her thus in the third person, and in all the common business and conversation of life to allude to her as now out of the way and insensible to what we are doing (as is indeed the case) is to me the most distressing circumstance perhaps attending our loss.'[43]

Here we find Newman, a man of deep and refined sentiment, yet always the writer, struggling to put experience, memory, the loved one into words. Five months on, still grieving, he would write of riding out to the village of Cuddesdon near Oxford, thinking of Mary:

I wish it were possible for words to put down those indefinite vague and withal subtle feelings which quite pierce the soul and make it sick. Dear Mary seems embodied in every tree and behind every hill. What a veil and curtain this world of sense is! beautiful but still a veil.

He wrote a poem for Jemima, which he sent on that day: 'would they came up to my feelings', he remarked:

This is the room, and this the bed,
    Whence at the awful word
Of high command once upward sped
    A saint to meet her Lord.

These curtains closing round her death
    Last met her failing eye
This pillow laid my head beneath
    Heard her last gentle sigh.[44]

The final verses would find their echo in a poem he would write near forty years hence: 'The Dream of Gerontius.' There are allusions, moreover, to a Catholic sense of faith in angels and sainthood:

Till that new world's first dawning bright
    When faith shall have its end,
Heaven's angel ladder beam in light
    And saints to heaven ascend.

Meanwhile, where last on earth she trod,
    This grace to faith is given,
There to discern the house of God
    There find the gate of heaven.[45]

He would grieve for her all his life. Aged 76 he would write: 'I have as vivid feelings of love, tenderness, and sorrow, when I think of dear Mary , as ever I had since her death JHN.'[46] Even aged eighty the very thought of her would bring tears to his eyes.

As with many of his relationships, within and outside of the family, he had betrayed hints of self-reference in his professed fraternal love. On her previous birthday he had sent his good wishes not to Mary direct, but via Harriet: 'I love her very much; but I will not say (as she once said to me) I love her better than she loves me.'[47] He may well have remembered that comment and felt remorse for it. Following her death he had sent a pedestrian poem about her to Harriet, with a self-referential reflection that was not uncharacteristic: 'It goes to my heart to think that dear Mary herself, in her enthusiastic love of me, would so like them, could she see them, because they are mine. May I be patient. It is so difficult to realize what one believes, and to make these trials, as they are intended, real blessings.'[48]

ROLE OF COLLEGE TUTOR

If the fellows of Oriel were famous for their intellectualism, many of the high-born students were notorious for their dissolute behaviour. In addition to getting drunk nightly, riding to hounds, and gambling, Oriel students were keen boxers and wrestlers; not at all sports that Newman would have relished. Matches were held several nights a week in college rooms under the supervision of a prize fighter, known as 'the Flying Tailor'. One undergraduate, James Howard Harris, who became the Earl of Malmsbury and Lord Privy Seal, has left an impression of Newman's trials in the classroom with these sons of the gentry: 'He used to allow his class to torment him with the most helpless resignation; every kind of mischievous trick was, to our shame, played upon him – such as cutting his bell-rope, and at lectures making the table advance gradually till he was jammed into a corner. He remained quite impassive, and painfully tolerant.'[49]

With Hurrell Froude, and another fellow tutor, William Wilberforce (son of the famous anti-slave trade campaigner Samuel Wilberforce) Newman sought to improve the educational and spiritual tone of the college. He aimed to reorganize the tutorial relationship so as to make it more personal, and pastoral. According to Thomas Mozley, 'The tuition revolutionized an exacter regard to the character and special gifts of each undergraduate, and closer relation between him and his tutor'. No doubt with thoughts of his own wayward brother in mind, Newman insisted that the ideal tutor would stand 'in the place of a father, or an elder and affectionate brother'.[50] Tutors, according to Newman's policy, would spend their time teaching serious students, and caring for their moral and religious direction, in small groups or one to one; whereas the young grandee socialites would receive their education in large, occasional lecture groups.

One such aristo, Sir Charles Murray, was to leave a reminiscence that tells us as much about Murray and his Gentleman Commoner cronies as about Newman, while giving further evidence of the behaviour of the young Oriel gentlemen of class:

We were a merry set of youngsters, fond of singing late into the night over suppers. The songs were not classical, but, I am ashamed to say, generally very noisy. They disturbed Newman, who liked quiet; but instead of coming himself and asking us to be earlier and quieter, he sent a porter, whom we sent to the devil.[51]

Newman no doubt sensibly realized that had he tried to discipline them he would have been sent to the devil too.

It would be anachronistic to view Newman's reform of tutorials as the policy of a sanctimonious martinet. The colleges were religious foundations, and most of the tutors were clergymen. When he was offered the position of tutor in 1826, he resigned his curacy at St Clement's and his role at Alban Hall. He saw his tutorial role as in part at least the fulfilment of his ordination vow: as a 'species of pastoral care', as 'a great undertaking', and with the risk of certain temptations. He wrote to his sister Harriet: 'There is always the danger of the love of literary pursuits assuming too prominent a place in the thoughts of a College Tutor, or his viewing his situation merely as a secular office, a means of a future provision when he leaves College'.[52] Four weeks into the job he wrote a memorandum: '*Unless* I find that opportunities occur of doing spiritual good to those over whom I am placed, it will become a grave question whether I *ought* to continue in the Tuition.'[53]

Provost Hawkins, who was elected at the point at which Newman's reforms began to bite in 1828, was anxious not to alienate the young gentry. He was not pleased with Newman's attempts to rewrite the teaching policies of the college. Hawkins was insistent, moreover, that the role of tutor should be largely secular. The conflict over policy ended with Hawkins declining to assign students to Newman and his reformer colleagues.

By default therefore Newman had more time for the Fathers, and he was spurred on by the encouragement of the editors of the *Theological Library* series to write a book on the early Councils of the Church. His former students (the serious and assiduous ones) and supportive fellows banded together to purchase more volumes of the Fathers, 36 in all, which were now arrayed on the shelves of his college rooms. In the event, he restricted the scope of his first book, published in July 1832, to the Council of Nicea, with the title *The Arians of the Fourth Century*.

Nicea constituted an outstanding instance of the Church's need to clarify doctrine for the sake of converts to Christianity. The early Church, he argued, had kept back the teaching of the Our Father, the Creed, and crucial doctrines such as the nature of the Trinity, until a spiritual discipline had been inculcated: a *disciplina arcane*. Newman had in his sights contemporary Evangelicalism and 'much of that mischievous fanaticism' that 'at present abounds from the vanity of men, who think that they can explain the sublime doctrines and exuberant promises of the Gospel, before they have yet learned to know themselves and to discern the holiness of God'. [54]

Arianism, went on Newman, was equivalent to Wesleyan style Evangelicalism which put Christians and those seeking to become Christians (known as catechumens) on an equal footing, allowing women to preach, teach and baptize. Indeed, among the 'present perils' of Anglicanism, he found 'a marked resemblance to those of the fourth century … of an Heretical Power enthralling [the Church], exerting a varied influence and a usurped claim in the appointment of her functionaries, and interfering with the management of her internal affairs'. [55] That heretical power, moreover, in his view, was an enemy within the Church, rather than outside it.

CHAPTER 5

To the Mediterranean

'Oh that Rome were not Rome; but I seem to see as clear as day that a union with her is *impossible*. She is the cruel Church – asking of us impossibilities, excommunicating us for disobedience, and now watching and exulting over our approaching overthrow.'

J. H. NEWMAN LETTER TO HIS SISTER JEMIMA, 11 APRIL 1833

Of Newman's six hundred or more published sermons, more than half were preached before 1832 while he was a young Anglican minister at Littlemore and in St Mary's Church, Oxford. During a preaching ministry that spanned more than five decades there would be developments in his preaching both in content and style at each stage of his life. His early homilies, contained in the first three volumes of his *Parochial Sermons*, were mainly preoccupied with individual spiritual growth, and were strikingly severe in tone and language.

He wrote his sermons, and read them word for word. He did not declaim or gesture. His most effective oratorical device was an occasional dramatic pause. He read calmly, quietly, in simple language, rarely looking up from the page before him. William Wilberforce would recollect:

[He] never moved anything but his head. His hands were literally not seen, from the beginning to the end. The sermon began in a calm musical voice, the key slightly rising as it went on: by-and-by the preacher warmed with his subject; it seemed as if his very soul and body glowed with sternly-suppressed emotion. There were times, when in the midst of the most thrilling passages he would pause, without dropping his voice, for a moment which seemed long, before he uttered with gathered force and solemnity a few weighty words. The very tones of his voice seemed as if they were something more than his own.[1]

Wilberforce went on to describe the 'breathless' and 'expectant attention' of the congregation. He described the 'gas-light, just at the left hand of the pulpit, lowered that the preacher might not be dazzled'. The congregation was invariably packed, many of them 'standing in the half-darkness under the gallery'.

Newman deplored earnest preaching, and made this interesting comment when he was in his fifties:

We may of course work ourselves up into a pretence, nay, into a paroxysm, of earnestness; as we may chafe our cold hands till they are warm. But when we cease chafing, we lose the warmth again; on the contrary, let the sun come out and strike us with his beams, and we need no artificial chafing to be warm. The hot words, then, and energetic gestures of a preacher, taken by themselves, are just as much signs of earnestness as rubbing the hands or flapping the arms together are signs of warmth.[2]

According to many of his listeners, Newman's developing sense of charisma owed much to the impression that he was living according to the words he preached. We have seen in the opening chapter the effect he had on his congregation. Matthew Arnold's famous description speaks of 'words and thoughts which were a religious music, – subtle, sweet, mournful'. The beguiling musicality of his voice matched the elegant cadences of his prose.

Richard Church, friend of Newman and later Dean of St Paul's, wrote of the early sermons that they preached the 'Holiness necessary for future Blessedness':

They showed the strong reaction … against the poverty, softness, restlessness, worldliness, the blunted and impaired sense of truth, which reigned with little check in the recognised fashions of professing Christianity; the want of depth both of thought and feeling; the strange blindness to the real sternness, nay the austerity of the New Testament.[3]

In these sermons of the late 1820s and early 1830s he stressed the hardship of the Christian life, the difficulty of obeying the call to perfection, while warning against both complacency and Evangelical enthusiasm. There are all too many Christians, Newman said, 'who have rejected the austerity aspect of the Gospel, considering it enough to be benevolent, courteous, candid'. Newman's youthful sermons insisted on the small daily acts of consistent self-denial and self-discipline. He believed that the holiness of the most eminent saints was a result of their consistency, which he saw as form of religious obedience:

Nothing is more difficult than to be disciplined and regular in our religion. It is very easy to be religious by fits and starts, and to keep up our feelings by artificial stimulants; but regularity seems to trammel us, and we become impatient.[4]

It was not necessary to indulge in self-wounding mortification, he insisted. We are not called to 'literally bear Christ's Cross', or to live on 'locusts and wild honey'. The Christian obligation is to carry the everyday burdens that come our way, such as overcoming temptation to anger. He was no Calvinist, however. His spirituality was both that of Good Friday and of Easter Day: suffering tempered by joy and hope.

The Holy Spirit works through human nature, he declared. That is why persistent examination of conscience is crucial for growth in spirituality: 'For it is in proportion as we search our hearts and understand our own nature, that we understand what is meant by an Infinite Governor and Judge.'[5] In this way it might be possible to conquer 'deceitfulness of the heart'. Pride, hypocrisy, affectation, 'unreality', and lack of simplicity are major drawbacks from progress in holiness. Feelings and words must be matched by action; otherwise our lives are a mere fiction – like a novel, he observed. Those who speak of love without practising it in their every day lives and relationships are spiritually dislocated:

The real love of man *must* depend on practice, and therefore, must begin by exercising itself on our friends around us, otherwise it will have no existence.[6]

Newman at times addressed his mainly student congregation on the special temptations of youth, when good habits should be formed and bad habits eradicated. He warned of the assumption that conversion of life can be put off to be dealt with later by the power of free will. For bad habits 'clog' the exercise of the will. The characteristic toughness of his preaching can be savoured in the following passage on the importance of timely repentance:

I do not speak of the dreadful presumption of such a mode of quieting conscience (though many persons really use it who do not speak the words out, or are aware that they act upon it), but, merely, of the ignorance it evidences concerning our moral condition, and our power of willing and doing....

So very difficult is obedience, so hardly won is every step in our Christian course, so sluggish and inert our corrupt nature, that I would have a man disbelieve he can do one jot or tittle beyond what he had already done; refrain from borrowing aught on the hope of the future, however good a security for it he seems to be able to show; and never take his good feelings and wishes in pledge for one single untried deed. Nothing but *past* acts are the vouchers for *future*.[7]

The metaphor conjured from the world of banking – borrowing, futures, securities, pledges, vouchers – would have come with feeling from the son of a man whose bank had gone under.

Sin is not only a matter of outward actions and deeds, but of private thoughts too. 'Evil thoughts', he declared, 'do us no harm if recognized; if repelled, if protested against by the indignation and self-reproach of the mind. It is when we do not discern them, when we admit them, when we cherish them, that they ripen into principles.' Hence he preached the existence of the individual soul, impressing on his congregation that sense he had felt since boyhood of the contrast between inner and outer worlds.

In these early sermons on personal strivings for holiness, Newman frequently employed the language of guilt, sin, repentance, passions, the Devil, temptation, seductions of the world, and even 'hell fire'. The imagery is intense, yet disciplined: sin acts like a 'poisoned garment' which eats into the flesh: the Devil's temptations inflame 'the wounds and scars of past sins healed'.

J. A. Froude, Hurrell's brother, would praise Newman's genius for giving the impression that he was looking into the hearts of each member of his young congregation:

While so much of our talk is so unreal, our own selves, our own risings, fallings, aspirings, resolutions, misgivings, these are real enough to us; these are our hidden life, our sanctuary of our own mysteries … It was into these that N's power of insight was so remarkable. I believe no young man had ever heard him preach without fancying that some one had been betraying his own history, and the sermon was aimed specially at him. It was likely that, while he had possession so complete of what we did know about ourselves, we should take his word for what we did not.[8]

Yet preaching cannot be an end in itself, he counseled; it is a prelude to the Church's salvation – a theme that he would develop, expand, and take in new directions, in the next stage of his Oxford ministry. Preaching, he insisted, is no substitute for the sacraments – 'means and pledges of grace, – keys which open the treasure-house of mercy'. Through the influence of Hurrell Froude, he was beginning to nurture a special devotion to the Eucharist. And he had a growing regard for the role of the Virgin Mary, also a token of Froude's influence. On the Feast of the Annunciation, 1832, he preached a sermon in praise of Mary that drew criticism for its warmth towards the Mother of God:

Who can estimate the holiness and perfection of her, who was chosen to be the Mother of Christ? … For truly, she is raised above the condition of sinful beings, though she was a sinner; she is brought near to God, yet is but creature … We cannot combine in our thought of her, all we should ascribe with all we should withhold.

JOURNEY SOUTH

Late in 1832 Newman preached a sermon he entitled 'Wilfulness the Sin of Saul',[9] in which he insisted on the role of revealed as opposed to philosophical religion: 'Revelation provides us with an important instrument for chastening and moulding our moral character', he said, but 'the so-called philosophical Christians' want to rid themselves 'altogether of the shackles of a Revelation.' The sermon was delivered against the background of the passing of the Reform Act in Britain's parliament, demonstrating for Newman the relentless advance of secularism and relativism. As he would write in the *Apologia*, 'Great events were happening at home and abroad, which brought out into form and passionate expression the various beliefs which had so gradually been winning their way into my mind'.[10] The Reform Act aimed to increase and broaden the British electorate, diversifying representation in parliament and creating new constituencies in the rapidly expanding industrial cities. There were other reforms within the Act, including bids to eliminate bribery of voters and the existence of 'pocket boroughs', constituencies that were 'owned' by great landowners, giving the aristocracy the right to control representation in the House of Commons. But Newman, like many Anglican priests and bishops, had opposed the Act for ecclesiological rather than political reasons. Since parliament ultimately governed the Church of England, the enlargement of representation signalled a House of Commons open to candidates of any creed and of none. Meanwhile the Whig government was set to reform the established Church – a prospect Newman believed would lead to the final destruction of Anglican claims to apostolic continuity and authority. None of this concerned Dissenters, of course, but even clergy of the Church of England, Newman maintained, appeared unaware of the disastrous implications: 'What is most painful', he would write to his aunt, 'is that the clergy are so utterly ignorant on the subject. We have no *theological* education.' [11]

At a point when he felt drawn to enter the fray, however, he took an extended break from his Oxford duties. Hurrell Froude, with advanced tuberculosis of the lungs, believed that another winter in England would prove the death of him. He and his father, Archdeacon Froude, had decided on wintering abroad, and they asked Newman to join them. The journey would change his life.

On 8 December they boarded the *Hermes* at Falmouth. With the prospect of several months travel, a weight seemed to lift from his shoulders. His talent for lively observation was about to enjoy free rein. He wrote to his mother: 'Fowls, Ducks, Turkeys, all alive and squatted down under the legs of beef, hampers, and vegetables. One unfortunate Duck got away, and a chase ensued – I should have liked to have let him off, but the poor fool did not know how to use his fortune and instead of making for the shore, kept quacking with absurd vehemence close to us.' [12]

They saw Portugal from out at sea. At Cadiz they took on passengers, but were unable to land. They arrived in Gibraltar on Monday, 18 December, and after a day in quarantine Newman set foot for the first time on 'foreign land'. They were in Malta on Christmas Day, but stayed on board because of a cholera scare, reaching Patras in Greece by the New Year. He relaxed into the role of tourist: he noted the traditional dress worn by men, Greek coffee, Orthodox churches, Turkish confectionary (honey, otto of roses, almonds), and the wine of Ithaca. On to Messina and Palermo, Newman was enthralled with a journey by mule to Segesta: 'From the moment I saw Sicily, I kept saying to myself "This is Sicily".' He longed to breathe it in, 'as one smells again and again at a sweet flower'. [13]

In Naples, his Anglican sensibilities were offended by pictures of the souls in Purgatory and other 'pagan' items of 'popular and exoteric religion'. He was aghast at the universal habit of spitting, even among ladies of fashion, and on one occasion witnessed a priest spitting 'at altar in the most sacred part of the service'.

It was in Naples that he heard news of the plan to abolish ten dioceses of the Church of Ireland (the established extension in Ireland of the Church of England), at the same time levying taxes on bishoprics, and rich parishes. The proposal had been written into the draft of an act of parliament known as the Church Temporalities Bill. Up to this time Church revenues had been extracted from the Irish population, who were mainly of course Roman Catholic. Where would it end? He wrote to his mother. 'We have just heard the Irish Church Reform Bill – well done my blind Premier, confiscate and rob, till, like Samson, you pull down the political structure on your own head, tho' without his deliberate purpose and good cause!'[14]

Arriving finally in Rome, he wrote to one of his pupils this remarkable first impression with its metaphor of separated body and soul:

We arrived at this wonderful place only Saturday last … the effect of every part is so vast and overpowering – there is such an air of greatness and repose cast over the whole, and, independent of what one knows from history, there are such traces of long sorrow and humiliation, suffering, punishment and decay, that one has a mixture of feelings, partly such as those with which one would approach a corpse, and partly those which would be excited by the sight of the spirit which had left it. It brings to my mind Jeremiah's words in the Lamentations, when Jerusalem, or (sometimes) the prophet, speaks as the smitten of God.[15]

His thoughts, still pervaded by a Protestant perspective, continued to run on the corruptions of the Church of Rome, intermixed with forebodings for the Church back home: 'It is a beautiful flower run to seed … I am impressed with a sad presentiment, as if the gift of truth, when once lost, was lost for ever. And so the Christian world is gradually becoming barren and effete, as land which has been worked out and has become sand. We have lasted longer than the South, but we too are going, as it would seem.'

He did the round of the churches and ruins. He was astonished at the splendid sight of St Peter's illuminated, and was enraptured by the Raphael paintings on a visit to the Vatican museum. He was tempted to consider whether the Churches of Rome and England could unite, but decided that it was impossible as things stood. 'A union with Rome, while it is what it is, is impossible; it is a dream.' This did not mean that he could not nourish admiration of individual Roman Catholics: 'As to the individual member of the cruel church, who can but love and feel for them?'[16]

He came to admire an individual Catholic clergyman in the person of Nicholas Wiseman, Rector of the Venerable English College which he visited with Froude. The three discussed prospects for greater union between the English and Roman Churches, but Wiseman himself was not sanguine. He could see little progress unless the Church of England accepted the decrees of the Council of Trent, which had set out the principles of the Counter-Reformation. Nevertheless, perhaps sensing that his two visitors had potential for 'coming over', he 'courteously expressed a wish' that they might find their way back to Rome, or stay longer. Newman recollected later that he had replied, by way of expressing his regrets, that they had 'work at home'. Union with Rome, he concluded at the time, would remain a 'dream'.

SICILY AND ILLNESS

The Froudes departed for Marseilles in early April, but Newman decided to travel back to Sicily via Naples alone. The trip had found him ambivalent about his travelling companions. Much as he loved Hurrell, he cherished control of his own solitude. There had been an occasion on the journey when he had written of himself as being in the constant company of 'strangers'. Yet, on parting with the stricken Hurrell, Newman may well have felt a pang of emotion. In the previous year in England, he had taken Hurrell's hand on one such parting and 'looked into his face with great affection'. Later, in Sicily, he would write that verse of extraordinary feeling – 'fond adoring gaze' – with echoes of another parting look.

He saw his initiative to travel alone as an act of crucial self-fulfilment. There had been something of the 'grand tour' about their trip so far, something too of the classical scholar's exploration of antiquities. But Newman realised that his desire to return to Sicily was fairly located in Romantic yearnings – of creative and imaginative renewal, which he must experience alone.

It will be a vision for my whole life; and, though I should not choose, I am not sorry to go alone, in order, as Wordsworth would say, to commune with high nature.[17]

And yet he was not entirely alone; he took, as behoved an English gentleman, a servant in the form of Gennaro, a Neapolitan who had served on board the *Victory* at the Battle of Trafalgar, and had been in service for some years with an English family. They landed in Messina off an English sailing brig, hired mules and muleteer, and set off into the interior.

Sicily was 'Eden', and the view from Taormina was more than anything he 'had conceived possible'.

It realized all one had read of in books of the perfection of scenery – a deep valley – brawling streams – beautiful trees – but description is nothing – the sea was heard in the distance. I felt for the first time in my life with my eyes open that I must be better and more religious, if I lived there ... [18]

Yet down-to-earth reality was intervening in the form of blisters, sleepless nights, filthy lodgings, hunger, and fleas. As his journey progressed bad weather, discomforts, and poor food, began to tell on him. He became feverish, and with the fever he pondered his character – in particular his self-willed nature. Then he contracted typhoid. He was bled by a local doctor, with whom he had communicated in Latin, and certainly should have died had it not been for the trusty Gennaro, who remained by his side day and night despite his own hardships.

He recounted his delirium in simple, powerful language, while suggesting a sense of destiny, which he professes to find incomprehensible:

My servant thought that I was dying, and begged for my last directions. I gave them, as he wished; but I said, 'I shall not die'. I repeated, 'I shall not die, for I have not sinned against light, I have not sinned against light.' I never have been able to make out what I meant.

I got to Castro-Giovanni, and was laid up there for nearly three weeks. Towards the end of May I left for Palermo, taking three days for the journey. Before starting from my inn in the morning of May 26th or 27th, I sat down on my bed, and began to sob violently. My servant, who had acted as my nurse, asked what ailed me. I could only answer him, 'I have a work to do in England'. [19]

Newman would record that during the worst of his illness he could not bear Gennaro to be absent from the room even for five minutes. Whenever he went out Newman would call out: 'Gen-na-rooo.'

After the crisis had passed he began to enjoy the scenery again, but he was now homesick for England and for Oxford. In retrospect, Newman wondered whether Satan himself had not sought to destroy him in Sicily in order to frustrate his destiny and vocation.

As he waited in Palermo for a boat to start his journey back to England he wrote some of the poems that would appear in the volume of verse to be called *Lyra Apostolica*, by members of his circle in Oxford. He also wrote a curiously ambivalent verse occasioned by his visits to the city's churches where he had sought respite from the 'city's sultry streets':

O that thy creed were sound!
For thou dost sooth the heart, Thou Church of Rome,
By thy unwearied watch and varied round
Of service, in thy Saviour's holy home. [20]

At sea, he wrote what would become one of the most famous hymns in the English language: 'Lead kindly Light', which he entitled 'The Pillar of the Cloud' – an allusion from Exodus to the guidance of God to the people of Israel as they wandered in the desert. 'Neither the pillar of cloud by day nor the pillar of fire by night left its place in front of the people.' As the Newman scholar Ian Ker writes:

The words which are most characteristic of Newman come at the end of the first stanza: 'I do not ask to see/the distant scene, – one step enough for me.' It was a thought which was always to be at the heart of his spirituality, namely, that light is only given to us gradually bit by bit, but that we are always given enough to see what we have to do next, and that when we have taken that step which has been lit up for us, we shall see the next, but only the next, step illuminated – while to attempt to see several steps ahead or the end of the path is not only futile but also self-defeating.[21]

The hymn embodies a profound personal resolution and insight: the abandonment of his own will, and surrender to God's will. It would become the watchword of his future spiritual life: '… we are in God's hands, and must be content to do our work day by day, as He puts it before us, without attempting to understand or to anticipate His purposes.'[22] Then again:

The Providence of God has been wonderful with me all through my life…. Everyone doubtless is so watched over, and tended by Him that at the last day, whether he be saved or not, he will confess that nothing could have been done for him more than had been actually done; and everyone will feel his own history as special and singular.[23]

The illness and the consequent second conversion would remain with him for the rest of his life. 'It made me', he would write, 'a Christian.'

The Mediterranean trip also seemed to have awakened and expanded in Newman a capacity for perceiving in literary terms the sensuous concrete, an ability to keep his eye steadily focused on immediate specific objects. It was in Sicily that he observed with exquisite sensitivity the gentleness of Gennaro's massive finger-tips while the man was applying vinegar to his nostrils. At sea, describing the noises above his cabin, he could pen passages of impressively refined observation, his senses and imagination fully engaged:

It is like half a hundred watchmen's rattles … mixed with the squeaking of several Brobdingnag pigs, while the water dashes dash dash against the sides. Then overhead the loud foot of the watch, who goes on tramping up and down the whole night more or less. Then (in the morning) the washing of the deck … Rush comes an engine pipe on the floor – ceases, is renewed, flourishes about, rushes again – then suddenly 1/2 a dozen brooms, wish, wash, wish, wash, scrib, scrub, roaring and scratching alternately. Then the heavy flump, flumps of the huge dabbing cloth which is meant to dry the deck in a measure instead of a towel or duster.[24]

The Mediterranean interlude may well have been a crucial prelude to his developing skill in clothing abstract ratiocinations with precise and powerful metaphors.

Newman arrived in Oxford on Tuesday, 9 July 1833. The following Sunday, July 14, as Newman would write in the *Apologia*, 'Mr Keble preached the Assize Sermon in the University Pulpit. It was published under the title "National Apostasy". I have ever considered and kept the day, as the start of the religious movement of 1833.'[25] The movement was the Oxford Movement.

CHAPTER 6

The Oxford Movement

'Every feeling which interferes with God's sovereignty
in our hearts, is of an idolatrous nature ...'

J. H. NEWMAN LETTER TO BISHOP RICHARD BAGOT, 29 MARCH 1841

'Scoundrels must be called scoundrels!'[1] That's how Newman's friend, the pious John Keble, denounced in 1833 those he believed were destroying the Church of England, the established religion of the nation. Preaching in St Mary's University Church on the biennial occasion of the opening of the Oxford Assizes, the local law courts, he seized the opportunity to launch an attack on what he called the 'National Apostasy'. Like so many would-be religious reformers and revivalists, before and since, Keble insisted that the nation's religious decline must be reversed with the renewal of each individual human heart:

... the surest way to uphold or restore our endangered Church, will be for each of her anxious children, in his own place and station, to resign himself more thoroughly to his God and Saviour.[2]

But he had wider political and ecclesiastical concerns, familiar among the devout and orthodox of every Faith in the modern period in Europe: how to combat the effects of encroaching secularism, doubt, and indifference. For years he had deplored the lukewarm practices of Anglican clergy and laity. Bishops, he complained, were all too often selected with regard to secular and political considerations; clergy were more intent on leading comfortable lives than tending their flocks.

The political background to Keble's sermon was the perception that the established Church was increasingly in the grip of Dissenters, agnostics, atheists, and even Roman Catholics. The Tory Government, Keble asserted, had in 1828 forfeited its right to influence the Church by repealing the Test Acts, so allowing dissenters to enter public office. The following year the Catholic Relief Act was passed, allowing Catholics into Parliament. Then came the Reform Act of 1832, creating new constituencies in industrial areas and allowing broader categories to vote than property owners. And now the Church of Ireland episcopate was about to be taxed, turned upside down, and decimated.

Opposition to electoral reform appeared on the face of it a reaction to the liberalizing aspirations of an expanding industrial society; but there were deeper, institutional insecurities nagging within the ranks of the more devout clergy. The Church of England seethed with conflicting affiliations: 'High', 'Low', 'High and Dry', 'Broad', 'Evangelical'. The Low Church, cherishing the legacy of Puritanism, adhered strictly to the Thirty-Nine Articles defining the essential Protestantism of an Anglican in contrast to a Roman Catholic. For example, the Articles rejected the 'fond' belief in Purgatory, and scorned transubstantiation, the Roman Catholic belief that the bread and wine change 'substantially' into the flesh and blood of the living Christ. The High Church, flirting with Romish practices, had inclined towards Catholic liturgy, incense, vestments, miracles, veneration of the Virgin Mary and the saints. The Broad Church welcomed all shades of opinion and practice, risking the charge of relativism. Meanwhile diverse Evangelical movements espoused individual feeling, primacy of Bible reading, and preaching, rather than sacraments, priesthood, and the divinely ordained authority of bishops.

Keble's sermon resonated feebly in the country at large, but it galvanized the circle of Oxford clerical dons, and former dons, that included Newman, Pusey, Keble, Henry Wilberforce, and Hurrell Froude. There were excited meetings near and far from Oxford. Groups were formed, and yet not a 'party' as such (nor any association, as Newman put it, 'in which a majority bound a minority'). Eventually they called themselves 'Friends of the Church' and determined to publish a series of campaigning pamphlets known collectively as 'Tracts': hence they would come to be known as the Tractarians. The first, entitled *Tract for the Times*, just three pages in length, was dedicated to 'my England, ordained by the Holy Spirit and by the laying-on of hands'. While attacking the intrusion of the government in the ambit of the Church, it insisted that the bishops owed their authority not to the King but to the unbroken succession that went back to the first apostles, and to Jesus himself. The anonymous author was John Henry Newman. The Oxford Movement was launched. The closest historic precedent for such a hiatus in the Church of England had been the group of non-juring bishops and clergy who refused to swear allegiance to William of Orange following the 'Glorious Revolution' in 1688. Those refuseniks of the late seventeenth and early eighteenth centuries had speculated on the notion of the Church of England as a local branch of the Catholic Church.

Newman was a whirl of activity. His *Arians of the Fourth Century* was published, and the first volume of *Parochial and Plain Sermons*. Now he was writing on the apostolic succession for the *British Magazine*, now on church discipline for the *Record*. He was frequently on the road, drumming up Tractarian support; yet hurrying back to Oxford to hold daily services. At the same time, he was becoming pastorally rigorous, and getting a name for it. He was derided in the national press for refusing to marry a certain Miss Jubber and her betrothed. The unfortunate lady could not produce a baptismal certificate;

Newman refused to marry them. A report of the episode published in the *Weekly Dispatch* (6 July) gives an impression of the tensions generated by Newman's rigorism:

The Vicar of St Mary the Virgin parish Oxford, in his hyper-anxiety to signalize his zeal against dissent and in favor of 'orthodoxy' refused on Tuesday last to marry a young couple of very respectable connexions in that City solely because the blooming to be Bride had not been christened, and was in the rev: bigot's phraseology an *outcast*, the matrimonial knot was however tied directly afterwards by the more tolerant and less pharisaical minister of a neighbouring parish-church, and the happy pair were very properly relieved from the cruel disappointment which threatened them.[3]

The Bishop of Oxford directed Newman in future to marry the unbaptised, laying the responsibility on his own episcopal conscience.

As the movement developed and thrived, the members set out to make good a deficiency in devotional works in print. They recommended or republished with new prefaces works by Anglican writers such as Christopher Sutton's *Godly Meditations upon the Most Holy Sacrament*, and Thomas Wilson's *Sacra Privata*, which encouraged silent prayer, or meditation, and examination of conscience. Newman had been reading the *Imitation of Christ* since 1822, but he now turned to the seventeenth-century bishop Lancelot Andrewes' book of meditations as suited to the spiritual renewal of the times. Newman translated the text from the Latin and published it as a tract. The simplicity of the prayers, sourced in Scripture, and the recommendation to pray at regular intervals of the day, seven times between rising and retiring, indicated devotional resonances from Roman Catholic monastic and priestly practices. It would go through several editions to 1873, and Newman would always keep a copy by him.

Meanwhile a parliamentary bill to admit Dissenters into the universities had been passing through both Houses. Newman and the religious conservatives in Oxford had been energetic in their opposition. As it happened, the bill failed in the Lords. The issue returned the following year when Oxford University's Convocation met to vote on a liberal motion that would allow university entrants merely to declare their conformity to the Church of England (as opposed to declaring subscription to the Thirty-Nine Articles). Again it was defeated by the conservatives. Among those present was Hurrell Froude. It was to be his last public act in Oxford. Soon afterwards he returned home to Devon, his TB having worsened. Nothing had worked, neither wintering in the Mediterranean nor spending time on the island of Barbados in the Caribbean.

Froude died at home on 28 February 1836, aged thirty-three. Newman was grief-stricken. He wrote to his undergraduate friend Bowden: 'He has been so very dear to me, that it is an effort to me to reflect on my own thoughts about him. I can never have a greater loss, looking on for the whole of life – for he was to me, and he was likely to be ever, in the same degree of continual familiarity which I enjoyed with yourself in our Undergraduate days.' [4] The reflection reveals sentiments that could be construed as youthful close companionship – 'continual familiarity … in our Undergraduate days'. And yet, there was that stanza to Froude, when Newman had written of his 'adoring gaze' and 'yearning heart'. Choosing a book from Froude's library, Newman's hand hovered over a copy of Butler's *Analogy*, then he chose his dead friend's Roman Breviary which he would treasure for the rest of his life. 'I took it', he would write in the *Apologia*, 'studied it, wrote my Tract from it [75, June 24, 1836], and have it on my table in constant use till this day'. [5]

The death of Froude was not the only loss Newman bore that year. His mother died after an illness that had undermined her very personality. He took it with fortitude:

My dearest Mother is taken from us [he wrote to his aunt Elizabeth]. If you knew how dreadfully she has suffered in mind, and how little her wanderings left her like herself, you would feel, as we do, that it really is a release. Who would have thought it! Every thing is strange in this world – every thing mysterious. Nothing but sure faith can bring us through. [6]

Then, within a year, both his surviving sisters, Jemima and Harriet married his friends – the brothers Tom and John Mozley.

'CREDO IN NEWMANUM'

By the time of Hurrell Froude's death, Newman was entering the prime of his Oxford charisma. J. F. Russell, visiting Oxford from Cambridge in 1837, summarized his impression of Newman's reputation:

all the men of talent in the University come to hear him, although at the loss of their dinner. His triumph over the *mental* empire of Oxford was said to be complete! [7, 8]

Newman's tracts, combined with his preaching, exerted a powerful double effect. As Richard Church put it: 'While men were reading and talking about the Tracts, they were hearing the Sermons; and in the sermons they heard the living meaning, and reason, and bearing of the Tracts, their ethical affinities, their moral standard.' [9] Contemporary accounts and recollections returned repeatedly to the moral and spiritual impact of Newman's preaching rather than its doctrinal arguments. Church again noted the appeal 'to conscience with such directness and force … a passionate and sustained earnestness after a high moral rule, seriously realized in conduct'. [10] Arthur Penryn Stanley, writing in the *Edinburgh Review* ('The Oxford School', April 1845), comparing Newman to Thomas Arnold of Rugby, thought that Newman's congregations were drawn by 'chiefly the grasp of ethical precepts, the appeals to conscience, the sincere conviction of the value of purity and generosity'.[11]

James Froude, Hurrell's historian brother, wrote an impression of the critical targets of Newman's sermons at this time:

A foolish Church, chattering, parrot-like, old notes, of which it had forgot the meaning … selfishness alike recognized practically as the rule of conduct, and faith in God, in man, in virtue, exchanged for faith in the belly, in fortunes, carriages, lazy sofas, and cushioned pews.[12]

Newman was fired up. He deplored the decline of piety and devotion, the physical decay of many churches. People, he said, came into church for gossip, to scoff at the sermons in pleasant vein. Non-believers were appointed to lay church positions, coats and hats and coats were dumped in the fonts; sanctuaries became orchestral stages. He referred to ritualists, those who fall in love with sanctuary choreography and vestments for their own sake, as 'gilt gingerbread' men.

Newman's reputation as a scholar and superior Oxford mind had never been in doubt since he had settled in at Oriel twelve years before the Oxford Movement got underway. 'But now', according to his first biographer, Wilfrid Ward, son of one of his principal proselytes, William George Ward (W. G. Ward) 'the character of a prophet and leader of men was added. And the movement in Oxford of which he was the life and soul aroused all the enthusiasm of the time.'[13] James Froude, brother of Hurrell, noted 'a clearness of intellectual perception, a disdain for conventionalities, a temper imperious and wilful, but along with it a most attaching gentleness, sweetness, singleness of heart and purpose'. James Froude remembered:

I had then never seen so impressive a person. I met him now and then in private; I attended his church and heard him preach Sunday after Sunday, … He was … the most transparent of men. He told us what he believed to be true. He did not know where it would carry him…. Newman's mind was world-wide. He was interested in everything which was going on in science, in politics, in literature. Nothing was too large for him, nothing too trivial, if it threw light upon the central question, what man really was, and what was his destiny … Thus it was that we, who had never seen such another man, and to whom he appeared, perhaps, at special advantage in contrast with the normal college don, came to regard Newman with the affection of pupils (though pupils, strictly speaking, he had none) for an idolized master. The simplest word which dropped from him was treasured as if it had been an intellectual diamond. For hundreds of young men *Credo in Newmanum* was the genuine symbol of faith.[14, 15]

And yet, was Newman himself entirely beyond reproach? If there was a note of egotism and oddity in Newman's life at this time it was his occasional, jaundiced attitude towards the marriages of his friends.

Fellows of colleges, excepting heads of house, gave up their fellowships on marriage, and it was the norm for a clerical don to find a bride and a parish living by his late twenties or early thirties. For Newman, who had admitted to confirmation of an option for life-long celibacy by the age of 28, it was not simply an idiosyncratic lifestyle choice. From time to time he felt the marriage of his close male friends like a betrayal. At times he sulked. When his sister Harriet married Tom Mozley, Newman wrote to Albany Christie (who would later join him in the monastic-style community he was to establish at Littlemore): 'Be sure of this, that every one when he marries is a lost man – a clean good for nothing – I should not be surprised to be told that Mozley would not write another letter all his life.' [16] And this was his brother-in-law. It was in character for him to be disgruntled, even angry, on the occasion of his male friends' nuptials, including Pusey's, and even Keble's, which, Isaac Williams remarked, caused Newman 'great annoyance'.

When Henry Wilberforce, one of the inner Oriel circle, got engaged, he was so anxious about Newman's reaction that he funked telling him. Newman heard rumours, but refused to believe them. He wrote to Frederic Rogers, 'By-the-bye, talking of H.W., do not believe a silly report that is in circulation that he is engaged to be married … I am spreading my incredulity, and contradicting it in every direction, and will not believe it, though I saw the event announced in the papers, till he tells me'. [17] Newman was devastated when he was finally apprized of the fact of the marriage and appears to have poured out his anger and disappointment in every direction. Wilberforce then wrote to Newman what he thought to be an assuaging letter, insisting on his continuing affection, but Newman seemed determined to behave the jilted lover. He penned a letter, which he never sent. Perhaps he never intended sending it, and it was a means of letting off steam; but he kept it while destroying many others. It reveals, as does no other document, the complex layers of Newman's affections towards his close male friends, as well as his attitude towards women and marriage:

You surely are inconsiderate – you ask me to give my heart, when you give yours to another – and because I will not promise to do so, then you augur all sorts of illtreatment towards you from me. – Now I do not like to speak of myself, but in selfdefence I must say, it is a little hard for a friend to separate himself from familiarity with me (which he has a perfect right, and perhaps lies under a duty to do,) and then to say, 'Love me as closely, give me your familiar heart as you did, though I have parted with mine'. Be quite sure that I shall be free to love you, far more than you will me – but I cannot, as a prudent man, forget what is due to my own comfort and independence as not to look to my own resources, make my own mind my wife, and anticipate and provide against that loss of friends which the fashion of the age makes inevitable. [18]

The telling phrase is his resolve to '*make my own mind my wife*': written, it would seem, more in peevishness than determination. The anger, the injured feelings, the jealousy ('give your heart to another'), are expressed in the language of a disappointed lover:

You know very little of me, if you think I do not feel at times much the despondence of solitariness…. Why must I give my heart to those who will not (naturally, it would be a bad bargain for them) take charge of it? … My dear H. – you really have hurt me – You have *made* a *difficulty* in the very beginning of our separation. You should have reflected that to remove it, you would not only have to justify it to yourself but to explain it to me.[19]

Apart from the self-pity, there is the bitterness of betrayal, of wasted emotional investment, a strong impression of distaste for the marriage state – 'fashion of the age'. Newman was behaving as if he had rights over those to whom he had given his heart; and it is tempting to believe that, at times, his extravagant endearments were stratagems of control as much as heartfelt affection. Father Henry Tristram, an Oratorian Father of the first half of the twentieth century, wrote an entire book comprising Newman's ornate dedications to friends. The dedications, published prominently for all the world to read, speak of affections that clearly, for Newman, contained no inappropriate sentiment. And yet, this was not entirely how the recipients saw such outpourings. Frederic Rogers (a 'dear and intimate friend … that dear and familiar companion') had earlier tried to talk some sense into Newman over Henry Wilberforce's marriage. He declined to be the dedicatee of Newman's *The Church of the Fathers* in 1839, since he believed that its sentiments might be taken amiss outside their circle. 'If I knew the "dearest, sweetest, etc" was to be contained in those two little volumes I should never be able to see their very backs without colouring up to the eyes.'[20] In the event, Newman dedicated the book, without permission, to Isaac Williams, whom he had loved for years, ending his letters to him 'ever yours affectionately', or with 'most lovingly and affectionately'. The dedication was, for Newman, so toned down as to prompt a cynical aside from his brother-in-law, John Mozley, to his sister: 'How do you like the dedication to *The Church of the Fathers*? … It seems to me as if it were a translation of some old patristic dedication rather than an original one.'[21] The lapidary dedication stated: 'To my dear and much-admired Isaac Williams … the sight of whom carries back his friends to ancient, holy, and happy times.'

THE OXFORD MOVEMENT AND CELIBACY

The ideal of priestly or clerical celibacy, meaning an obligation on the part of ordained priests not to marry, was a norm within the Western tradition of Christianity from at least the eleventh century. Celibacy is not to be confused with continence, which means avoidance of all sexual activity, including 'impure' thoughts, and masturbation; although continence is often interpreted as a requirement of celibacy. Nor is celibacy to be confused with the virtue of chastity, which means avoidance of impurity for both single and married people – avoidance of adultery, for example.

Celibacy as an ideal, if not an obligation, among the Anglican priesthood, as expounded by Newman and Hurrell Froude, became an aspect of the Oxford Movement that would draw criticism and suspicion. There were widespread insinuations that celibacy would lead to fornication, a prejudice widely entertained about Roman Catholic priests in the confessional as a result of luridly anti-Catholic popular novels of the *Maria Monk* variety. There have been retrospective suggestions of a link between Anglican celibacy and the intense same-sex relationships that have been leveled against Catholic priests and religious: that young men troubled by unacknowledged homosexual feelings are attracted to celibacy as a form of sublimation.

Central to the Tractarian ideals was the aim to restore the sacred nature of priestly ordination as an estate higher not only than common humanity but even that of the angels. If the sacraments were the means of grace and salvation for all, then this privileged the priesthood and those on whom it was bestowed; in contrast to the Evangelical clergy, who controlled their faithful through preaching.

In their initial polemic in 1864, leading to the writing of the *Apologia*, Kingsley would accuse Newman of preaching that 'a Church which had sacramental confession and a celibate clergy was the only true Church'.[22] Newman, in those early exchanges, would hotly deny that he had intimated any such thing: in fact, he wrote, he would have been 'the dolt to say or imply that celibacy of the clergy was a part of the definition of the Church …'[23] Yet in 1840, he would write to a friend arguing that the texts stating that 'concupiscence has the nature of sin', and 'in sin hath my mother conceived me', indicated that celibacy was a 'holier state than matrimony'. And was not a priest, as he constantly insisted, called to holiness? More important, however, was Newman's expression of self-knowledge: his admission of a consistent repugnance towards the ties of marriage and connubial domesticity. He would also write in 1840:

All my habits for years, my tendencies, are towards celibacy. I could not take that interest in this world which marriage requires. I am too disgusted with this world — And, above all, call it what one will, I have a repugnance to a clergyman's marrying. I do not say it is not lawful – I cannot deny the right – but, whether prejudice or not, it shocks me.[24]

The self-examination appears to be going in three directions. He appears celibate by force of inclination – a happily confirmed bachelor; yet he also presents a rationale based on his self-professed unworldliness – an argument for celibacy that he would urge in his historical sketch on monasticism some years later. Yet mention of 'repugnance' and 'shock' at a clergyman marrying suggests disgust at what he sometimes termed 'sensuality' or 'carnal indulgence'.

At the very least Newman gives the impression that celibacy, and indeed chastity, never involved, for him, a sacrifice or struggle. It came naturally like his talent for writing. Newman's isolation, despite his fervid professions of intimacy with male friends, is at times reminiscent of the sense of artistic independence of ties expressed by others in his era (William Godwin's *St Leon*, for example: 'a limb torn off from society') who struggled to come to grips with what separated the artist from the common run of human beings. And Keats, who was prepared to live like a 'hermit' in the world, put up with anything 'any misery, even imprisonment – so long as I have neither wife nor child'. Yet this was not so much Keats's misogyny and a dislike of children as the writer's need for freedom from sexual intimacy and domesticity alike. Such isolation, however, would not preclude Newman's need for close, devoted friends; nor later, for a faithful companion-servant, such as Ambrose St John, who served a wide scope of practical needs, as well as offering a measure of emotional comfort, affection, and support, albeit non-sexual.

It is in Newman's persona as literary artist that one begins to understand his emotional attachments and dependence on particular individuals – known in Catholic ascetical theology as special or particular friendships. These attachments, in Newman's case, are less suggestive of preludes to a homosexual relationship than to the strong same-sex literary intimacies of the previous generation, such as existed, for example, between Wordsworth, Coleridge, and Southey, who employed epithets of affection between each other that might appear suspect in the twenty-first century.

During the early years of the Oxford Movement, the impression of the group as a circle of artists, of poets, was reinforced by their enthusiasm for publishing verse together. The existence of an aesthetic dimension to the group has led some commentators to draw parallels with homosexual aesthetes later in the nineteenth century, rather than the Romantic circles of the previous generation, or deep Victorian same-sex intimacies – such as Tennyson and Hallam. The versifying of the Oxford Movement, however, is less aesthetic than catechetical. John Bowden, Hurrell Froude, John Keble, Henry Wilberforce, Isaac Williams, and Newman came together in the *Lyra Apostolica*, published in 1836. The fact that many of their contributions were penned with a palpable spiritual design upon the reader explains perhaps the poor quality. Newman's 'Lead Kindly Light' is by far the best of the inclusions; but a typical example of the rest can be gathered from another verse of Newman's entitled 'Discipline' which feebly parallels the greater hymn:

So now, whene'er, in journeying on, I feel
The shadow of the Providential Hand,
Deep breathless stirrings shoot across my breast,

Searching to know what He will now reveal,
What sin uncloak, what stricter rule command,
And girding me to work His full behest.[25]

Two poems in the *Lyra* collection by Newman clearly allude to his friendship with Hurrell Froude who had died before publication: 'David and Jonathan', and 'James and John'. The 'David and Jonathan' verses[26] are headed with a line from Samuel: 'Thy love to me was wonderful, passing the love of women.' It ends with the line: 'he bides with us who dies, he is but lost who lives.'[27] A stanza in 'James and John' reads:

Brothers in heart, they hope to gain
   An undivided joy,
That man may one with man remain,
   As boy was one with boy.[28]

James dies young, falling to 'Satan's rage', while John lingers out his fellows all, and dies 'in bloodless age'. Newman's aptitude for intimate same-sex friendship finds expression in these verses against the background of the death of Hurrell, yet the imagery lacks eroticism to the point of desiccation.

INTIMATIONS OF HOMOEROTICISM
IN THE OXFORD MOVEMENT

Ever since the publication of Geoffrey Faber's *Oxford Apostles* (1933), the Oxford Movement has been linked in the minds of some commentators with homosexuality. If there were indications of the homoerotic in Newman's circle, they more properly attach to the early writings of Frederick Faber who would be closely involved with Newman after they became Catholics and Oratorians. It is an appropriate point at which to explore Faber's early homoeroticism in order to contrast him with Newman.

When Faber came up to Balliol College in 1833, a fellow undergraduate, Roundell Palmer, wrote of him: 'The attraction of his looks and manners ... soon made us friends, and our affection for each other became not only strong but passionate. There is a place for passion, even in friendship; it was so among the Greeks; and the love of Jonathan for David was "wonderful, passing the love of women".'[29] It is the fusion of the Biblical and Classical references that distinguishes him from Newman's citation of Samuel, and confirms the ambivalence of religiosity and homo-sentimental.

Faber won the Oxford University Newdigate poetry prize in 1836 and began to specialise in writing verses that expressed highly emotional male intimacy.

Exchanges between Faber, already in Holy Orders, aged 24, and one of his close friends, George Smythe, bordered typically, and queasily, on the homoerotic.

We pulled each other's hair about,
   Peeped in each other's eyes,
And spoke the first light silly words
   That to our lips did rise.

Ah, dearest! – wouldst then know how much
   My aching heart in thee doth live?
One look of thy blue eye – one touch
   Of thy dear hand last night could give
Fresh hopes to shine amid my fears,
And thoughts that shed themselves in tears.[30]

Smythe wrote to Faber after a holiday together in the Lake District:

Dear Master – I do love thee with a love
Which has with fond endeavour built a throne
In my heart's holiest place. Come sit thereon
And rule with thy sweet power, and reign above
All my thoughts, feelings, they to thee will prove
Loyal and loving vassals, for they burn
With a most passionate fire and ever yearn
And cleave to thee as ne'er before they clove,
Dearest, to others.[31]

Faber's brother Francis wrote to him at about this time suggesting that such sentiments between male friends were not healthy. Faber responded: 'I feel what they express to *men*: I never did to a born woman. Brodie [a Harrow friend] thinks a revival of chivalry in male friendships a characteristic of the rising generation, and a hopeful one.'[32]

Faber's early verse would anticipate the scores of hymns he would write with a mix of saccharine piety and sensuality: for example his hymn to the Child Jesus:

Dear Little One! how sweet Thou art! Thine eyes how bright they shine!
So bright they almost seem to speak When Mary's look meets Thine!
How faint and feeble is Thy cry, Like plaint of harmless dove,
When Thou dost murmur in Thy sleep Of sorrow and of love![33]

Thirty years after Faber left Balliol, Gerard Manley Hopkins came up to Oxford. Hopkins, influenced at Balliol by Benjamin Jowett and Walter Pater, fell in love with Digby Augustus Stewart Mackworth Dolben who felt drawn to Pusey's spirituality and had a taste for Faber's versifying. He walked around in a Benedictine habit, and was contemplating going over to Rome when he was drowned aged 19 in the River Welland.

Hopkins became a Catholic, and a Jesuit, and would end his life teaching at the university Newman founded in Ireland. It is arguable that Dolben made available to Hopkins, under the influence of Faber, the realisation of a mix of the religious and the homoerotic. In his 'The Lantern Out of Doors', Hopkins observes men walking in the night – 'either beauty bright/In mould or mind or what not else'. All these men are cherished, he reflects, by Christ as if by an intimate friend:

Christ minds: Christ's interest, what to avow or amend
   There, eyes them, heart wants, care haunts, foot follows kind,
Their ransom, their rescue, and first, fast, last friend.[34]

Towards the end of the nineteenth century, with links via Faber and Hopkins, Roman Catholicism would attract a constituency of writers and poets who were homosexuals: Oscar Wilde and Alfred Douglas; Lionel Johnson, author of the 'Dark Soul'; the extraordinary Frederick Rolfe, aka Baron Corvo of *Hadrian VII* fame who spent time at Oscott College and the Scots' College in Rome (being turned out of both – from the Scots' College while still in his bed); John Gray, who studied at the English College in Rome, and his lover André Raffalovich who saw connections between Catholicism and homosexuality – unisexisme, he called it, or the third sex. Raffalovich distinguished between those who were born homosexual, and those who chose homosexuality. The ideal life for the born homosexual was to transcend his tendencies through sublimation, aided by art and the nurturing of spiritual relationships. Those non-congenital homosexuals, he asserted, who chose such a life style were guilty of vice and beastliness. While Faber to an extent anticipated something of the mood and sentiments of this circle, the attempts to make connections with Newman are ill-conceived.

NEWMAN ON POETRY

Newman's ideas about the art of poetry and religion found expression during the era of his Oriel fellowship in an essay he wrote as a contribution to a new magazine edited by an ex-Catholic priest called Blanco White. White was one of the more bizarre individuals in the Oriel circle. Something of a verse writer him-self (his sonnet 'Night and Death' was deemed by Coleridge 'the finest and most grandly conceived sonnet in our language'), he was famously anti-Catholic, the author of an essay entitled 'Evidences against Catholicism'. He was clearly an entertaining and plausible conversationalist since he was allowed the run of the Oriel Senior Common Room as if he were an elected fellow. Blanco's spiritual journey had brought him from Catholicism, via agnosticism, and Unitarianism, to Anglicanism (he would end an atheist). Hence he was an object of some fascination to Oriel's dons: a source of insider knowledge on fallacious arguments of Romanism and Non-Conformism, as well as a redeemed apostate from unbelief. He had studied theology in Oxford and made friends with Thomas Arnold and Newman after being offered a home at Oriel.

In November of 1828 White was invited to edit a start-up periodical, *The London Review*, and appealed to Newman for an article for the first issue. White asked him to write on a non-religious theme with a secular treatment. 'Give me any article on any subject you like', he wrote to Newman, 'Divinity excepted for the present, for of that I expect a flood.'[35] With a fast approaching deadline, White begged Newman to put down his thoughts as they came. 'I should strongly advise you to venture upon the strength of your *household stuff* – on the reading and reflection of many years. Write without much concern; you are sure to write well … imagine yourself in our Common-Room, myself in the corner, Dornford passing the wine, etc, etc, and tell us your mind on paper.' Newman responded enthusiastically with an article entitled 'Poetry with Reference to Artistotle's Poetics', which he delivered to White on 8 November 1828. The theme is an ancient problem that poets and critics were exploring with renewed interest in the nineteenth century: is the poet a different kind of person from the rest of humankind? Newman argues that Aristotle was wrong to teach that poetry exists in the work, rather than in the poet. For Newman, poetry is the rhapsodic or prophetic gift itself – the genius or talent that separates and isolates the artist from the common run; whereas a poem is 'no essential part of poetry, though indispensable to its exhibition'. The isolation of the poet, Newman goes on, finds parallels in the interior life of religion and a sense of God. The Christian spends 'the greater part of his time by himself, and when he is in solitude, that is his real state'. Hence Newman suggests that each Christian is a kind of poet:

With Christians, a poetic view of things is a duty, – we are bid to colour all things with hues of faith, to see a Divine meaning in every event, and a superhuman tendency. Even our friends around are invested with unearthly brightness – no longer imperfect men, but being taken into Divine favour, stamped with His seal, and in training for future happiness. It may be added, that the virtues peculiarly Christian are especially poetical – meekness, gentleness, compassion, contentment, modesty, not to mention the devotional virtues; whereas the ruder and more ordinary feelings are the instruments of rhetoric more justly than of poetry – anger, indignation, emulation, martial spirit and love of independence.[36]

This does not mean that Newman expected every poet to be a Christian, but, according to his view of the matter, the good person should strive to be a poet.

After he became a Catholic, Newman would review a collection of Keble's poems, *Lyra Innocentium*, in the *Dublin Review*, arguing that 'the Church herself is the most sacred and august of poets'. What is the Church, he would ask, if not a channel through which emotion finds expression. She is 'a discipline of the affections and passions … She is the poet of her children; full of music to soothe the sad and control the wayward, wonderful in story for the imagination of the romantic; rich in symbol and imagery, so that gentle and delicate feelings, which will not bear words, may in silence intimate their presence or commune with themselves. Her very being is poetry …'[37]

If Newman saw the religious life as parallel to the life of a poet, the comparison stopped short of the poet as a person of aesthetic pretensions. He was averse to art for art's sake and he found the literary type unattractive. 'I am hard hearted', he wrote three years after his conversion to Catholicism, 'towards the mere literary ethos, for there is nothing I despise and detest more'.[38]

CHAPTER 7

Parting of friends

'My sole ascertainable reason for moving is a feeling of indefinite *risk*
to my soul in staying … shall one bear to live, where die one cannot?
J. H. NEWMAN LETTER TO JOHN KEBLE, 21 NOVEMBER 1844

While members of the Oxford Movement promoted their ideas in the tracts, Newman continued to lecture small groups in a chapel within Oxford's university church. He was like a man torn between two loves. Increasingly he felt attracted to the Roman Mother Church. As one of his characters, drawn to Catholicism yet still unable to make the plunge, puts it in Newman's novel *Loss and Gain* (written in 1847):

She is our mother – oh, that word 'mother!' – a mighty mother! She opens her arms – oh, the fragrance of that bosom! She is full of gifts – I feel, I have long felt it. Why don't I rush into her arms? Because I feel that she is ruled by a spirit which is not she. But did that distrust of her go from me, was that certainty which I have of her corruption, disproved, I should join her communion tomorrow.[1]

For the time being he felt that he could not abandon the Church of England despite the doubts he entertained about the authenticity of her traditions. He was still looking for that reliable connection back to God's true Revelation. He was looking for guarantees.

Newman throughout this period had been pondering a Via Media or middle way, that drew on what seemed to him the most authentic aspects of both Churches, while rejecting the evident shortcomings of each. Was that middle way not Anglo-Catholicism, the Catholic Church in England? And was this not the Church that would bring England back to the one, true, holy, catholic and apostolic Church, while loosening the stranglehold of a Parliament and Government comprised of Evangelicals, Dissenters, and Papists?

The lectures that lay the ground for this Via Media had been published in March 1837 in a volume entitled *The Prophetic Office of the Church viewed relatively to Romanism and Popular Protestantism*. The Tractarians had adopted the term Anglicanism (originating from the time of King James I) with its resonances of Gallicanism – the French experiment with a Catholicism of strong local discretion. Then the coinage 'Anglo-Catholicism' gradually came into vogue. Yet Newman was soon openly admitting that, despite its growing popularity, Anglo-Catholicism existed, alas, only in theory. It had no substance: it was a 'paper Church'. But he remained optimistic that the Christians of England, led by the bishops and pastors, might still awaken to its claims and make it a Church in reality.

By 1839, however, he was assailed by a serious scruple. Absorbed in his readings of long forgotten religious quarrels, he was shocked to discover that fourteen centuries earlier a similar compromise in a doctrinal controversy had resulted in a Catholic anathema. The Latin and the Greek wings of the Church, East and West, had insisted that Jesus Christ possessed two distinct natures, human and divine: Jesus Christ was God and he was Man. Whereas the West talked of two natures 'in' Christ, the East spoke of the two natures 'of' Christ: but two natures, nevertheless. While the recondite bickering continued as to how this should be expressed, a group of North African Christians, known as Mono-physites, aimed to resolve the dilemma by positing a middle way: a coalesced single nature of Christ. For this they were roundly condemned. As Newman reviewed the episode, he was stunned by the parallel with Anglo-Catholicism and himself: 'I saw my face in that mirror', he wrote, 'and I was a Monophysite … there was an awful similitude, more awful, because so silent and unimpas-sioned, between the dead records of the past and the feverish chronicle of the present.'[2] Theologising adrift from history landed one in heresy.

There was more to come. Nicholas Wiseman, Rector of the English College, whom he had met in Rome with Hurrell Froude, had written an article for the *Dublin Review* in which he compared the Church of England with a fourth century schismatic sect known as the Donatists. They claimed that the Catholic Church was out of step with doctrinal orthodoxy in declaring that a priest in mortal sin could nevertheless administer valid sacraments. Newman was at first unimpressed by the article, but a friend emphasized Wiseman's quotation of the words of Saint Augustine '*Securus judicat orbis terrarum*' – the entire world is the secure judge. In other words, in seeking authentic doctrine one does not merely hark back to antiquity; one listens to the echoing judgment of the contemporary faithful majority of Christendom. Newman could now see the mer-its of the parallel Wiseman had drawn between the Church of England and the Donatists. With aid of an uncharacteristically atrocious mixed metaphor, he wrote to Frederick Rogers in September 1839 that Wiseman's argument was 'the first real hit from Romanism which has happened to me … it has given me a stomach-ache. You see the whole history of the Monophysites has been a sort of alterative, and now comes this dose at the end of it. It does certainly come upon one that we are not at the bottom of things. At this moment we have sprung a leak …'[3] The term 'alterative' refers to a medicine that affects the process of digestion. A little later, on a walk in the New Forest, he compared his situation to one who has been presented with a landscape 'to the end of which I do not see'. In the *Apologia* he would write that the words '*securus judicat orbis terrarum*' struck with a 'power which I never had felt from any words before … they were like the "Turn again Whittington" of the chime; or … the "Tolle lege, – Tolle, lege" of the child, which converted St. Augustine himself … By those great words of the ancient Father, interpreting and summing up the long and varied course of ecclesiastical history, the theory of the *Via Media* was absolutely pulverized.'[4] The 'Tolle lege' – 'take up, read' – refers to the incident in Augustine's *Confessions*, when he hears the voice of a child repeatedly asking him to take up his Bible. He opens the book on Paul's Epistle to the Romans, 13: 13–14, and is converted.

Newman nevertheless hung on uncomfortably within the Anglican communion, attempting to assuage his scruples while still hoping to discover a way to bring the Churches of Rome and England closer together. But by now his heart was not in it. As he would write in the *Apologia*: 'I was on my death-bed, as regards my membership with the Anglican Church.'[5] But, yet again, he attempted to solve the contradictions in an essay arguing that the fundamental principles of his Church, as stated in the Thirty-Nine Articles, could still be reconciled, partially at least, with the 'old Catholic Truth'. The essay would be published as *Tract 90* in February of 1841, and would prove the last of the tracts; but first he was drawn into another controversy.

TAMWORTH READING ROOM

Ahead of the publication of *Tract 90* Newman, signing himself CATHOLICUS, wrote a series of anonymous letters to *The Times* objecting to what he judged a strident reformulation of utilitarian ideas. The occasion was a speech published as a pamphlet by Sir Robert Peel to mark the opening of a reading room for working-class men and women at Tamworth in the industrial Midlands. The institute provided instruction manuals for such work-skills as building, engineering, and agriculture, and a wide range of literary and historical reading matter. The library committee, however, would not allow works of religious and political 'controversy' on its shelves.

On the face of it, the initiative seemed praiseworthy and progressive – recognising the need for inclusive adult education among the poor. What incited Newman's scorn, however, was Peel's assumption that science leads people naturally and inevitably towards happiness, higher moral standards, and belief not only in a theistic creator God but even in the claims of Christian revelation. The concerns on both sides – those of Peel and those of Newman – are as familiar and relevant today as they were in the mid-nineteenth century. For Newman, the initiative was tainted with the same secularist fallacy that had been evident at the foundation of London University. A library without religious books, he believed, was as culturally unacceptable as a university without a faculty of theology. His most interesting and powerful arguments focus on the relationship between science and religion. Newman challenged Peel's assertion that science and rational philosophy alone provide an ideal basis for the creation of a good society – 'that an increased sagacity', as Peel put it, 'will administer to an exalted faith; that it will make men not merely believe in the cold doctrines of natural religion, but that it will so prepare and temper the spirit and understanding, that they will be better qualified to comprehend the great scheme of human redemption'. Newman was not attacking science or natural theology as such, nor claiming that reason and science are opposed to religion. He was saying that scientific conclusions and deductions do not, as Peel was arguing, encourage morality and religion. 'This is why science', he writes, 'has so little of a religious tendency; deductions have no power of persuasion.' Then comes a remarkable plea for the engagement of a person's total humanity in religious conviction and practice. 'The heart is commonly reached', he writes, 'not through the reason, but through the imagination, by means of direct impressions, by the testimony of facts and events, by history, by description. Persons influence us, voices melt us, looks subdue us, deeds inflame us.'[6]

Nor, by invoking imagination, is Newman drawing an equivalence between religion and literature. 'A literary religion is so little to be depended upon; it looks well in fair weather, but its doctrines are opinions, and when called to suffer for them, it slips them between its folios, or burns them at its hearth.' He is emphasising the multi-faceted, multi-dimensional lived nature of what it means to be a complete human being capable of religious belief and expression: 'Man', he insists, 'is not a reasoning animal; he is a seeing, feeling, contemplating, acting animal. He is influenced by what is direct and precise. It is very well to freshen our impressions and convictions from physics, but to create them we must go elsewhere.'[7]

As for religious belief based on philosophical reasoning:

I have no confidence … in philosophers who cannot help having religion, and are Christians by implication. They sit at home, and reach forward to distances which astonish us; but they hit without grasping, and are sometimes as confident about shadows as about realities. They have worked out by calculation the lie of a country which they never saw, and mapped it by a gazetteer; and like blind men, though they can put a stranger on his way, they cannot walk straight, and do not feel it quite their business to walk at all.[8]

LITTLEMORE

Newman's former curate at Littlemore, J. R. Bloxam, recalls paying a visit to the village and looking through the window of his former dwelling where he saw a figure 'kneeling in prayer'. It was Newman, who had spent the Lent of 1840 experimenting with a semi-eremitical life, following devotional practices more familiar within mainstream Catholicism than Anglicanism. Newman's journal entries for this period reveal a measure of self-absorption reminiscent of the diaries of Hurrell Froude; although both echo the ascetical retreat 'notes' of Catholic spiritual exercises:

I have this Lent abstained from fish, fowl, all meat but bacon at dinner; from butter, vegetables of all sorts, fruit, pastry, sugar, tea, wine, and beer and toast. I have never dined out. I have not worn gloves … On Wednesday and Friday I abstained from all food whatever to 6 P.M. when I added a second egg to my usual supper. I sometimes drank a glass of cold water in the morning for a particular reason …[9]

The refinement of examination of motive and conscience betrays the scrupulosity of a monastic novice: '[I] have felt very little fatigue, very little pain, and no languor or lowness of spirits.'[10] He writes that he has kept quinine pills by him, and taken them from time to time. He admits to have indulged himself in a minor way: 'I have happened to see two newspapers, not more; I have seen my friends who now and then called, and Bloxam and Rogers once or twice stayed a while.'[11] On Sundays, and on a feast day, he confesses, 'I wore gloves'.[12]

Newman had purchased an L-shaped block of stables and cottages in Little-more village which he aimed to turn into a simple community residence where he could settle to pray and study. It stands to this day, much as it was, a single-storeyed simple building in College Lane, just off the Eastern by-pass south of Oxford, in an area that has become part of the suburban fringe extending down from the city to Iffley and Cowley. As the building was undergoing necessary preparations, the reception of *Tract 90* had raised a storm of protest in Oxford. 'The main thesis of the Essay', Newman wrote, 'was this: – the [39] Articles do not oppose Catholic teaching; they but partially oppose Roman dogma; they for the most part oppose the dominant errors of Rome.'[13] He was clearly offering a final recipe for reconciling the best of Catholicism with fundamentals of Anglicanism in the vain hope of remaining within the Church of England in good faith. Many leading clerical dons were having none of it. Open letters were published and circulated throughout the university, accusing Newman of seducing members into violating their 'solemn engagements'. Heads of colleges published a condemnation; and, finally, his bishop, Richard Bagot, signalled disapproval. Newman decided that the ninetieth tract was to be the last. The Oxford Movement was in effect at an end. With a chorus of criticism ringing in his ears, he plunged again into the Early Fathers and reviewed the details of the Arian heresy, which doubted the equivalence of God the Father and God the Son. He fixed on the relationship between different shades of Arianism and the Catholic Church at large. Newman saw that in his own contemporary parallel 'the pure Arians were the Protestants, the semi-Arians were the Anglicans, and that Rome now was what it was then'.[14] The Eternal City beckoned.

Then, in 1841, came another blow to any remaining hope Newman might have entertained of finding a safe haven in the Church of England. That year saw the proposal to establish an Anglo-Prussian bishopric of Jerusalem. Michael Solomon Alexander was a former Jewish Rabbi, who was intended as a bishop to represent Protestants of a variety of confessions, as well as converts from Judaism. As Newman put it:

What a miserable concern this Jerusalem Bishoprick is! We have not a single member of our Church there, except travellers and officials. It is a mere political piece of business, to give our government influence in the country, such as the Russians have through Greeks and the French through Latins. We are to head the Protestant Church – which I fear too truly will be composed of Jews (whether converted or not) Lutherans etc. whether conformed [conforming] or not, Druses who are half Mahometans, and the Monophysites of Mesopotamia etc. – a remarkable collection of Jews, Turks, Infidels and Heretics. It is deplorable.[15]

His principal anger was against a Church that could gather together such a random collection of Christian hybrids of dubious apostolic provenance. Newman later commented with relish: 'I never heard of any good or harm [the Jerusalem bishopric] has ever done, except what it has done for me; which many think a great misfortune, and I one of the greatest of mercies. It brought me on to the beginning of the end.'[16]

By the Spring of 1842 Newman had moved into the community residence at Littlemore and begun a style of living that included the reading of the Roman breviary, meditation, rigorous fasting, and the study of Athanasius, the scourge of those Arian heretics. Newman's journal for March 6, noting the date in Romish style, '*Dominica Quarta in Quadragesima*' (the Fourth Sunday in Lent), records renewed absorption in his ascetical practices, and concern about his bowel movements:

I have eaten nothing between breakfast & tea, besides eating no meat except on Sundays, but on the other hand I have eaten more eggs and taken tea. However my relaxations have been these, & for these reasons. The addition of milk (not in tea) I have already mentioned. I have lately added butter, because it enabled me to eat more bread, because it seems to contribute to relieve the more inconvenient effect of (eggs), because it enables me to take powdered rhubarb with my meal, which seems to succeed better than anything else… I am very much exhausted – & from exhaustion have not been regular sometimes in the Breviary Offices.[17]

He was now joined by the first members of his embryonic community. There was John Dalgairns, an excitable, pious young man who had failed to be elected to an Oxford fellowship because of his Roman tendencies. Next came William Lockhart, with family links to Sir Walter Scott; his stay at Littlemore appears to have been a substitute for going over to Rome. Then Frederick Bowles from

Abingdon in Oxfordshire. Finally, came Ambrose St John, 28 years of age, a linguist ancient and modern. Other visitors, such as Mark Pattison, James Anthony Froude, and David Lewis would drop by or stay briefly.

The day was organized along monastic lines. The community observed a 'greater silence' from seven-thirty in the evening until two in the afternoon the following day. Rising at five in the morning, four hours were set aside for 'devotions', including Matins, Lauds and Compline, and nine hours for study. The rumour went around that the members of the Littlemore group, excepting Newman, were already Catholics. A newspaper asserted that Newman had founded an 'Anglo-Catholic Monastery' comprising a chapel, 'cells of dormitories', cloisters, and a refectory. Newman wrote to his bishop insisting that this was pure fantasy: 'There is no chapel; no refectory, hardly a dining room or parlour. The "cloisters" are my shed connecting the cottages.' [18] 'I do not understand what "cells of dormitories" means.' The Littlemore experiment was clearly monastic by any standard, yet there was another crucial motive, of which Newman wrote as follows: 'I am almost in despair of keeping men together. The only possible way is a monastery.' Was this not an acknowledgment of his disappointment with former 'men' who had departed to get married? But the monastic regime, in his view, was also an expression of a religious impulse: 'Men want an outlet for their devotional and penitential feelings – and if we do not grant it, to a dead certainty they will go where they can find it.' [19]

While it seemed more obvious to outsiders that Newman was moving inexorably, by sheer power of the logic, towards Rome, he appeared to be taking an inordinate amount of time about it. He seemed conscious of the impatience of others. 'I had a great dislike of paper logic', he wrote.

For myself, it was not logic that carried me on; as well might one say that the quicksilver in the barometer changes the weather. It is the concrete being that reasons; pass a number of years, and I find my mind in a new place; how? The whole man moves; paper logic is but the record of it. All the logic in the world would not have made me move faster towards Rome than I did; as well might you say that I have arrived at the end of my journey, because I see the village church before me … Great acts take time.[20]

Newman continued to experiment with 'Catholic' spirituality using a medley of books of devotion. In *Loss and Gain* he registers the stock Anglican objections to Roman Catholic works. 'But look at their books of devotion', insisted Carlton, 'they can't write English.' Then Reding, Newman's young alter ego, smiles and responds: 'They write English, I suppose, as classically as St John writes Greek.' [21] But coming around to that view point, written in 1847, took some time. The Littlemore retreats, lacking an experienced retreat director, proceeded with an amalgam of the *Ignatian Spiritual Exercises*, Rosmini's *Manual*, and Stone's *Spiritual Retreat*. We know that by 1841 he was reading St Francis de

Sales's *Love of God*, and, later, his *Introduction to the Devout Life*, expurgated of the 'Errors of the Popish Edition'.

Meanwhile he was energetically writing and publishing. Among the new publications was his *Essay on the Miracles recorded in the Ecclesiastical History of the Early Ages*. The book falls into two parts, the first, on miracles in Scripture, was written in his early Oriel days (1825–1826), the second, on miracles throughout the history of Christianity (following the death of the last Apostle), was written later at Littlemore. Newman aimed to combat the Protestant rejection of miracles outside Scripture as typical of Romish decadence. In this sense it is an anti-Protestant, pro-Catholic essay. His logic is impeccable, at least for a believer: 'What God did once', he writes, 'He is likely to do again.' [22] He judges authentic miracles to be phenomena, with a deep religious connection, that defy natural explanation.

And while he had espoused the power of the religious imagination in the Tamworth letters to *The Times*, there is no place for the role of imagination in his essay on the authentically miraculous. 'The force of imagination may also be alleged to account for the supposed visions and voices which some enthusiasts have believed they saw and heard; for instance, the trances of Montanus and his followers, the visions related by some of the Fathers, and those of the Romish saints.' He speculates moreover that 'Mahomet's pretended night-journey to heaven' might not unreasonably be 'referred to the effects of disease or of an excited imagination'. [23] The essay was widely castigated by Protestant critics, not least for the examples of miraculous authenticity he cited in the final chapters: the prayers by the Thundering Legion that relieved a drought; St Helena's discovery of the True Cross; St Gregory Thaumaturge's miraculous alteration of the flow of a river.

If Newman's interest in ecclesiastical miracles indicated his taste for Roman Catholic culture, so did a new preoccupation with the lives of the saints. During this time he encouraged his young men, following the cue of Frederick Faber, who had been translating the hagiographies of Continental saints, to write up the lives of the British saints as way of exploring the ancient and authentic Catholicism of the island race. Signs, wonders and miracles mingled in the thoughts and conversations of the community at Littlemore. Newman himself wrote the lives of Saint Ediwald and St Gundleas, and co-authored a life of St Bettelin. James Froude, younger brother of Hurrell, took on the life of St Neot, a task that may well have sown the seeds of his later agnosticism, as pointed out in Herbert Paul's biography of him (*Life of Froude*, 1905). In his *Eminent Victorians* Lytton Strachey would exploit gleefully Paul's account, including Froude's remarks about his researches into Saint Patrick: 'St Patrick I found once lighted a fire with icicles', Froude had written, 'changed a French marauder into a wolf, and floated to Ireland on an altar stone. I thought it nonsense. I found it eventually uncertain whether Patricius was not a title, and whether any single apostle of that name had so much as existed.' [24] At the end of his version of the life of St Neot, Froude famously added: 'this is all, and perhaps rather more than all that is known of the life of the blessed St Neot.'

MARY, PATTERN OF FAITH

On 23 May 1842, in St Mary's Church, Bishop Richard Bagot of Oxford had declared publicly against Newman's *Tract 90*, which had sought to remove any deep and permanent enmity between the Church of Rome and the Church of England. It was not the first explicit attack on the Tractarians. Pusey, for example, had been banned from preaching to the university because of a sermon he had delivered promoting the doctrine of transubstantiation – the belief that the bread and wine changes substantially into the body, blood, soul and divinity of Christ at the words of the consecration in the Eucharist.

Now Bishop Bagot tackled head on Newman's claim that there was nothing in the 39 Articles that drove a wedge between the two Churches:

I have already expressed my opinion, that [Tract 90] was objectionable, and likely to disturb the peace of the Church. I thought so last year, and I think so still. I deeply regret its publication … and I cannot reconcile myself to a system of interpretation, which is so subtle, that by it the [39] Articles may be made to mean anything or nothing.[25]

Newman, who was present during the bishop's charges, was deeply upset since the bishop had assured him that no further criticism would be made of the tract provided that it was to be the last.

On the Feast of the Purification (also known as Candelmas), 2 February 1843, in the second year of his Littlemore retirement, Newman preached a sermon that proved to be the last of the series published as *Fifteen Sermons Preached Before the University of Oxford*. Its theme was 'the theory of developments in religious doctrine', and it contained important seeds of ideas on faith and reason that he would work up into an entire book the following year. Development of doctrine would be the key to understanding how later beliefs, that appeared to be accretions and corruptions, had existed in embryo form in Scripture and antique Christianity.

His text, taken from Luke 2:19, was 'But Mary kept all these things, and pondered them in her heart'. Taking Mary as his exemplar, was of course, a tribute to Roman Catholicism, and a significant indication of his Romeward tendency. 'St Mary', he said, 'is our pattern of Faith, both in the reception and in the study of Divine Truth.' None are spared the obligation, as Mary taught, of balancing belief with reason, reason with belief, assenting, developing, loving, reverencing, investigating, weighing, defining belief, as does the Church, its theologians, and doctors down the ages – and as should the 'unlearned': nobody, he is saying, is spared the responsibility of approaching faith with one's whole being – or one's whole imagination:

She does not think it enough to accept, she dwells upon it; not enough to possess, she uses it; not enough to assent, she developes it; not enough to submit the Reason, she reasons upon it; not indeed reasoning first, and believing afterwards, with Zacharias, yet first believing without reasoning, next from love and reverence, reasoning after believing. And thus she symbolizes to us, not only the faith of the unlearned, but of the doctors of the Church also, who have to investigate, and weigh, and define, as well as to profess the Gospel; to draw the line between truth and heresy; to anticipate or remedy the various aberrations of wrong reason; to combat pride and recklessness with their own arms; and thus to triumph over the sophist and the innovator.[26]

Deep in this richly textured sermon is the proposal that we imagine religious truths quite differently from the way in which we know the tangible world about us. While echoing the thought in the Tamworth letters – 'the heart is commonly reached not through reason but the imagination' – he appeals to the idea of a powerful religious symbolism which partakes in what it renders intelligible: 'The metaphors by which [supernatural truths] are signified are not mere symbols of ideas which exist independently of them, but their meaning is coincident and identical with the ideas.'[27]

As Newman sees it, the Church, like Mary, 'ponders' Scriptural utterance in its heart. With remarkable elasticity of thought and imagination, he analogously expands the idea of authentic doctrinal development to parallels in physics, music and even mathematics. 'While [*calculi*] answer', he writes, 'we can use them just as if they were the realities which they represent, and without thinking of those realities; but at length our instrument of discovery issues in some great impossibility or contradiction, or what we call in religion, a mystery.'[28] In the ambit of physics he notes that its laws, 'as we consider them, are themselves but generalizations of economical exhibitions, inferences from figure and shadow, and not more real than the phenomena from which they are drawn':

Scripture, for instance, says that the sun moves and the earth is stationary; and science, that the earth moves, and the sun is comparatively at rest. How can we determine which of these opposite statements is the very truth, till we know what motion is?[29]

In a final reflection, he considers music as an instance 'of an outward and earthly form, or economy, under which great wonders unknown seem to be typified'. He asks: 'What science brings so much out of so little?' He goes on:

Is it possible that that inexhaustible evolution and disposition of notes, so rich yet so simple, so intricate yet so regulated, so various yet so majestic, should be a mere sound, which is gone and perishes? Can it be that those mysterious stirrings of heart, and keen emotions, and strange yearnings after we know not what, and awful impressions from we know not whence, should be wrought in us by what is unsubstantial, and comes and goes, and begins and ends in itself? It is not so; it cannot be. No; they have escaped from some higher sphere; they are the outpourings of eternal harmony in the medium of created sound; they are echoes from our Home; they are the voice of Angels, or the Magnificat of Saints, or the living laws of Divine Governance, or the Divine Attributes; something are they besides themselves, which we cannot compass, which we cannot utter, – though mortal man, and he perhaps not otherwise distinguished above his fellows, has the gift of eliciting them.[30]

PARTING OF FRIENDS

Newman's retirement at Littlemore had become a matter of fascination and no little scandal to the dons and students of Oxford. He would recollect how he could not walk in or out of the cottages without people staring at him. 'One day when I entered my house, I found a flight of Undergraduates inside. Heads of Houses, as mounted patrols, walked their horses round those poor cottages. Doctors of Divinity dived into the hidden recesses of that private tenement un-invited, and drew domestic conclusions from what they saw there.'[31] And what they concluded, of course, was the establishment of a monastic settlement for young men preparing to go over to Rome.

And much as he protested to the contrary, for a time at least, there was a large measure of truth in that conclusion. In March of 1843 he wrote to John Keble: 'What men learn from me, who learn anything, is to lean towards doctrines and practices which our Church [of England] does not sanction. There was a time when I tried to balance this by strong statements against Rome ... But now, when I feel I can do this no more ... I am in danger of acting as a traitor to that system, to which I must profess attachment or I should not have the opportu-nity of acting at all.'[32] Later he wrote to Keble on 4 May 1843, in a letter he pub-lished in the *Apologia*, announcing with great clarity and simplicity the final, drastic decision of heart and mind that had consumed him for so many months: 'I am very far more sure that England is in schism, than that the Roman addi-tions to the Primitive Creed may not be developments, arising out of a keen and vivid realizing of the Divine Depositum of Faith.'[33] As for his young men at Littlemore, in August 1843 William Lockhart disappeared from the cottages and was later received into the Roman Catholic Church by the Rosminian priest and missionary, Luigi Gentili. Others were going over too, or considering their positions, including the young Frederic Faber whom Newman counselled to take his time – recommending at least three years of contemplation and prayer.

Meanwhile friends of a life time, close members of the Oxford Movement, and family members, not least his sister Jemima and ageing Aunt Elizabeth, made known their distress as the signs of his defection to Rome became ever more apparent. This was hard enough, but he also had to contend with suspicions that he was a Catholic renegade while continuing to enjoy the status and privileges of an Anglican priest. The break with most of his family was sealed in September 1843 when his brother-in-law, Harriet's husband, Tom Mozley, converted, abandoning a parish living to do so and threatening his domestic security. Blaming her brother, sister Harriet would never speak to Newman again, and already he was estranged from his brothers Charles and Francis. Jemima, a remarkable woman, with echoes of their late mother, wrote a letter of understanding and sympathy: 'Whichever way you decide, it will be a noble and true part, and not taken up from any impulse, or caprice, or pique, but on true and right principles, that will carry a blessing with them.' Newman's response revealed an element of self-centredness: 'Am I not providing dreariness for myself? if others, whom I am pierced to think about, because I cannot help them, suffer, shall not I suffer in my own way?'[34]

That same month he resigned his position as Vicar of St Mary's, although still clinging to his membership of the Anglican Church, while alluding to his unjust treatment at its hands. His last sermon, preached at a Eucharistic Service at Littlemore church on 25 September, was entitled 'The Parting of Friends'. An element of self pity pervades the oration, which contained such strange, outlandish even, parallels with David's departure from Jonathan at the court of Saul. He also invoked the story of Ruth and Naomi. He received communion on that occasion from Pusey amidst sobs and pregnant pauses. At this symbolic parting of the ways, despite his own long and tortuous path, he could not disguise his disappointment at having failed to persuade the Church of England to move with him towards acceptance of the maternal Catholic origins of the authentic, legitimate Church.

There was more than a hint of bitterness and recrimination in his letters at this time. He had been badly and unfairly treated, as he assured the tractarian Archdeacon Henry Manning: 'No decency has been observed in the attacks upon me from authority: no protests have appeared against them … the English Church is showing herself intrinsically and radically alien from Catholic principles, so do I feel the difficulties in defending their claims to be a branch of the Catholic Church.'[35] Manning responded that it was unreasonable to expect 'the living generation to change the opinions, prejudices, and habits of a whole life in a few years at one bidding'.[36] Newman, however, was not to be appeased. Meanwhile, William Gladstone (whose Roman Catholic convert sister used the pages of Protestant books as lavatory paper), having viewed the Newman-Manning correspondence, judged that Newman was staggering 'to and fro, like a drunken man' at his 'wits' end'.[37]

That November, 1843, Archdeacon Manning, as if to distance himself publicly from the direction in which Newman was heading, preached virulently against

Popery on Guy Fawkes day. The next day he went to Littlemore in order, it seems, to reassure Newman (who had obviously received report of the sermon) of his personal regard. Newman, however, refused to be 'at home'. This was Newman's obstinate high-dudgeon side.

The new year of 1844 brought harsh winter weather and Newman suffered a series of heavy colds as well deepening anxiety and perplexity. He was beginning to feel a stranger in his own university and college. Even the college servants were looking at him as if he were a stranger, he thought. Then his friend Bowden died of tuberculosis. 'He introduced me to College and University', wrote Newman. 'He is the link between me and Oxford. I have ever known Oxford in him. In losing him I seem to lose Oxford. We used to live in each other's rooms as Undergraduates, and men used to mistake our names and call us by each other's.' Then he recollected that strange circumstance recorded in the prologue to his book. 'When he married, he used to make a similar mistake himself, and call me Elizabeth and her Newman. And now for several years past, though loving him with all my heart, I have shrunk from him, feeling that I had opinions that I dared not tell him.' [38]

Newman reflected by Bowden's corpse on the consolations of Anglican prayer. He wrote: 'there lies now my oldest friend, so dear to me – and I with so little of faith or hope, as dead as a stone, and detesting myself.' Bowden had had an easy death, prompting Keble to invoke George Herbert's notion of death as 'going from earth to paradise as from one room to another'. [39] Newman sobbed bitterly over Bowden's coffin, 'to think that he had left me still dark as to what the way of truth was, and what I ought to do in order to please God and fulfil His will'. He bought books with the legacy of a hundred pounds left him by his dead friend, and with the remainder felt he could afford to fund the purchase of hair shirts and scourges for the Littlemore community: a rare hint of the Catholic ascetical rigours he had discreetly undertaken.

CHAPTER 8

How doctrine develops

'But one aspect of Revelation must not be allowed to
exclude or to obscure another.'
J. H. NEWMAN, *ESSAY ON DEVELOPMENT*

In early 1845 matters were coming to a head. The impetuous W. G. Ward had written a book, *The Ideal of a Christian Church*, blatantly asserting the right of an Anglican to profess Roman Catholic spirituality and doctrine, and yet to remain within the Church of England. While exposing Ward to widespread opprobrium for its anti-Protestantism, Newman was also in the firing line for his authorship of *Tract 90*. As Ward put it, 'in subscribing the [39] articles I renounce no one Roman doctrine'.[1]

The difference between the impetuous Ward and the careful, slow moving Newman, was never more succinctly put (despite many distortions in other matters) than by Lytton Strachey:

'The thing that was utterly abhorrent to [Ward]', said one of his friends, 'was to stop short.' Given the premises he would follow out their implications with the mercilessness of a medieval monk, and when he had reached the last limits of argument be ready to maintain whatever propositions he found there with his dying breath … Captivated by the glittering eye of Newman, he swallowed whole the supernatural conception of the universe which Newman had evolved, accepted it as a fundamental premise and began at once to deduce from it whatsoever there might be to be deduced.[2]

On 13 February Ward was deprived of his Oxford degrees, having declined to withdraw six extracts from the book that offended the spirit of the Thirty-Nine Articles. Oxford's Sheldonian Theatre was packed to hear Ward defend himself, many MAs arriving in Oxford on the newly opened railway line from London. The vote to take away his degrees went against him by a mere 58 out of twelve hundred. A further motion to censure Newman's *Tract 90* was vetoed by the Proctors.

Newman's sense of injustice at Ward's treatment was exacerbated, in his mind, by what he saw as the many 'atrocious heresies' of the Church of England, whereas others were being treated 'so severely for being over-Catholic'. The following month he advised Jemima that he was going to resign his Oriel fellowship. She responded that it was like hearing of the imminent death of a friend. 'I have a good name with many; I am deliberately sacrificing it', he replied on 15

March 1845. 'I have a bad name with more; I am fulfilling all their worst wishes, and giving them their most coveted triumph. I am distressing all I love, unsettling all I have instructed or aided … Pity me, my dear Jemima. What have I done thus to be deserted, thus to be left to take a wrong course, if it is wrong?' He added that he feared travelling lest he should die suddenly while in his present state; that if he were in danger would send for a priest.[3]

All the while he had been in the final stages of a work that was to justify his path to Rome, *An Essay on the Development of Christian Doctrine*. In the 'advertisement' he wrote that the book's thesis was directed towards the removal of the obstacle to 'communion with the Church of Rome'. Yet the theme – how and why primitive Christianity should have developed such beliefs and practices as Purgatory, invocation of saints, popes, veneration of the Virgin Mary, and traffic in indulgences – required, and would continue to require, explanations not only for Anglicans, but for Catholics too. He must show, in particular, how the Council of Trent, which defined the counter-reforming stance of Rome, could have been a continuation of the great earlier Councils, rather than a historic discontinuity. At the heart of the book, moreover, is Newman's dissociation of authentic Christianity from liberalism – which he would later characterize, on being made a Cardinal, as 'an error overspreading, as a snare the whole earth'. In the *Essay on Development* he enlarged on his definition and repudiation of liberalism in religion in this way:

That truth and falsehood in religion are but matter of opinion; that one doctrine is as good as another; that the Governor of the world does not intend that we should gain the truth; that there is no truth; that we are not more acceptable to God by believing this than by believing that; that no one is answerable for his opinions; that they are a matter of necessity or accident; that it is enough if we sincerely hold what we profess; that our merit lies in seeking, not in possessing; that it is a duty to follow what seems to us true, without fear lest it should not be true; that it may be a gain to succeed, and can be no harm to fail; that we may take up and lay down opinions at pleasure, that belief belongs to the mere intellect, not the heart also; that we may safely trust to ourselves in matters of Faith, and need no other guide, – this the principle of philosophies and heresies, which is very weakness.[4]

Newman's theory of the Church's development contrasts with perspectives that would emphasise the absolutely unchanging nature of the Church. Ian Ker describes the essay as 'comparable to Darwin's *On the Origin of Species*',[5] which is fair; although the late Avery Dulles comments, perhaps unnecessarily, that Newman's theory is 'not a brief' for a kind of 'dogmatic Darwinism'. 'Newman', Avery continues, also fairly, 'opposes the "transformist" view that Christianity is ever in flux and accommodates itself to the times'.[6]

Such developments as occur, Newman argues, must be shown to be in accord with the Christianity of the Apostles, and antique Christianity. To probe the authenticity of these developments, he invokes seven tests based on his vast reading in the Early Fathers, while significantly avoiding citation of any of the later Catholic authorities such as Suarez and Thomas Aquinas.

He asks that developments should be such that the Church would remain recognisably the same to an Early Father who returned to earth. He lists a number of principles, such as the 'sacramental principle' and the primacy of faith over reason, indicating that there should be a 'continuity' of these original features down to the present. Far from the Church being changed by the cultures it encounters, it is the Church that assimilates and transforms cultures. And there should be logical inferences to be drawn from fundamental truths: for example the cleansing of original sin in baptism implies further satisfaction in the sacrament of penance for sin committed after baptism.

The final three tests pay tribute to the imaginative dimension of continuity, which Newman signals by emphasizing signs of vitality and growth. There is, in the fifth test, the insistence that 'when an idea is living', in other words, 'influential and effective', it develops 'according to its own nature, and the tendencies, which are carried out on the long run, may under favourable circumstances show themselves early as well as late'.[7] And he gives a lively comparison:

Nothing is more common, for instance, than accounts or legends of the anticipations, which great men have given in boyhood of the bent of their minds, as afterwards displayed in their history, so much so that the popular expectation has sometimes led to the invention of them. The child Cyrus mimics a despot's power, and St. Athanasius is elected Bishop by his playfellows.[8]

In the sixth test, 'conservative action upon its past', Newman argues that a corruption, or heresy, is a reversal of vital creativity, whereby a development, like a cancerous growth 'ceases to illustrate, and begins to disturb, the acquisitions gained in its previous history'. He goes on:

A true development, then, may be described as one which is conservative of the course of antecedent developments being really those antecedents and something besides them: it is an addition which illustrates, not obscures, corroborates, not corrects, the body of thought from which it proceeds; and this is the characteristic as contrasted with a corruption.[9]

An example of this, according to Newman, is that the doctrine of the Holy Trinity, the doctrine of the existence of three persons in one God, does not, properly understood, undermine monotheism, but reinforces it.

The final test, 'chronic vigour', appeals to the persistence of vitality, of expanding, flourishing life; whereas corruption, heresy, tends to eventual dissolution. Heresy, he insists, is 'an intermediate state between life and death, or what is like death; or, if it does not result in death, it is resolved into some new, perhaps opposite, course of error which lays no claim to be connected with it'.[10] The tests are followed by Newman's 'application' of them through the history of the Church, making the essay an eclectic study of the history of Christianity. In his application of the seventh and final test, 'chronic vigour', he enlists a catalogue of the Faith's conflicts and struggles, external and internal, with this conclusion:

Is it conceivable that any one of those heresies, with which ecclesiastical history abounds, should have gone through a hundredth part of these trials, yet have come out of them so nearly what it was before, as Catholicism has done? Could such a theology as Arianism have lasted through the scholastic contest? Or Montanism [a second century heresy involving claims for new divine revelation] have endured to possess the world, without coming to a crisis, and failing? Or could the imbecility of the Manichean system, as a religion, have escaped exposure, had it been brought into conflict with the barbarians of the Empire, or the feudal system?[11]

Avery Dulles contends that Newman's teaching on the Virgin Mary is a working exemplification of the tests of authentic development. Mary is invoked, for example, in the principle of the conservative action on the past (does the new doctrine confirm or weaken past ancient faith?). Taking the Protestant objection that devotion to Mary draws the faithful away from Christ, Newman argues that the opposite is true. The title '*theotokos*' (God bearer), he argues, was bestowed on Mary 'to protect the doctrine of the Incarnation, and to preserve the faith of Catholics from a specious Humanitarianism'.[12]

The book's most challenging theme involves Newman's view of the Catholic Church as a single organic 'idea', invoking a notion that owed much to the Romantic common tradition on imagination. The previous generations of poets, Blake, Wordsworth, and Coleridge in particular, saw poetic imagination as productive, prophetic, self-authenticating, rather than merely mimicking nature. Newman's notion of 'idea' is much closer to their version of living symbolism than to an abstract thought. It is as if Newman is treating the Church itself as a living work of art. Indeed his tests of authenticity are reminiscent of principles borrowed from aesthetics. The 'logical sequence' test, moreover, suggests an awareness of the Church's essential harmonies, as if imaginatively alert to its complex musicality – the endless combining and recombining of the many and the one. The cultural historian Stephen Prickett writes of his correspondence with the theologian Nicholas Lash on this point, leading to Lash's suggestion that the metaphor of a musical fugue is perhaps the best way to understand 'logical sequence':

The various models [Newman] uses serve as basic structures for the fugue: historical, philosophical, and christological. The tendency to … treat [the 'idea' or Church] as if it were a person, which we find in some passages, [Lash] suggests, is partly due to the fact that one of the themes of the fugue is an explicit identification of the 'idea' with the person of the living Christ striding, as it were, through history.[13]

The Church is, of course, a 'fact', but its contents and evidences are perceived, Newman insists, through the imagination as if it were a living, changing, diverse, organic unity, in which its diversities are drawn into a whole. 'But one aspect of Revelation must not be allowed to exclude or to obscure another … Christianity is dogmatical, devotional, practical all at once; it is esoteric and exoteric; it is indulgent and strict; it is light and dark; it is love, and it is fear.'[14] It acts like all living entities in a non-stop process of growth.

While some authorities, such as Jacques-Bénigne Bossuet, the great seventeenth-century French preacher, had argued that change was the test of heresy (the Church being ever the same),[15] Newman turned the criterion on its head. 'The more claim an idea has to be considered living, the more various will be its aspects; and the more social and political is its nature, the more complicated and subtle will be its issues, and the longer and more eventful will be its course.'[16]

That was not the only notion he reversed. Exemplifying the dynamism of the Church with a river, he thwarted the expectations of his readers with a paradoxical rendering of the familiar metaphor. Whereas, for example, the distinguished translator of the Book of Isaiah, Robert Lowth, had employed the metaphor of a stream as in gradual deterioration, increasingly polluted, 'the stream generally becoming more impure, the more distant it is from its source',[17] Newman turns the expectation inside out with a striking conceit:

… the stream is clearest near the spring. Whatever use may fairly be made of his image, it does not apply to the history of a philosophy or belief, which on the contrary is more equable, and purer, and stronger, when its bed has become deep, and broad, and full. It necessarily rises out of an existing state of things, and for a time savours of the soil. Its vital element needs disengaging from what is foreign and temporary, and is employed in efforts after freedom which become more vigorous and hopeful as its years increase. Its beginnings are no measure of its capabilities, nor of its scope. At first no one knows what it is, or what it is worth. It remains perhaps for a time quiescent; it tries, as it were, its limbs, and proves the ground under it, and feels its way. From time to time it makes essays which fail, and are in consequence abandoned. It seems in suspense which way to go; it wavers, and at length strikes out in one definite direction. In time it enters upon strange territory; points of controversy alter their bearing; parties rise and fall around it; dangers and hopes appear in new relations; and old principles reappear under new forms. It changes with them in order to remain the same. In a higher world it is otherwise, but here below to live is to change, and to be perfect is to have changed often.[18]

The essay was challenged and criticized, most notably by Newman's contemporary, F. D. Maurice, theologian and socialist. Maurice noted that Newman's 'system' of 'generative powers, vital energies, in unceasing movement' is a kind of inflexible self-regulating process, more vegetable than human. It does not allow, he argued, for the conscious, interacting dialectical processes described by Coleridge within literary traditions, whereby tradition makes the writer and the writer in turn shapes the tradition. As Coleridge wrote in his *Lectures on Shakespeare*:

… few there have been among critics, who have followed with the eye of the imagination the imperishable, yet ever-wandering, spirit of poetry through its various metempsychoses, and consequent metamorphoses; – or who have rejoiced in the light of clear perception at beholding with each new birth, with each rare avatar, the human race frame to itself a new body, by assimilating materials of nourishment out of its new circumstances, and work for itself new organs or power appropriate to the new sphere of its motion and activity.[19]

Maurice, however, was convinced that Christianity's sure foundation was not so much the Church, and emphatically not the Bishop of Rome, but Scripture; Maurice being secure in a tradition of criticism that had been exploring the Bible as poetry. In the preface to his *Lectures on the Epistle to the Hebrews* Maurice deconstructs Newman's theory of development, insisting that Christianity's organic continuity has developed from the prophetic revelation running from the Old Testament to the New. The two thinkers nevertheless share in common an imaginative apprehension of the Church that is peculiarly English, literary, of its time, and alien to scholastic and Roman ways of thinking about development.

That very literary approach has failed to impress some subsequent critics, even Catholic ones. An example of which is the Oxford philosopher, and former Catholic priest, Anthony Kenny. While still a priest, albeit in the process of thinking himself out of the Church, Kenny criticized the explanatory force of Newman's essay when, in 1962, he was assigned to lecture on the topic of development of doctrine before a conference of diocesan clergy:

Catholics were taught that revelation had ceased with the death of the last Apostle, and that the Faith was unchanging. How was this to be reconciled with the manifest variation in the theological beliefs recorded during the long history of the Church? I set out the difficulties with gusto: the changing attitude of Catholic Christians to the imminent return of Christ, to the creation of the world in seven days, to the Pope's temporal sovereignty and deposing power, to the lawfulness of usury. Cardinal Newman had written a celebrated account of the development: all it offered, I complained, was metaphor in place of explanation.[20]

The drift of the book does indeed appeal to powerful metaphors rather than logical argument, and borders on the poetic rather than the philosophical. Newman had laboured over it as if it were a work of art. 'Perhaps one gets over-sensitive even about style, as one gets on in life', he informed Mrs William Froude. 'Besides re-writing, every part has to be worked out and defined as in moulding a statue. I get on, as a person walks with a lame ankle, who does get on, and gets to his journey's end, but not comfortably.'[21]

PART TWO

CHAPTER 9.

Rome at last

'I will not raise controversy in the Church, and it would
ill become a neo Catholic to be introducing views …'

J. H. NEWMAN LETTER TO J. D. DALGAIRNS, FEAST OF ST CECILIA, 1846

The writing of *An Essay on the Development of Christian Doctrine* was a crucial, life-changing process in the story of Newman's quest for the true Church. 'As I advanced', he would write, 'my difficulties so cleared away that I ceased to speak of "the Roman Catholics", and boldly called them Catholics. Before I got to the end, I resolved to be received, and the book remains in the state in which it was then, unfinished.'[1]

In September of 1845 Dalgairns left to enter the Catholic Church. On 2 October it was the turn of Ambrose St John. The next day Newman formally resigned his Oriel fellowship. Hawkins, the Provost of Oriel, wrote a sombre letter trusting that he would not sink into such Romish errors as worshipping statues.

Father Dominic Barberi, a member of the Passionist Congregation with a reputation for holiness, had received many converts into the Roman Catholic Church, and was due to visit Littlemore from Birmingham on 8 October. He was an Italian with poor English and no scholar or intellectual. He was a charismatic spiritual director, albeit of a different kind of charisma than Newman. Born into a peasant family near Viterbo, and orphaned at the age of six, Barberi's path to priesthood had been difficult as a result of his illiteracy well into boyhood. On arrival on the English 'mission' in 1842, aged 50, he had contended with resentment from 'old Catholics', suspicious of Italianate-style piety, as well as local Protestant attacks. He was once stoned by boys in the street; he picked up the rocks, kissed them, and placed them in his pockets.

He was met off the coach in Oxford by Dalgairns, whom Newman had told: 'When you see your friend, will you tell him that I wish him to receive me into the Church of Christ.' Father Dominic was soaked, having journeyed from Birmingham for five hours on the outside of a coach in a storm. They went by chaise to Littlemore, arriving at the cottages after eleven o'clock. Dominic later told his confreres that he was drying himself before the fire when Newman entered: 'The door opened – and what a spectacle it was for me to see at my feet John Henry Newman begging me to hear his confession and admit him into the bosom of the Catholic Church! And there by the fire he began his general confession with extraordinary humility and devotion.' The next day Father Dominic heard the rest of his confession.[2]

Newman had prepared for his confession all week. The following March he would write to Mrs Bowden, wife of his lately dead friend John, about the final period before his decision to be received into the Church:

Of course *I* should call them artifices of the enemy to hinder what seems inevitable. The moment before acting may be, as can easily be imagined, peculiarly dreary ... I could do nothing but shut myself up in my room and lie down on my bed.[3]

Newman had finally come home. And yet he was going into exile, not least from Oxford. He would write in the *Apologia* those famous lines of longing and nostalgia for Oxford: 'There used to be much snap-dragon growing on the walls opposite my freshman's rooms there [at Trinity College], and I had for years taken it as the emblem of my own perpetual residence even unto death in my University ... I have never seen Oxford since, excepting its spires, as they are seen from the railway.'[4]

His separations would extend to family members, many old friends, colleagues, and pupils: all that he had known and could call home. As the news spread throughout the country, and even overseas, the reactions to his 'perversion' to Rome was received with incomprehension, anger, and disgust. Gladstone would write that Newman's conversion 'has never yet been estimated at anything like the full amount of its calamitous importance'.[5] In the aftermath, others, Anglican clergy and lay people, would follow, but it would take time for the truly 'calamitous' repercussions of Newman's rejection of the Church of England to take effect.

OSCOTT AND MARYVALE

At a mid-point on the Chester Road, which connects industrial conurbations north of Birmingham – Brownhills and Stoke on Trent – with the leafy townships of Leamington Spa and Warwick, one passes a screen of tall trees, punctuated by gothic gatehouses. Beyond lies an impressive neo-gothic building, four storeys high with many towers and gables, and cloisters. There are well-stocked libraries, lecture halls, a museum, and a chapel built by Augustus Welby Pugin filled with late Medieval decorative treasures brought over from the Continent – the ecclesiastical casualties of the French Revolution. This is Oscott College, opened in 1838 as a school and seminary; it was also the headquarters for the revival of Catholicism in England in the mid-nineteenth-century. The historian Lord Acton, who was a boy in the school in the 1840s, wrote that 'we thought that Oscott was the centre of the world'.[6] The magnificent new college had in fact replaced a smaller house half a mile distant, known thereafter as Old Oscott.

Before the end of October 1845, Newman, newly received into the Catholic Church, visited Nicholas Wiseman, now President of Oscott College (having left the English College in Rome). Wiseman confirmed Newman and Ambrose St John in Pugin's chapel on the Feast of All Saints, 1 November 1845. Then he offered Newman and his Oxford converts the Old Oscott house which Newman promptly renamed Maryvale. There was a chapel and some twenty rooms, and here he could make his home, a 'Littlemore continued'. Yet first he must wind up his affairs at the old Littlemore. While pondering his future within the Catholic Church, he embarked on the task of 'burning and packing … reading and folding – passing from a metaphysical MS to a lump of resin or an ink-glass'. It was a typically self-conscious, literary flourish of the conceptual and the tangible. He did not finish until 22 February 1846: 'I quite tore myself away – and could not help kissing my bed, and mantelpiece, and other parts of the house.'[7]

Newman found his first Catholic home at Maryvale 'dismally ugly'. He confessed that he had little idea of what it meant to be a Catholic in daily practice. The impact of his 'going over' focused at first on that most Catholic of doctrines and devotions, belief in the Real Presence in the consecrated wafer, preserved and venerated in the ornate cupboard or tabernacle on the altar of most Catholic churches and chapels, attended by a hanging oil lamp. 'I am writing next room to the Chapel – It is such an incomprehensible blessing to have Christ in bodily presence in one's house, within one's walls, as swallows up all other privileges and destroys, or should destroy, every pain. To know that He is close by – to be able again and again through the day to go in to Him …'[8] Reflecting on his visits to Catholic churches in the past, he wrote: 'I did not know, or did not observe, the tabernacle Lamp – but now after tasting of the awful delight of worshipping God in His Temple, how unspeakably cold is the idea of a Temple without that Divine Presence! One is tempted to say what is the meaning, what is the use of it.'[9]

Yet all was not unsullied joy. The spiritual consolation, he wrote, 'destroys, or should destroy, every pain'. It did not. Oscott College, where he was obliged to spend much of his day, with its 'hosts of visitors', he found a 'place of dissipation'. And while he had been nurturing a circle of female friends, mainly as correspondents, he deplored the 'tribes of women' that flocked to the college. He was soon to taste a lack of respect and consideration on the part of his new co-religionists, as well as unwarranted assurance from a constituency of converts, and old Catholics, who took it upon themselves to deliver him lectures. There was scant 'delicacy towards my feelings', he would complain. He recollected some years later:

How dreary my first year at Maryvale ... when I was the gaze of so many eyes at Oscott, as if some wild incomprehensible beast, caught by the hunter, and a spectacle for Dr. Wiseman to exhibit to strangers, as himself being the hunter who captured it! [10]

Six years on he would write to his friend T. W. Allies, a married man who found it hard converting to Catholicism: 'Your trial ... is a most exceedingly great one, but those who are unmarried have their own. They are solitary and thrown among strangers more intimately and intensely than married people can be ... We have been (necessarily) located as children being grown men.' [11]

It went hard with him, moreover, that even young Dalgairns, of the generation that had idolised him at Oxford, now considered himself on the same level and qualified to 'lecture' him. Meanwhile, Wiseman, the President of Oscott, whether to give him a lesson in humility, or from thoughtlessness, made him stand at his door 'waiting for Confession amid the Oscott boys'. [12]

And yet, he had suggested to Wiseman that he wanted to be 'strictly under obedience and discipline for a time'. [13] His wish was granted in the form of a period of seminary training in Rome at the College of Propaganda. Founded in the seventeenth century, and under the teaching authority of the Jesuits, the college was a power-house for intending missionaries to distant lands. The choice signalled the expectation that Newman would head a new evangelisation thrust in England.

While deciding on his future, and that of St John, Dalgairns and the other recent Littlemore converts, he would get a dose of *Romanità*. He had been considering entering one of the great religious orders: the Vincentians, perhaps, the Dominicans, or the Jesuits. Wiseman had already suggested the Oratorian congregation for its 'external secularism with a gentle inward bond of asceticism'. [14] The Oratorians, founded by Philip Neri in Rome in the sixteenth century, were communities of secular priests, living together without vows in city locations, dedicating themselves to scholarship, writing, and pastoral work. There was no Oratory in England, and Wiseman evidently thought that such a community led by Newman in London or Birmingham, or perhaps both, could have a significant missionary influence in England.

Newman and St John set off for Italy, reaching Milan on 20 September. Again he was struck by the glimmering sanctuary lamps in all the churches. 'It is really most wonderful to see this Divine Presence looking out almost into the open streets ... I never knew what worship was, as an objective fact, till I entered the Catholic Church ...' [15] He would write that 'there is nothing which has brought home to me so much the Unity of the Church, as the presence of its Divine Founder and Life wherever I go – All places are, as it were, one ...' [16] At the Duomo he was struck by the devotional buzz typical of Catholic cathedrals on the continent: 'groups of worshippers, and solitary ones – kneeling, standing – some at shrines, some at altars – hearing Mass and communicating – currents of worshippers intercepting and passing by each other – altar after altar lit up for worship, like stars in the firmament …'[17] So unlike an Anglican cathedral!

His sensibilities were nevertheless affronted by Italian manners. 'They spit everywhere – they spit on the kneeling boards – they encourage it, and as if for amusement go on every ten seconds … They spit over the floors of their rooms – their floors are filthy principally with dust … if you drop your coat or stockings in undressing, it is far worse than if you dropped them in the street.'[18]

Newman's first impression of his hotel in Rome was of 'a palace of filth'. He was disgusted by the Romans' 'horrible cruelty to animals – also with their dishonesty, lying and stealing apparently without any conscience – and thirdly with their extreme dirt'.[19] Yet he was also struck by '*every where* a simple certainty in believing which to a Protestant or Anglican is quite astonishing'.[20] He had preferred, however, that they revealed a faith that leads to 'sanctity of character' rather than a faith that can 'disjoin religion and morality'.

PAPAL AUDIENCE

Visitors to Rome wishing to summon a fleeting sense of Newman's presence should mount the steps from the famous Via dei Condotti with its international boutiques and turn right along the Piazza di Spagna passing the façade of the Propaganda College on the left and walk to the end of the street. There on the left is the church known as San Andrea delle Fratte, ministered by a Franciscan community. Within the church is the side-altar where a Jewish businessman, Alphonse Ratisbonne, claimed to have received a vision of the Virgin Mary. He subsequently converted to Catholicism in 1842 and became a priest (today the shrine is also celebrated as the place where Father Maximilian Kolbe – who gave his life up for a fellow inmate at Auschwitz – said his first Mass). If one looks from the nave of the church up through the high clerestory windows it is possible to see the windows of the apartment created for Newman and St John at the rear of the Propaganda building. They, in turn, could look down from their windows into the shrine of the Virgin.

A portrait by Maria Giberne hangs outside Newman's room at the Birmingham Oratory, depicting Newman and Ambrose sitting at a table in their study at the Propaganda. They are dressed in cassocks and cloaks. Newman appears to be gazing pensively at the young, slim, blonde-haired St John, widely referred to by the Roman monsignori as an 'Angel Guardian'; the younger man sits staring at the floor, as if in shock. Behind them is depicted the image of Our Lady of the Miraculous Medal, or Our lady of the Immaculate Conception (the result of another apparition, to Catherine Labouré in the convent chapel in Rue du Bac, Paris, in 1830), which is commemorated in the church below.

Newman and St John were granted an audience with Pius IX, known familiarly as Pio Nono, who was in the first year of his pontificate and only 54 years of age. Pio had declared that he wished to see Newman 'again and again'. As Newman genuflected to kiss the pontifical ring, he stumbled and banged his head against the papal knee. The Pope was evidently pleased with the prize conversion, referring to him as a 'recovered sheep'. There were high hopes in the papal palace of the conversion of England to its old faith and His Holiness entertained the visitors with a story about a convert Anglican clergyman. But when St John – somehow failing to appreciate the avuncular drift of the anecdote – asked for specific details, including the man's name, the pope laughed, took him by the arm, and replied that he could not pronounce English names.

Newman noted that the Holy Father was 'a vigorous man with a very pleasant countenance, and was most kind'.[21] He also thought he had the most 'English face' in Italy: this evidently being intended as a compliment. But there was to be an early frisson as a result of an item of gossip winging its way around Rome and back to the Apostolic Palace. Newman was asked at short notice by a leading Roman nobleman to preach at the funeral of the niece of the Earl of Shrewsbury, the noted Catholic philanthropist and supporter of Pugin. The congregation included many members of the English nobility, including Protestants who were wintering in Rome. Newman's friend Maria Giberne, who was also present (she had tried to kiss the Pope's foot a few days earlier and nearly sent him flying), conceded that the preaching was rather 'deliberate' – a token of his 'deep feeling'. Evidently his Oxford charisma was not working in Rome. He told the distinguished congregation that the Eternal City was 'not the place for them, but the very place in the whole world where Michael and the Dragon may almost be seen in battle'. He lambasted the English tourists for 'prying like brute animals into the holiest places'.[22] The congregation spilled out of the church angrily asserting that Newman had referred to them as 'dogs'. Ambrose St John noted in his diary that a group of glowering Protestants looked as if they would 'eat' Newman. One was heard to say that Newman should be tossed into the Tiber. Newman remarked later: 'O, I was a sort of sucking child, just as much knowing what I should say, what I should not say, and saying nothing right, not from want of tact so much as from sheer ignorance'.[23] Matters were made worse by a meddlesome Vatican official and former Anglican, Monsignor George Talbot, who had at first professed warm friendship with Newman on his arrival in Rome. Talbot, a relative of the Earl of Shrewsbury, was a favoured advisor and toady in the court of Pio, with title of Papal Chamberlain. Talbot, who was present at the sermon, and even admitted to liking it at the time, subsequently tittle-tattled to the Pope that it was a disaster and gave offence. Whereupon Pio remarked that Mr Newman should apply honey rather than vinegar in his pastoral work, and that he was evidently more of a philosopher than a preacher. Monsignor Talbot will return to our story as an influential antagonist in years to come.

TO BE AN ORATORIAN

The sermon debacle was less of a concern to Newman, however, than the negative reception in Rome of his *Essay on Development*. An American newspaper editor, and well-known recent convert from Unitarianism to Catholicism, Orestes Brownson of Boston, had charged in an article in his own newspaper that Newman had given comfort to those who denied the doctrine of the Trinity. The Unitarians, he claimed, had seized on the book to claim that belief in the Trinity did not belong to 'primitive' Christianity, but was a development of the third century. Surely Newman's book should be put on the Index of forbidden books. Newman was at first inclined to dismiss the attack as the work of 'a half-converted Yankee',[24] but he was concerned by the news that America's bishops were up in arms against him, and that doubts about his orthodoxy were gaining purchase in Rome, particularly among the Jesuits. The problem was that the Roman theologians did not know English, and the Jesuits were receiving bits of mistranslation from America. They did not understand him, and their terms were at variance. On a particular point: where Newman talked of 'probability' based on demonstrative and circumstantial evidence, the Jesuits took this as a denial that certainty could be attained in matters of doctrine. So Newman appealed to the authority of the theologian De Lugo on the contrast between reason and faith; but De Lugo, it appeared, cut little ice among the Roman professors. Father Carlo Passaglia, a leading theologian in Rome, opined that Newman was attempting to replace certainty with probability. Meanwhile Father Giovanni Peronne, a professor at the Jesuit Collegio Romanum, had plucked a quotation from one of Newman's earlier Anglican anti-papal texts expressing the opinion that the Pope was Satan. It got back to Newman that the teachers at the Collegio were consequently plundering his Essay to teach the students the difference between orthodoxy and heresy. This was particularly irritating to Newman as Father Peronne himself was writing a book in defence of the imminent declaration of the dogma of the Immaculate Conception (a belief that had once been opposed by such great figures as St Bernard and St Thomas Aquinas); the Immaculate Conception, Newman declared, was a classic instance of development of doctrine in action. Remembering the case of Lamennais, the French philosopher and priest, who had once been welcomed in Rome, only to be later denounced by Gregory XVI, Newman was anxious lest it should be whispered that here was another Lamennais in the Eternal City.

Newman's dismay was not a matter of authorial pride, nor even of personal anxiety lest he should find himself, as in England, at the centre of controversy. He was convinced that Rome's theologians were not equal to countering the difficulties of Anglicans, on the one hand, and the growing atheism of the age, on the other. He was convinced that it was his vocation to expound apologetics for a new era. As he would write to his friend J. M. Capes on the same theme in December 1849:

Italian divines … know nothing at all of heretics as realities – they live, at least in Rome, in a place whose boast is that it has never given birth to heresy, and they think proofs ought be convincing which in fact are not. Hence they are accustomed to speak of the argument for Catholicism as a demonstration, and to see no force in objections to it and to admit no perplexity of intellect which is not directly and immediately wilful.[25]

He decided nevertheless that it would be best to take things slowly, hoping that the *Essay on Development* would in time achieve its effect. In the event, after he wrote a summary of his development theory in Latin for Peronne, the Jesuit's doubts about Newman's theology began to evaporate and they became friends. Ambrose St John reported: 'N. has struck up quite a close friendship with F. Peronne: they embrace each other.'[26] Peronne's principal objection was now confined to Newman's expression 'new dogmas' instead of 'new definitions'. In principle they agreed. Both accepted that while the 'deposit of the Faith' was committed to the Church before the death of the last apostle, Christians were not explicitly conscious of all its intellectual implications. The 'dogma' was given once and for all, but the definitions would emerge, or develop, with time.

Meanwhile a visit to the great Oratorian house in Rome, adjoining the Chiesa Nuova (which can be viewed on the right of Corso Vittorio Emanuele II as one approaches the Vatican), finally won Newman over to the idea of establishing an Oratorian congregation in England. The domestic arrangements reminded him of an Oxford College, and he approved of the Oratorians being allowed to keep their money and property.

In January he wrote to Wiseman that he had now come round to his original suggestion that the Oratorian congregation would be an ideal choice of life for himself and his companions. The following month he put in a formal submission to the Vatican to establish a community in England, and it found immediate favour with the Pope. By May, he and St John had received Roman Catholic Holy Orders after a nine-day retreat with the Jesuits.

ORDINATION AGAIN

During his ordination retreat Newman wrote out an examination of conscience in Latin, translated by the Oratorian Father Henry Tristram in the posthumous volume: *Autobiographical Writings*. At the heart of this exercise is the admission:

I am querulous, timid, lazy, suspicious … I have not that practical, lively and present faith, against the persistent working and wiles of the evil spirit in my heart, which I ought to have….

When I was growing up, and as a young man, I had confidence and hope in God … But when I began to apply my intellect to sacred subjects, and to read and write, twenty years ago and more, then, although what I wrote was for the most part true and useful, nevertheless, first, I lost my natural and inborn faith … then too I have lost my simple confidence in the word of God … That subtle and delicate vigour of faith has become dulled in me, and remains so to this day…. What is more serious, I have for some years fallen into a kind of despair and gloomy state of mind.[27]

It appears indicative of a mild depression, an impression reinforced by a harsh image that follows. 'I have in my mind a wound or cancer', he wrote[28]; and as he reflected in circular mode, it appears that he was experiencing a sense of lethargy and dissatisfaction typical of the complaint familiar among religious, known as *accidie*, or what he called 'dreariness'.

Enlarging on his own modest attainments in the devout life, he confirms an assessment that he would make later of himself: 'I have nothing of a saint about me as everyone knows.'[29] He complains in his Rome self-assessment of lack of fervour. 'I creep along the ground, or even run – well enough for one who creeps or runs, but I cannot fly.'[30] He reveals himself as comfortable with routines of devotion and prayer: 'The Mass, visits to the Blessed Sacrament, the Rosary, litanies, the Breviary – all these give me pleasure.'[31] But he declares that anything beyond this distracts and terrifies his mind, because he is 'subject to scruples', or distracting obsessive thoughts. He goes on to write '… it is difficult to explain and strange even to myself, but I have this peculiarity, that in the movement of my affections, whether sacred or human, my physical strength cannot go beyond certain limits'.[32]

It is a remarkable admission, since he regards this as permanently limiting the scope of his spiritual life. He confesses that he is 'always languid' in his thoughts of 'divine things', and like a man 'walking with his feet bound together'.[33] It is, he writes, a physical thing which prevents him from being 'fervent in praying and meditating'.

While conscious that he had enthusiastically embarked on Catholic-style asceticism while still an Anglican at Littlemore, he notes that he no longer relishes such practices. His religious life is pedestrian. 'I cannot rise above it to a higher level.'[34] He accuses himself of mild self-centredness: 'I do not like poverty, troubles, restrictions, inconveniences … I like tranquility, security, a life among friends, and among books, untroubled by business cares – the life of an Epicurean in fact.'[35] He confesses to being unacceptably self-willed: 'In almost everything I like my own way of acting; I do not want to change the place or business in which I find myself, to undertake the affairs of others, to walk, to go on a journey, to visit others, since I prefer to remain at home.'[36] The comments are ironic in view of his activities five years hence, when he would found the Catholic university in Dublin, a city to which he would commute regularly from Birmingham while embroiled in a host of literary and vexing administrative tasks.

In the meantime, the self-examination shows him still smarting from what he saw as unjust treatment at the hands of the leadership of the Church of England; not unmixed with self-righteousness and self-pity – faults that he does not recognize in himself, at least at this stage of his life:

In the Church of England I had many detractors; a mass of calumny was hurled at me: my services towards that Church were misrepresented by almost everyone in authority in it. I became an exile in solitude, where I spent some years with certain of my friends, but not even in that retreat was I safe from those who pursued me with their curiosity. I believe and hope that I did not on that account give way to anger, indignation, or the like, for in that respect I am not especially sensitive, but I was oppressed and lost hope. And now the cheerfulness I used to have has almost vanished.37

After ordination into the Catholic priesthood, his spirits evidently revived during a trip to the Castelli region, Tivoli, and the lakes of Albano and Nemi, before meeting up with his young confreres at the Cistercian community of Santa Croce in Rome. Here were the future Oratorians of England, joining their 'Father' Newman and Ambrose St John to make a mandatory novitiate retreat before formal admission as Oratorians: Dalgairns, Stanton, Bowles, William Coffin and Robert Coffin who had come out from England. But again, Newman sank back into his mild *accidie* under the novitiate regime, which he found 'dreary' in the absence of the 'scouts' and college servants of his Oxford days – 'room-sweeping, slop-emptying, dinner-serving, bed making, shoe blacking'.[38] But he broke the routine to visit Naples and the great Oratory there.

While touring the city's churches and shrines he gave cautious credit to the variety of liquefaction 'miracles', of which there were some fifty within ten miles of the centre; but he was unable to attend the most famous one of all, the liquefaction of the blood of San Gennaro (Saint Januarius). Gennaro was a fourth century bishop and martyr whose blood was collected in an ampule from the sand of the amphitheatre where he was killed. The blood remained black and solid until the occurrence of its liquefaction phenomenon, first reported in the fourteenth century, and a regular event on the commemoration of the saint's martyrdom, 19 September.

Newman made a distinction between doctrine and devotion, and the cult of Januarius was emphatically devotional although, describing it to Henry Wilberforce, he gave qualified credence to the supernatural nature of the event:

Catholics, till they have seen it, doubt it – Our [Oratorian] father director here tells us that before he went to Naples, he did not believe it. That is, they have vague ideas of natural means, exaggeration etc, not of course imputing fraud. They say conversions often take place in consequence … it is not simple liquefaction, but sometimes it swells, sometimes boils, sometimes melts – no one can tell what is going to take place. They say it is quite overcoming — and people cannot help crying to see it. I understand that Sir H. Davy attended every day, and it was this extreme variety of the phenomenon which convinced him that nothing physical would account for it. Yet there is this remarkable fact, that liquefactions of blood are common at Naples – and unless it is irreverent to the Great Author of miracles to be obstinate in the inquiry, the question certainly rises whether there is something in the air. (Mind, I don't believe there is – and, speaking humbly, and without having seen it, think it a true miracle – but I am arguing). We saw the blood of St Patrizia, half liquid, i.e. liquefying, on her feast day.[39]

By November the new English Oratorians came out of their retreat and prepared to return to England. Newman bade farewell to Pio Nono at the Quirinal Palace, the papal summer residence, on 3 December and set off for England via Loreto – to visit one of the most famous, and, for Protestants, most suspect of devotional shrines, the Holy House of Mary. Legend had it that the house in which the Virgin Mary was born, and received news of her pregnancy from the Angel Gabriel, was carried by Angels from Nazareth in three stages, to be deposited, finally, at its present site (nowadays Our Lady of Loreto is the patron of airline pilots!). Writing again to Henry Wilberforce, he noted: 'We went there to get the Blessed Virgin's blessing on us.' As if to boast his new Catholic credentials, Newman went on to emphasise his devotion to the Virgin, and his consciousness of her protection, as a feature of his adult life: 'I have ever been under her shadow, if I may say it. My College was St Mary's, and my Church; and when I went to Littlemore, there, by my own previous disposition, our Blessed Lady was waiting for me. Nor did she do nothing for me in that low habitation, of which I always think with pleasure.'[40]

LOSS AND GAIN

During his sojourn in Rome Newman found time to write a novel that carried him back to his early Oxford years, although its central theme explored more recent preoccupations and decisions. *Loss and Gain: The Story of a Convert*, depicts the hero, Charles Reding, as an undergraduate on the path from Anglicanism to Roman Catholicism. His spiritual journey, with its hesitations, scruples, and questionings, is described in a series of conversations at his home (his father is a parson) and on walks around Oxford, and in college rooms. The principal foil for Charles's quest is Sheffield, a clever fellow undergraduate. Newman would claim in later years that he wrote the novel to help out his publisher, James Burns, who was sustaining financial loss as a result of Newman's going over to Rome. That does not tell the whole story. The book is clearly autobiographical, and expresses a languorous nostalgia for a world of innocent male intimacy, where there was time to walk and talk the days and weeks away; endless breakfasts, luncheons and dinners, long vacations when time stood still.

In *Loss and Gain* Newman describes young men walking and talking two by two, when 'a soft melancholy came over us, of which the shadows fall even now …'[41]; young men walking 'arm-in-arm along Broad Street, evidently very intimate'. The diffidence towards women is pointed up in the discussion between Charles and Sheffield on the topic of dancing:

It makes me laugh to think what I have done, when a boy, to escape dancing; there is something so absurd in it; and one had to be civil and to duck to young girls who were either prim or pert. I have behaved quite rudely to them sometimes, and then have been annoyed at my ungentlemanlikeness, and not known how to get out of the scrape.

'Well, I didn't know we were so like each other in anything', said Charles, 'oh, the misery I have endured, in having to stand up to dance, and to walk about with a partner! – everybody looking at me, and I so awkward. It has been torture to me days before and after.'[42]

The book opens with Charles's clergyman father declaring: 'No one on earth can know Charles's secret thoughts. Did I guard him here at home ever so well, yet, in due time, it would be found that a serpent had crept into the heart of his innocence.'[43] Newman the author, however, does know the secrets of Charles's heart, because he is clearly modeled on himself. In the course of the novel we find him searching for 'reality' in religion, but he is also seeking love. He had 'found very few friends' among his former school acquaintances: 'Some', he remarks, 'were too gay for him, and he had avoided them; others, with whom he had been intimate … had fairly cut him on coming into residence.'[44] He makes friends with Sheffield and they embark on discussions about the relative merits of Anglicanism and Catholicism – to which Charles is increasingly drawn.

One cannot help feeling sympathy with Sheffield, who soon grows weary of Charles's preoccupation with religion. And while Newman intends the reader to gather that Sheffield is a shallow individual, Charles's interest in ecclesiastical matters, crucial as they are to the purpose of the story, border at times on the superficial: comparative liturgies, rood screens, Gregorian versus Gothic architecture, credence tables, holy water stoups, vestments, styles of church music.

Newman would claim that the book was not apologetic; yet he has a strong design on the reader. The underlying theme is the contrast between religionists who have no sense of history, and those that do. Newman portrays a contrast familiar among the dons of Oriel between 'viewiness' and having a 'view'. 'Viewiness', according to this parlance, is to be 'impatient to reduce things to a system'. A true view is gained by a process of development. Writing to a correspondent in 1845 about the reasons he had written the *Essay on Development*, Newman asserts: 'When we have lost our way we mount up to some eminence to look about us', [45] rather than diving 'into the nearest thicket to find out his bearings.' [46] Those guilty of 'viewiness' rather than views

hear of men, and things, and projects, and struggles, and principles; but everything comes and goes like the wind, nothing makes an impression, nothing penetrates, nothing has its place in their minds. They locate nothing; they have no system. They hear and they forget; or they just recollect what they have once heard, they can't tell where. [47]

Charles is depicted as one who comes to Catholicism not as a 'conclusion from premises' but through a process of gradual experience, process, growth. 'All the paper-arguments in the world are unequal to giving one a view in a moment.' [48] Newman was evidently pondering the nature of faith, or assent, as a process of many strands; and there is an impressive moment when a priest tells Charles: 'A man's moral self is concentrated in each moment of his life; it lives in the tips of his fingers, and the spring of his insteps.' [49] Yet, while a work of fiction, with its narrative progression, might have demonstrated this idea, so replete in Newman's own life, and powerfully to be argued in his *Grammar of Assent*, the novel fails to exemplify the conviction.

There are nevertheless glimpses of his powerful literary imagination at work. Here he is, dealing with the great paradox of conscience versus dogma and Church authority. Of 'private judgement' as a guide for converts, he writes:

they use it in order ultimately to supersede it; as a man out of doors uses a lamp in a dark night, and puts it out when he gets home. What would be thought of his bringing it into his drawing room? … if he came in with a great-coat on his back, a hat on his head, an umbrella under his arm, and a large stable-lantern in his hand? [50]

Loss and Gain was written, evidently, with Anglican waverers in mind, and the Tractarians and Anglo-Catholics Newman had left behind had plenty to waver about by the time Newman had returned from Rome.

That year an Evangelical parson of the Church of England, George Cornelius Gorham, had been promoted to a new parish, but the Bishop of Exeter, the High Anglican Henry Phillpotts, had rejected the appointment because he considered the incumbent-to-be's position on the theology of baptism tainted by Calvinism. Gorham appealed to the Archbishop of Canterbury's Court of Arches, which confirmed the bishop's decision. So Gorham next took his case to the secular Privy Council, which found in his favour. Here again was proof that the supposedly apostolic Church of England was run by lay politicians. Among those who left the Established Church for Rome at this time was Archdeacon Henry Manning.

Ironically, while High Anglicans continued to agonise over the conundrum as to how an Established Church could at one and the same time be the one true Church of the apostles, the sister Church of the Episcopalians in the United States of America had shown how its members could thrive as a disestablished community that was both sacramental and apostolic. Bishop John Henry Hobart of New York had proved himself a great leader of his Church in America, initiating worldwide missions. While the Churches in England continued to suffer fragmentation and erosion Episcopalian and Anglican efforts redoubled to take the Gospel into every continent on earth. The Tractarian movement and its followers had made available to the Church of England a deeper understanding of the dignity and authority of bishops. At the same time the Episcopal authority gave impetus to new, more independent Church structures such as the resumption of the Convocations of York and Canterbury. The new sense of confidence and identity would sustain the Anglican and Episcopalian Churches in colonies throughout the world. In New Zealand Bishop George Selwyn encouraged lay participation that would in time influence practices in England.

Newman had delivered a blow to the Church of his birth; but while he was followed by some notable former Tractarians and stragglers, and while there would be a steady stream down the years, it was not to be a grand walk-out. As Professor Diarmaid MacCulloch puts it succinctly: 'Newman's background in intense Evangelical religiosity meant that his years as a Tractarian were a staging post on an unstable lurch away from his roots, but the existing High Church party, much caricatured by callow Tractarians as "High and Dry", was not so easily tipped towards Rome, and beyond the shores of Britain, there were other sources of strength.'[51]

PIO NONO'S TRIBULATION

If the depth of Newman's Catholicism was marked by his new, fervent devotion to the Virgin Mary, it was revealed equally in his professed regard for the papacy, and the Pope in person, Pio Nono, who had shown an interest and concern for him. Indeed the Pope had given a considerable amount of his time to Newman and his confreres' welfare and future, despite a host of mounting political crises in Italy and Rome that year. The relationship between spiritual and temporal powers was at once complex and perilous.

On his accession in 1846, Pio had instituted a raft of liberal reforms in reaction to the authoritarianism of his predecessor Gregory XVI. He curbed the power of the papal police, abolished the Jewish ghetto in Rome, and declared a general amnesty. Newman, with his anti-liberal instincts, referred to the opening of the papal prisons as the release of 'scum of the earth'. Pio announced the introduction of lay participation in the government of the papal states, reforms in education, greater freedom of the press, and the introduction of such modern amenities as gas-light and railways. For a year or two, spanning Newman's time in Rome, Pio appeared to support the unification of Italy and even the formation of lay advisory and, later, executive, bodies. He appeared to toy with the idea of becoming a constitutional monarch in so far as his temporal power was concerned; some optimists even thought that he might preside over a federal united Italy. Yet he rejected the idea as unfeasible in view of the disjointed state of the peninsula. Meanwhile progressive factions in Rome grew stronger by what they fed on, leading to calls for republicanism and revolution. Pio, who started out, according to Britain's *Morning Post,* as 'the most enlightened of modern sovereigns', would within two years become a Pope of intransigence whose attitude towards unification was emphatically '*non possumus*' – or in our contemporary parlance: 'no way!' The effective issue was his refusal to side with King Charles of Piedmont when war broke out with Austria, the traditional military ally of the Popes. In October 1848 revolutionaries in Rome murdered Count Pellegrino Rossi, lay government minister of the papal states, and besieged the papal Quirinal palace. Pio escaped disguised in a priest's simple cassock, fleeing to the seaside fortress of Gaeta within the safety of the neighbouring kingdom of Naples. From this fastness Pio hurled denunciations against the 'outrageous treason of democracy' and threatened prospective voters with excommunication. Only with the help of French troops and a loan from Rothschilds, did Pio contrive to return to the Vatican a year later to resume his reign over the city of Rome and what was left of the papal territories. A council of censorship was charged with investigating those implicated in the republican plot. The new papal regime was not beneficent. Writing to William Gladstone in 1852, two years after Pius's return to the Eternal City, an English traveller characterized Rome as a prison house: 'There is not a breath of liberty, not a hope of tranquil life; two foreign armies, a permanent state of siege, atrocious acts of revenge, factions raging, universal discontent; such is the Papal government at the present day.'[52] The Jews were made a target of post-republican reprisal. Although his return to Rome had been paid for by a Jewish loan, the Roman Jews were forced back into the ghetto and made to pay, literally, for having supported the revolution.

These events occurred after Newman returned to England to establish his Oratory. Despite his manifold troubles, Pio had proceeded with the formation of a hierarchy for England, a deeply threatening move in the view of non-Catholics, and began work on the definition of the dogma of the Immaculate

Conception – a belief that provoked Protestant antipathy towards the papacy and Catholicism in general. Newman's personal devotion to Pio, his newly established Romanism, and his sympathy for the Pope's recent political troubles, moved him to write a remarkably energetic and imaginative defence of the supernatural power of the papacy:

Behold, the mighty world is gone forth to war, with what? with an unknown something, which it feels but cannot see; which flits around it, which flaps against its cheek, with the air, with the wind. It charges, and it slashes, and it fires its vollies, and its bayonets, and it is mocked by a foe who dwells in another sphere, and is far beyond the force of its analysis, or the capacities of its calculus…. Whom have you gone out against? a few old men, with red hats and stockings, or a hundred pale students, with eyes on the ground and beads in their girdle; they are as stubble; destroy them; – then there will be other old men and other pale students instead of them. But we will direct our rage against one; he flees; what is to be done with him? Cast him out upon the wide world. But nothing can go on without him. Then bring him back: but he will give us no guarantee for the future. Then leave him alone; his power is gone, he is at an end, or he will take a new course of himself: he will take part with the world. Meanwhile, the multitude of influences in active operation all over the great Catholic body, rise up all round, and hide heaven and earth from the eyes of the spectators of the combat; and unreal judgments are hazarded, and rash predictions, till the mist clears away, and then the old man is found in his own place, as before, saying Mass over the tomb of the Apostles.[53]

Twenty years on, Newman would take a very different view of Pio Nono's papacy. He would write that the dogma of papal infallibility had been conducted 'very cruelly, tyrannically, and deceitfully'.[54] He would temper his earlier, largely sentimental, view of the papacy with a perspective based on personal experience.

For myself, I think that a new world is coming in, and that the Pope's change of position (which in spite of any temporary re-action which may come, is inevitable) will alter matters vastly. We have come to a climax of tyranny. It is not good for a Pope to live 20 years. It is anomaly and bears no good fruit; he becomes a god, has no one to contradict him, does not know facts, and does cruel things without meaning it.[55]

Nevertheless that early devotion to the Real Presence in the Blessed Sacrament, his first sense of being a Catholic, would remain as strong as ever. He would write in November 1870:

For years past my only consolation personally has been in our Lord's Presence in the Tabernacle. I turn from the sternness of external authority to Him who can immeasurably compensate trials which after all are not real, but (to use a fashionable word) sentimental. Never, thank God, have I had a single doubt about the divine origin and grace of the Church, on account of the want of tenderness and largeness of mind of some of its officials or rulers.[56]

CHAPTER 10

Oratory

'Catholicism is a deep matter – you cannot take it up in a teacup.'
J. H. NEWMAN LETTER TO J. SPENCER NORTHCOTE, 8 FEBRUARY 1846

By New Year of 1848, back in England, Newman was seeking a suitable site for his Oratory in Birmingham. The fledgling community included five fellow priests – Fathers St John, Dalgairns, Penny, Coffin, and Stanton; but an opportunity had now arisen to join forces with Frederick W. Faber's recently founded group, known as Brothers of the Will of God, or Wilfridians. Faber, who was of the generation of Oxford students that had idolised Newman during his Oriel days, was a self-willed egotist, but he nourished a romantic ideal of obedience to a religious superior and spiritual director. As Faber would put it later, he wanted to be 'a cadaver in the Superior's hands'.[1] Newman at first acquiesced and welcomed Faber in. The decision would give rise to personality clashes, as well as problems over finance, property and authority. In the final analysis, the conflict would reveal profound differences about the nature of spiritual life and Catholicism in England in the nineteenth century.

Newman's intent was to find a property that would house the expanded community. But Faber and his Wilfridians had recently settled in a rural location at Cotton Hall (renamed St Wilfrid's) in North Staffordshire, where he had made commitments to his generous patron, John Talbot, Earl of Shrewsbury, and was already successfully converting the local population to Catholicism. Faber had somehow hoped that Newman and his group would make St Wilfrid's the motherhouse of the English Oratorians, or at least keep the house going as a country retreat, or novitiate. Newman knew that St Wilfrid's would not do as a principal residence since the Oratorian ideal was to work and live in cities. St Wilfrid's moreover would be too expensive to maintain in addition to two city houses. Nevertheless, while preparing a Birmingham location, Newman and his five priests came to live at St Wilfrid's as a temporary measure in October of 1848.

St Wilfrid's was situated on the side of a remote glen below the North Staffordshire moors. The main house was a fine regency mansion facing out across steep woods. The Earl of Shrewsbury, with help of the architect Augustus Welby Pugin, had been attempting to create a romantic medieval enclave in the surrounding district – a sort of religious theme park along the valley of the River Churnet. At one end Pugin was constructing a bizarre family seat for the Shrewsburys – part gothic folly, part residence, with galleries and banqueting halls, known as Alton Towers (later to become a twentieth century secular theme park). On a cliff above a neighbouring ravine, with the River Churnet below, Pugin had designed a Rhineland-style 'castle' known as St John's. At the other end of the valley, on the site of Cotton Hall, the Earl had envisaged a picturesque monastery, and had made funds available for a suitable church and extensions to house the Wilfridians.

Faber, Lord Shrewsbury and Pugin had been busy. In Cotton village arose a free and, crucially, gothic elementary Catholic school; in the local town of Cheadle, a church decorated with brilliant Medieval-style colours and an elaborate rood screen. Newman attended the dedication of the church, and would four years later let slip his true early impressions of some of his new co-religionists, and the sharp side of his tongue. 'Dr Gillis … at the opening of Cheadle Church he preached a sermon half screaming and bellowing, half whining – and Lady Dormer and other ladies of quality were in raptures with it. The same is seen in a parallel way in the after dinner conversation of priests, and the recreations of nuns. They are to be cheerful and they have *nothing* to be cheerful upon. So they are boisterous or silly.' [2]

At St Wilfrid's, Pugin had built a curious twisting cloister with leaded windows, a romantic sacristy, and the foundations of a neo-gothic church. Faber had designed for his Wilfridians flowing soutanes and cloaks; on their breasts were sewn in red the letters VD, Volente Deo, by the will of God. Rosaries and crucifixes dangled from deep waist bands. Pugin's idea, promoted in his best-selling book *Contrasts*, ordained that gothic architecture and Italianate Catholic emblems and banners made people better, happier, more religious – more *Roman Catholic*. Faber's idea of pre-Reformation Catholicism thrived entirely in his imagination; and central to his Catholicism was a keen devotion to the Virgin Mary (whom he liked to address as 'Mamma').

In keeping with his enthusiasm for Southern European piety, Faber had embarked on an edition of the *Lives of the Saints*, based on a translation of the more extravagant accounts of Latin saints. One of the hagiographies that drew vehement criticism was the life of Saint Rose of Lima, a seventeenth-century Peruvian saint, famous for her fasts and self-mutilation – she disfigured her face, which in babyhood had transformed itself miraculously into a rose bloom, in repudiation of her own beauty. Newman, as Faber's new superior, supported the series, but his doubts about the project were palpable. He submitted the texts to Bishop William Ullathorne, who had succeeded Wiseman as Vicar Apostolic of the Midlands. Ullathorne, in the event, supported the publication, but with considerable unease.

Ullathorne, a former Benedictine Abbot, in common with other Catholic bishops in England at the time, was increasingly embroiled in tensions between different Catholic factions, especially recent converts like Faber and the so-called 'Old Catholics', whose Catholicism had endured, despite persecution and hardship, ever since the Reformation. The new converts believed that the Old Catholics were a snobbish, self-satisfied, stagnant group, resistant to evangelising zeal. The Old Catholics, meanwhile, despised the newcomers for their extravagant devotions and excessive enthusiasm.

Newman, taking a middle position, did not see eye to eye with Faber on ways of prayer and styles of asceticism. Faber's group was attached to indulgences, saint's relics, imagined struggles with the devil. On one occasion Faber practised the rite of exorcism over a recalcitrant Irish lay brother. There were quarrels about rood screens, statuary, vestments. Faber favoured outdoor processions along newly laid paths at St Wilfrid's with swaying banners, incense, and chants. Newman was happier with silent prayer on his knees, in solitude or in chapel.

Faber was a strange mixture of harshness, mawkishness and exaggerated feelings. He suffered from poor health, exacerbated by ascetical practices such as wearing a horse-hair cord around his bare waist, and fasting in a haphazard fashion. Often his cures were worse than his illness. We learn of his falling ill with a 'most impetuous diarrhoea'. He took 'doses of laudanum … every hour as well as some astringents'. Finally he arranged for his back passage to be stopped up with 'three large suppositories … forced in one after another before the fury of the purging would give way'. The stoppage caused his body to swell. Then 'horrid perspirations' came on after his request that he be caked all over with 'atrociously smelling' cod liver oil. At length, after the community had prayed a novena to St Philip, his health rapidly improved, and he allowed that the 'terrible oil' be removed, 'to the inexpressible relief of all the community'.[3]

Then serious tensions and high feeling arose over Newman's 'particular friendship' with St John. Petty personal envies evidently lay beneath the anger, as well as the perception that Newman had offended Tridentine discipline in the matter. Having accused Newman of ignoring the younger members of the new community, Faber wrote to him:

Then here is another grief: advise me about it. Several of them have what amounts to a positive dislike of F. Ambrose [St John] … they cannot get on with him; for his manner is either a series of snubs or 'a condescension' … which is quite 'insulting'. You would think I exaggerated if I told you how strong this feeling really was and still is. Then they consider him as identified with you – they say he colours your view of them, and if they can't get on with both, they think it useless to try with one – that you are different with him from what you are with others – that he stands between them and you.[4]

Faber went on to say that when he spoke to young members of his former Wilfridian community 'about a particular friendship growing up between them', there came the answer that Newman had scandalised the younger community by his friendship with Father Ambrose [St John]. Faber himself, Newman riposted, had shown special affection for a younger confrere called Father Anthony.

'Special' or 'particular' friendships were clearly avoided in order to reduce the possibility of homosexual relationships as well as to inculcate charity towards all members of a community. Over many years Newman had fostered deep friendships at Oxford, especially towards Hurrell Froude, and he was not about to alter an inclination for such intimacies on becoming a priest. Newman wrote back at length in terms that revealed his rejection of the entire 'particular friendship' principle:

As to particular friendships, I have much wished a *definition* of what is meant. St James and St John had a sort of particular friendship among the Apostles – so must brothers in a Congregation ever – i.e. there *must* be feelings between them which are not between others. The point, I conceive, is that they should not *show* it, – should not *act* upon it. The only way of hindering the *fact*, is for them to be in separate Congregations … Again what is more striking, think of our Lord's love for St John…. To me *now* the hopeless thing is this, that when the idea has *once got* into people's minds, it *cannot* get out; for if from circumstances I *have* been brought closer to F. Ambrose than to others, let me *hide* the fact as I will, I can do nothing to *undo* it, unless I actually did cease to love him as well as I do.[5]

Newman, much as he had chosen to live his life in all-male communities, was not a gregarious person, try as he might. And much as he was aware that Catholic ascetical theology forbade the formation of particular friendships, he was determined to continue funnelling his affections and emotional needs into relationships that suited him.

BIRMINGHAM AND LONDON

While still searching for a suitable London site, Newman purchased and renovated a former 'gloomy gin distillery' on Alcester Street in Birmingham to serve as their first city chapel and Oratory house. He had brought with him his collected volumes of the Fathers, spraining his wrists with the task of hauling them into the building.

The chapel opened for Mass on 2 February 1849 with a congregation of six hundred. Newman's first sermon was 'The Salvation of the Hearer the Motive of the Preacher'. It was a strict homily, reminding his hearers of the reality of mortal sin and the need for the Church to combat the Devil. The Catholic baroque *coloratura* and content is unmistakable:

If the world has its fascinations, so surely has the Altar of the living God; if its pomps and vanities dazzle, so much more should the vision of Angels ascending and descending on the heavenly ladder; if sights of earth intoxicate, and its music is a spell upon the soul, behold Mary pleads with us, over against them, with her chaste eyes, and offers the Eternal Child for our caress, while sounds of cherubim are heard all round singing from out the fulness of the Divine Glory.[6]

While the pioneer Oratorians under Newman's leadership were now hard at pastoral work in Birmingham, Faber remained behind at St Wilfrid's as novice master, and Robert Coffin as Rector. Faber was not happy with the separation, and continued to urge that the Oratory should be in London rather than in Birmingham. He believed that Newman should be in the nation's capital, evangelising the social elite, while he, Faber, should be engaged in wider pastoral care of the ordinary people, conducting missions in London parishes. Newman was keen on a London Oratory, but he was determined that having made his start in Birmingham, he would continue there. It looked certain that there would be two Oratories rather than one. In April Newman bought a 21-year lease for £400 on premises in King William Street (now William IV Street), off the Strand in London. Faber was to be 'the acting Superior', and the London Oratory was accordingly founded on 31 May 1849, Wiseman preaching in the morning, and Newman in the evening. In a note on the 'colonisation' from Birmingham to London, Newman declared that the Faber group would get 'the *Metropolis*, the centre of political and ecclesiastical influence, instead of factory youths and snobbish intellects'.[7] St Wilfrid's, Cotton, after long drawn-out acrimonious discussion with the Earl of Shrewsbury, would be handed over eventually to the Passionist Order.

Newman continued as Superior of both the London and Birmingham Oratories which led to tensions between him and Faber. Directing and administering affairs in London from Birmingham, with frequent visits between the two cities and his own energetic programme of preaching and writing, was never going to be easy; nor was the task of managing Faber. Faber and his confreres soon became a familiar sight in central London, parading around in their soutanes and sweeping clerical cloaks. A comment of Newman's about the effect of an Oratorian novice spreading out 'his cloke [*sic*] like a peacock's'[8] in the street, suggests an awareness of potential for clerical high camp as well as unnecessary provocation of Protestant sensibilities.

Meanwhile Faber's volatile personality made him a difficult head of house and an impossible subordinate to manage at a distance. He had a catalogue of bigotries. An example was the case of two Irish priests in his charge – Robert Whitty and James McQuoin. Newman was keen that the London Oratory should include men who were Irish-born Catholics as well as converts. Faber, however, had a deep prejudice against Hibernians, as he liked to call them. He whinged about the smells and lice of the Irish poor deterring 'respectable' members of the congregation in the confessional. Faber insisted that 'weakness and treachery are next door to each other; in an Hibernian they are synonyms … Why even the civility of an Irish man riles me.'[9] In the event Whitty and McQuoin (whom Faber characterised as 'fickle and shilly shallying') departed. The tensions would continue between the Father Superior Newman and Acting Superior Faber, as Faber swung between abrasive complaints and obsequious gestures of affection. A frustrated Newman wrote to him: 'Save me from such affection and devotion, and give me a little more tenderness for others, and a little less self will.'[10]

Newman, while mainly irenic and reluctant to be firm, was capable of decisiveness when pressed to his limit: 'I am quite conscious always of not liking to tell people how keenly I feel things, both from tenderness to them, and again from a consciousness that, when I once begin, I am apt to let out and blow them out of the water.'[11]

We get an insight into Newman's manner of dealing, in last resort, with individuals in his community, as well as a flavour of the teething problems at Alcester Street in a letter written in April 1849. He is complaining to Father Dalgairns, who was about to depart for London to join Faber, about his indulgence towards a gang of larky teenage 'converts' who had made free of the Birmingham Oratory house, stealing and causing damage. Dalgairns had written to Newman on the previous day: 'I wish you now as an act of charity to tell me plainly where I have been wrong.' Newman obliged him, frequently addressing him as 'charissime', yet with an undisguised iciness, given the context:

I think then, Charissime, that you have a great fault, which, if I put it harshly, I should call, contempt of others … You never asked my advice from the first in any thing. You took up certain youths … You filled the rooms with them … I went into the guest room soon after we came, and to my surprise saw a party of them by themselves; I rushed into Chapel and told you, thinking you did not know of it; you told me to let them alone … I was obliged to take the carpet up; you laughed, when you heard I was putting locks on the closets and advised locking the doors … I found them strumming on the Piano, they ate the sugar and the jam and stole the candles; you laughed when it was complained of. F. Ambrose ran up to me, 'What *am* I to do? I can't hear a confession in my room, for the noise of the boys in F. Bernard's'. They flung about the ink in the guest room, broke the chairs, squandered coal and gas, broke into the closet, took out the Crucifix, and put it back head downwards … You gave them the lay brothers' books, and they made away with them … They took to playing tricks with the gas. I say nothing of their rudeness to me personally which you would naturally try to prevent …[12]

On settling in London, Dalgairns would make common cause with Faber in resisting Newman's view that Oratorians should be men of learning and teachers as well as pastors. Faber had roundly informed Newman that intellectualism in the Oratorian movement was a 'French' aptitude, which would end in

Jansenism. Faber and Dalgairns insisted that Oratorians were more at home hearing confessions than reading in a library. Dalgairns wrote to Newman: 'Since I have been a priest my intellect is gone; gradually what was once a pleasure has become a pain. I loathe literature; I am not even easy if I dip into a modern historical book. It troubles my mind, and I am forced to mention it in confession. Saints' lives on the contrary fill me with peace. In a word my intellect has disappeared.' [13]

The difference between Newman and Faber who had come to Catholicism from the Oxford Movement was that Newman saw the religious life in terms of growth and development, while Faber was moved by nostalgia, manifesting itself in authoritarianism. It is interesting that they disagreed even over the ideal number for an English Oratorian house. Newman insisted, contrary to Faber's idea of a large community, that twelve should be the limit (and would have preferred even less – '6 children form a fair fire side' as love 'cannot exist among many').[14] Long before the split Newman had declared to Faber, 'I can't command people about like so many soldiers or pieces of wood'.[15] He had advised Faber that they should let 'Providence, gently to work our separation ... as fruit ripens on the tree and falls; you all force me to take a knife and cut it off. I repeat, I cannot fight with facts.'[16]

Here at the outset of his religious life as a Catholic Newman was setting out principles that would guide his practical, intellectual and spiritual life. As he would put it in the *Idea of a University*, 'I should not rely on sudden, startling effects, but on the slow, silent, penetrating, overpowering effects of patience, steadiness, routine, and perseverance'.[17]

The two Oratories were shearing apart, yet Newman, despite a busy schedule in Birmingham, continued to make frequent visits to the capital to preach and to lecture. In May of 1850 he gave the first of a series of lectures *On Certain Difficulties felt by Anglicans in submitting to the Catholic Church*.

DIFFICULTIES OF ANGLICANS

The lectures on *Certain Difficulties* were principally aimed at Anglo-Catholics, and, as he explained, were intended 'to remove impediments to the due action of the conscience, by removing those perplexities in the proof, which keep the intellect from being touched by its cogency, and give the heart an excuse for trifling with it'.[18] Newman was demonstrating the multidimensional nature of conversion, emphasizing the role of imagination. In his letter to *The Times* on the Tamworth Reading Room quarrel, he had urged that 'the heart is commonly reached not through the reason, but through the imagination'. Newman now developed the argument further, warning that imagination in aid of religious understanding should be restrained in its exploitation:

We must not indulge our imagination, we must not dream: we must look at things as they are … we must not indulge our imagination in the view we take of the [Church of England] National Establishment. If we dress it up in an ideal form, as if it were something real … as if it were in deed and not only in name a Church, then indeed we may feel interest in it, and reverence towards it, and affection for it, as men have fallen in love with pictures, or knights in romance do battle for high dames whom they have never seen. Thus it is that students of the Fathers, antiquaries, and poets, begin by assuming that the body to which they belong is that of which they read in time past, and then proceed to decorate it with that majesty and beauty of which history tells, or which their genius creates.[19]

He goes on to explain that it is not so much imagination itself which is at fault, as its misdirection. In other words, his readings in Christian antiquity, leading to the formation of a shining idea of the Church, had originally been mistakenly applied to the Church of England, rather than to their true object – the Roman Catholic Church. It is not enough, he is saying, to nurture religious imagination in the search for truth; we must employ reason, to ensure that there is a correspondence between imagination and reality. Newman had worked through this process by drawing analogies between the present and the way in which the early Church strived to separate heresy from orthodoxy.

Newman's purpose was to bring over to Rome the constituency of Anglicans who believed that they had found Catholicity within the English established Church. With a series of skilful metaphors, he pities these attempts to linger in a Christian community separated from the Mother Church, typical of which:

there is no lying, or standing, or sitting, or kneeling, or stooping there, in any possible attitude … when you would rest your head, your legs are forced out between the Articles, and when you would relieve your back, your head strikes against the Prayer Book; when, place yourselves as you will, on the right side or the left, and try to keep as still as you can, your flesh is ever being punctured and probed by Episcopate, laity, and nine-tenths of the Clergy …[20]

But he had a wider argument for the nurturing of religious imagination at all times and in all circumstances. Religious conviction he was saying, yet again, was not derived from logic and reason alone, nor could it be demonstrated through objective apologetics. It is an 'ineffably cogent argument', combining subjective imagination, reason, and common sense.

Yet common sense, reason, and a sense of the relationship between social good and morality, deserted Newman when he attempted, with preposterous exaggeration, to contrast the sacred nature of the Church of Rome, with the secular nature of the established Church of England. The Catholic Church, he wrote:

holds that it were better for sun and moon to drop from heaven, for the earth to fail, and for all the many millions who are upon it to die of starvation in extremest agony, so far as temporal affliction goes, than that one soul, I will not say, should be lost, but should commit one single venial sin, should tell one wilful untruth, though it harmed no one, or steal one poor farthing without excuse … she would rather save the soul of one single wild bandit of Calabria, or whining beggar of Palermo, than draw a hundred lines of railroad through the length of Italy …[21]

As it happened, the tensions between Rome and England took a turn for the worse in 1850 when Wiseman was summoned to the Vatican to receive a Cardinal's hat and to plan the establishment of an English hierarchy that rivalled that of the Church of England. For those of a Protestant cast of mind it looked like an aggressive bid to infiltrate the country with Romanism. Ill-advisedly, perhaps, Wiseman issued in advance of his return a pastoral letter 'From out the Flaminian Gate', vaunting the restoration of the Catholic Church to its proper 'orbit in the ecclesiastical firmament'. On 14 October *The Times* poured ridicule on Wiseman as the 'newfangled Archbishop of Westminster'.[22] The Prime Minister, Lord John Russell, publicly condemned Rome's 'pretension of supremacy over the realm of England'. There were anti-Popery demonstrations, and effigies of the Pope were burnt in the streets. Priests were attacked, including Father Faber's Oratorians. The popular magazine *Punch* depicted Wiseman ('Wiseboy') bringing papal bulls into the country in full cardinal's fig, with Newman 'Newboy' holding his train.

To combat the surge of hatred against Catholics, Newman embarked on a series of talks (later published as *Lectures on the Present Position of Catholics in England*). He would one day consider it his 'best written book'.

LIBEL

Newman was overseeing the building of the Oratory in Edgbaston, at the same time contending with rumours prompted by a speech in parliament that Catholic religious houses were designing basement 'cells' for nefarious purposes. Richard Spooner, MP for North Warwickshire, had delivered a speech on the Religious Houses Bill, suggesting that a large religious convent in Edgbaston had 'fitted up the whole of the underground' with 'cells, and what were those cells for?' To which the House resounded with 'hear, hear'. The Mayor of Birmingham was accordingly called upon to inspect Newman's basement area, and confirmed that the site was quite innocent.[23]

In a bid to dampen anti-Roman prejudice, Newman again invoked wayward imagination as the reason for Protestant animus. Focusing on the cliché of Catholic institutions, such as convents and monasteries, as places of torture and sexual perversion, he turned the image against the Church's antagonists. It is the Protestant imagination that is a grim convent or workhouse where the 'thick atmosphere refracts and distorts such straggling rays as enter in'.[24]

On the difficulty of entering into dialogue or reasoned debate, he writes:

If, for instance, a person cannot open a door, or get a key into a lock, which he has done a hundred times before, you know how apt he is to shake, and to rattle, and to force it, as if some great insult was offered him by its resistance: you know how surprised a wasp, or other large insect is, that he cannot get through a window pane; such is the feeling of the Prejudiced Man when we urge our objections – not softened by them at all, but exasperated the more …[25]

Turning to the irrational Protestant classification of Catholics as a type, Newman conjures up a series of brilliant conceits, including

[In an] inquisitive age, when the Alps are crested, and seas fathomed, and mines ransacked, and sands sifted, and rocks cracked into specimens, and beasts caught and catalogued, as little is known by Englishmen of the religious sentiments, the religious usages, the religious notions, the religious ideas of two hundred millions of Christians poured to and fro, among them and around them, as if, I will not say, they were Tartars or Patagonians, but as if they inhabited the moon.[26]

In his fifth lecture, Newman ill-advisedly took the liberty of naming a name. His target was one Giacinto Achilli, a former member of the Dominican order who had left the Church after being indicted by the Roman Inquisition for sexual misconduct. While professor of philosophy at the seminary in Viterbo he had seduced two women. Three times he was moved on by the church authorities, but he continued his unpriestly behaviour in each new appointment, including the rape of a woman in the sacristy of St Peter's Church in Naples for which he was arrested by the local police. The Roman Inquisition (a milder institution than the notorious Spanish Inquisition) sent him to a remote retreat house to do penance, but he absconded to Corfu where he opened a Protestant chapel and had an affair with the wife of a tailor. In his new life, financed by the ultra-Protestant Evangelical Alliance, he preached and lectured against the Catholic Church, while conducting serial affairs. By 1850 he was in England delivering fiery anti-Popery lectures, arriving eventually in Birmingham where he came to Newman's notice.

Newman spoke against Achilli on 28 July 1851, unwisely, perhaps, referring to him as an 'infidel', and more to the point mentioning the allegations of his sexual misdemeanours, basing his facts on an article published by Cardinal Wiseman in a recent edition of the *Dublin Review*. His precise words were these, speaking, as it were, on Achilli's behalf – condemning himself from his own mouth:

I am that Achilli, who in the diocese of Viterbo in February, 1831, robbed of her honour a young woman of eighteen; who in September, 1833, was found guilty of a second such crime, in the case of a person of twenty-eight; and who perpetrated a third in July, 1834, in the case of another aged twenty-four …[27]

Wiseman had claimed that he possessed documentary evidence to back up these claims, as did Monsignor Talbot, who was in possession of Achilli's confession at the tribunal of the Roman Inquisition.

By September Achilli instituted criminal libel proceedings against Newman, which, should he lose, could result in an unlimited fine, or imprisonment. It was now crucial for Wiseman and others to produce the documentation that underpinned the Cardinal's original allegation. But Newman found himself in a nightmare of obstructional indifference. He wrote to his friend Capes at the end of November 1851: 'If the devil raised a physical whirlwind, rolled me up in sand, whirled me round, and then transported me some thousands of miles, it would not be more strange, though it would be more imposing a visitation. I have been kept in ignorance and suspense, incomprehensibly, every now and then a burst of malignant light showing some new and unexpected prospect.'[28] He went on: 'For three months I have been soliciting information from abroad – but I can't get people even to write to me.'

Wiseman said that he had mislaid the documentation, but Newman discovered that 'he never had looked for them' until it was too late to reverse the decision to go to trial. In the meantime Newman had sent two of his confreres, Father Nicholas Darnell and an ailing Joseph Gordon, to Italy to secure evidence, while his friend Maria Giberne travelled out to find and bring back witnesses.

In the event, the trial took place before a jury between 21 and 24 June 1852 and Newman lost. *The Times* attacked the verdict, judging it an unwarranted display of anti-Catholicism, confirming a belief that Catholics would now have good reasons for believing there was no justice for them in cases involving the 'Protestant feelings of judges and juries'.

The main casualty of the Achilli affair, however, was Father Joseph Gordon who fell seriously ill on his return from Italy and eventually died. Newman's sense of loss reveals the depth of his feeling for each of the small circle of companions who had served him loyally and selflessly. Referring to himself in the third person Newman wrote:

On S. Cecilia's day, November 22nd, the Father [Newman] was called up to London for judgement. It was too much for Father Gordon; faithful to his own loyal heart, on that very day he was seized with a pleurisy, and when the Father returned from London on the morrow with his process still delayed, he found him in bed. It was the beginning of the end. He languished and sank, got worse and worse, and at the end of nearly three months, on the 13th of February, 1853, he died at Bath. He is in the hands of his God. We all loved him with a deep affection; we lamented him with all our hearts, we keenly feel his loss to this day. But the Father's bereavement is of a special kind, and his sorrow is ever new.[29]

Newman himself was on the brink of collapse. Writing to his nun friend, Sister Mary Imelda Poole, he reported that the doctor had told him 'distinctly I shall have a premature old age, and an early death … He says my brain and nerves cannot bear it.'[30] The doctor prescribed a holiday, which Newman took in Scotland at Abbotsford for six weeks as a guest of John Gibson Lockhart, Walter Scott's son-in-law.

Troubles at the Oratory followed him on his convalescence, symptomatic of an overworked, highly-strung religious community with a lack of firm and experienced leadership. A lay brother called Bernard Hennin (lay brothers did the skivvying in religious houses, cleaning lavatories and so forth) had fallen for a Mrs Frances Wootten, a doctor's wife, who had come to live in Edgbaston and was making herself serviceable to the Oratorians. Mrs Wootten told the Oratorian Father Nicholas Darnell in confession that Bernard had attempted to kiss her four times on the face. Whereupon the shocked priest persuaded Mrs Wootten to make the same allegation outside of the seal of the confessional; which she did. The allegation was now shared with two other Oratorians, including Ambrose St John. On grilling Brother Bernard it was discovered that he had, in fact, just about kissed Mrs Wootten's hand and that he had got nowhere near her face. St John had decided, in Newman's absence, that Bernard should be sent to a Redemptorist retreat house near Liverpool. On learning of all this Newman became enraged, accusing Ambrose and his confreres of acting without proper authority. The first letter he sent to Ambrose on the matter demonstrates that much as he loved his younger friend, he could treat him harshly:

Charissime
I know that this letter will pain you … *Without* me you recommend a Brother of the Congregation to become a Trappist …[31]

Father Nicholas also received a broadside from Newman, lambasting him for virtually breaking the seal of confession: '… were I an Italian', he wrote, 'and a man of unsubdued mind, I should be sorely tempted, under circumstances, to use the stiletto against [such a] confessor'.[32] The hapless Brother Bernard, who was evidently mentally challenged and unsuited to an all-male community, eventually went to the Oratory in London whence he left the congregation and got married.

Newman received his sentence in the Achilli affair on 31 January 1853. The fine was £100, clearly a derisory figure; but Newman's costs amounted to more than £14,000 – at least a million pounds at today's value. Judge Coleridge left a remarkable diary note of the scene that day:

The immense crowd, the anxious and critical audience, his slender figure, and strange mysterious cloudy face. After all the speeches of Counsel he desired to say a few words. Oh! What a sweet musical, almost unearthly voice it was, so unlike any other we had heard.... I have a feeling that there was something almost out of place in my not merely pronouncing sentence on him, but in a way lecturing him. And yet as I could not avoid the one, so it seemed to me quite in course for me to do the other, when by breach of the law he had fairly been brought under me. Besides, in truth Newman is an *over-praised* man, he is made an idol of. [33]

In a manuscript note, Newman remembered that the judge was said to be 'very nervous', and that the contrast between them was 'great' – 'I looking so wooden'. Small wonder. Judge Coleridge, according to Newman, had rebuked him, saying, that 'I had been everything good when I was a Protestant – but I had fallen since I was a Catholic'. Coleridge ended by saying: 'I fear I make no impression on you.' [34]

An Achilli fund was instituted in England, Ireland, Canada and the United States to cover the phenomenal costs; the sum raised far exceeded the amount required. Three months later Newman was in a position to solicit funds from as far afield as Baltimore to help Bishop Ullathorne and Dr Moore, Rector of Oscott College who had been gaoled in Warwick prison as debtors. The pair had shares in a Welsh Bank which failed two years earlier. According to Newman, 'the Assignes [*sic*], witnessing the liberality of Catholics to me, determined, as they expressed it, to "put the skrew [*sic*] on Catholics", for the benefit of the creditors'. [35] The redoubtable bishop was relaxed since he had once worked as a missionary on Norfolk Island the penal colony. The debtors were let out after ten days.

CHAPTER 11

Idea of a University

'– there are no schools now, no private judgment (in the *religious* sense of the
phrase,) no freedom, that is of opinion. That is, no exercise of the intellect …'
J. H. NEWMAN LETTER TO EMILY BOWLES, 19 MAY 1863

While still in the anxious throes of the Achilli trial, Newman had travelled to
Ireland in early October, 1851. His first visit across the Irish Sea found him
apprehensive and impractical (as he himself admits) without his guardian angel
Ambrose St John, who had packed his case for him. From Thurles he had sent a
message to the Birmingham Oratory: 'We had a bad passage … I abjure Holyhead.
We got to bed at Dublin between one and two a.m … tell F. Ambrose, that I, with
my usual infelicity, spilt I can't say how much of my precious medicine over the
amice [part of the priestly Mass robes], and other contents of my portmanteau.' [1]

Newman was in Ireland at the invitation of Archbishop Paul Cullen of Armagh
who had asked initially for advice on the appointment of staff for a proposed
Catholic University. In fact, the bishop, who had got to know Newman at the
Propaganda College in Rome, had it in mind to organize the entire venture and
appoint him as the first Rector. As a prelude, and perhaps to get the measure of
how Newman would establish and run such an institution, Cullen asked him,
as if casually, to give 'a few lectures on education' to a specially invited audience
of ecclesiastics and distinguished Irish lay figures in Dublin. Newman's idea of
a university, expressed in those 'few lectures', would deal on the face of it with
how Catholic theology and philosophy of religion might survive in the face of
growing secularism. It would become, however, a master-class on the ideals of
university education across many cultural and political divides.

In the wake of the catastrophe of the Irish potato famine, which had devastated the social fabric of Ireland resulting in more than a million deaths – the
equivalent of a quarter of the population, sending an even greater number of
emigrants abroad, the country had become increasingly nationalist and turbulent. Some seventy per cent of Ireland's MPs were landed Protestants, and it
dawned on the British government that Catholic Ireland needed a proper university for the Irish Catholic majority if it was to emerge from its manifest and
mounting woes as a poverty-stricken, troubled and troublesome 'colony'.

The remoter background to Cullen's university proposal had been the original intention of English Protestants of Ireland to deprive the Catholic popula-

tion of education at any level after the final conquest of Ireland in 1691. For half a century Catholic children received an elementary education only in consequence of the 'hedge' schools, illegal classes held often in the open air by itinerant teachers. Catholic bishops were expelled from the country and only registered priests were allowed to minister to the faithful. Unregistered priests risked being hung, drawn and quartered. The provision of school education had improved by the middle of the eighteenth century, and by 1795 the British government had helped to fund St Patrick's College, Maynooth. Catholics were not admitted to Trinity College, Dublin, it being a Protestant foundation. In 1845 the governments decided to establish three secular Queen's Colleges in Belfast, Cork, and Galway, open to Catholics and Protestants alike. The degree giving body, founded in 1850, was to be known as the Queen's University of Ireland. Theology was not to be taught in any of the colleges. While a handful of Irish Catholic bishops favoured the Queen's plan, most were against it and so was the Holy See because of its lack of a faculty of Catholic theology. The Irish bishops and the Vatican wanted an institution comparable to the recently re-established Catholic University of Louvain in Belgium where theology held pride of place. Unfortunately the bishops envisaged something akin to a lay seminary (a circumstance Newman would discover when the bishops reproached him for allowing students to indulge in such licence as access to a billiard table and freedom to smoke).

But the detailed difficulties lay in the future. From the outset Newman was attracted to the idea. Perhaps, he suggested, such a foundation could be 'the Catholic University of the English tongue for the whole world',[2] or, at least, the British Empire, including Catholics of England who were deterred from entering Oxford and Cambridge. Perhaps he could recreate his beloved Oxford in Dublin, combining a university (with distinguished chairs) and a college system. Torn between enthusiasm for the project, and anxiety – prompted by his Oratorian confreres, who would be losing his presence in Birmingham – he agreed with some misgivings. But first there were the lectures. What should they be about, Newman asked, 'in order to be useful?' Cullen answered, 'What we want in Ireland is to persuade the people that education should be religious'.[3] Newman concurred, but his perspective on this question was decidedly different to Cullen's.

Newman's work to establish a Catholic University in Ireland would absorb him for much of the rest of the decade. It would be a period fraught with practical chores involving finance, administration, architectural plans, property deals, furnishings, fund raising, recruitment, annoying delays, and squabbles with the Irish hierarchy. He did not excel in understanding Irish politics, and the impression that he was a patrician district colonial officer from England was inescapable. His attitude – make the money available and allow me to get on with the job – was unrealistic, given the nature of Ireland's hierarchy and the temper of the times. He was never entirely comfortable as an administrator, and he was torn between Dublin and his community in Birmingham, requiring some sixty journeys between the two cities between 1851 and 1858.

His nemesis in Rome, Monsignor George Talbot, moreover, set about raising doubts about his capacity for such a task, prompting a stout rebuke from Newman's doughty friend Maria Giberne. Talbot had asked Giberne: 'Do you think Dr Newman capable of taking the management of the Irish University where he will have to battle continually with all the Paddies? I am afraid he will retire into himself and do nothing.' Giberne confessed to Newman that she had to bite her tongue for period, 'lest I should come down upon him like a thunder shower'. She eventually declared: 'Do nothing? If you knew Dr Newman as well as I do, you would know that he could move mountains, ay and men's wills too by sitting still and silent to all appearance, better than 1000 violent squabblers – Do nothing? Why who has done all that is doing in the Church the last 20 years and that without lifting up his voice?'[4]

A persistent problem would be Newman's lack of ecclesiastical authority and status in a country where the bishops were at odds with Archbishop Cullen, and Cullen himself eventually at odds with Newman. Three years into the project, after many delays, and questions about Newman's status, Cardinal Wiseman would tell Newman that he had taken up the cause of his lack of status in Ireland with the Pope himself. His Holiness, according to Wiseman, 'smilingly drawing his hands down from each side of his neck to his breast … added: "*e manderemo a Newman la crocetta, lo faremo Vescovo di Porfiorio, o qualche luogo* [and let us give Newman the crozier, we will make him the Bishop of Porphyrium, or some such place]". This was spoken in his kindest manner. Of course, Porphyrium was only an *exempli gratia*, as it is filled up. But I thought it would be pleasing to you to have the Pope's own words.'[5] He ended by asking Newman to treat the words of the Pope with 'your own discretion'. In the event, Newman would not be made a bishop.

The delays and the obstacles continued for a further three years. Despite Newman's unremitting toil in Dublin through 1854, Cullen sent him a letter in the depths of the summer vacation declaring '… there are complaints here, that no one is doing any thing for the university, and no one is charged to give information about what is to be done next'.[6] Newman responded that while on leave in Birmingham his assistant had been in attendance every day; but Cullen was determined to stir up trouble. He sent a letter out to the Propaganda in Rome:

For more than three months Father Newman has been in England, and has left a convert Englishman called Scratton here to take his place…. I have not therefore been able to find out how things stand, but they don't seem to me to be going in a way that can be defended. The continued absence of the Rector cannot be approved. Then the expenses have been very large, and furthermore the discipline introduced is unsuitable, certainly to this country. The young men are allowed to go out at all hours, to smoke, etc., and there has not been any fixed time for study. All this makes it clear that Father Newman does not give enough attention to details.[7]

It being the depths of the vacation, it was clear that Archbishop Cullen had more long-term quarrels with Newman than his summer absence. The university, as Newman struggled to establish it, seemed doomed to failure; but his published lectures and discourses on the ideal nature of a university remain one of his most prophetic and enduring legacies into the twenty-first century.

DISCOURSES

He gave the first 'discourse' in February 1852 in the Exhibition Room at the Rotunda building in Dublin, site of major public meetings in the city. Some 400 people turned up, and he was eminently audible despite his soft delivery. He could report that 'all the intellect, almost, of Dublin was there', including leading clergy, and women. He detected a frisson in the room, he wrote: 'when I said, not Ladies and Gentlemen, but Gentlemen.'

The *Idea of a University*, which grew out of the preparatory lectures or discourses, brings together Newman's expressed general and particular views on higher education against the background of Catholic Ireland's prevailing ecclesiastical culture. England had seen the challenge to Christian university foundations with the secular auspices of University College London, founded in 1826, which had opened its doors to both men and women, with a stress on science and technology, and with no requirement for Christian affiliation. The Queen's colleges were to be a continuation of this trend. And yet the question of secular versus religious was still in contention: in England, there had been new university foundations with an emphasis in the curriculum on theology, of which King's College, London (1829), and Durham University (1832), were examples. The abolition of great Catholic universities across Europe in a period of revolutions, the barring of Catholics from university education in England and Ireland, and the largely Protestant nature of university education in America, had stimulated the need for modern Catholic universities. Louvain had been refounded as a new Catholic University in Europe, and in the United States there had been Georgetown, Fordham and Notre Dame. Could Newman found a Catholic university not only for Ireland but for the entire Anglophone world of the British Empire? And what would be its special character and attraction? It had become clear to Newman, on conversion, that his vocation would be the education of Catholics rather than the conversion of Anglicans. He had come a long way since his time as reforming tutor at Oriel, or critic of Robert Peel's ideas on scientific and technical education at the opening of the Tamworth Reading Room. By 1851 he would source his idea for a Catholic university from a wide range of influences.

Newman's task in the first nine discourses was to keep Archbishop Cullen, and his paymasters, the Catholic bishops, happy. He agreed that theology must form a crucial part of any university worthy of the name, let alone a Catholic one; but he opposed the idea of a university dominated by religion, even Catholicism. A university, he believed, could not be a seminary for lay people; it must be a place in which each discipline reaches its own level of perfection unhindered and uninfluenced by any prevailing theology or ideology. Such a notion was in accord with aspects of secularization and liberalism that seemingly went against his own grain, let alone that of Catholic officialdom. The vision whereby he reconciled the apparent paradox is contained in the totality of the published texts that make up the *Idea of a University*.

Newman starts, however, by emphasizing the importance of Catholic theology, and thus setting out his credentials as a responsible Catholic Rector in whom the hierarchy could have confidence. Yet, as he wrote to Robert Ornsby in April 1852, those first lectures 'were suggested by high authority, and I think may please those whom I most wish to please, if I begin with them ... After these I shall go on to give a normal idea of a University.'[8] Not that Newman denied the importance of a faculty of theology in the university, but he was far from arguing for its pre-eminence as a subject or discipline. Nor did this mean that he was leaning towards a mainly secular ideal of education. The paradox is reconciled by his declaration that knowledge, or philosophy, or 'science' in its wider European sense, as an end in itself, is underpinned by a profound theological principle – that all being, all truth, is sustained by God; an altogether different consideration from the place of theology courses in a university curriculum.

He had argued in his letters on the Tamworth Reading Room that the sciences, technology, and the exercise of reason do not bring people to God, make people better. The *Idea* confirms, again, that the university does not contemplate a 'moral impression'. In a powerful metaphor he reinforces this insistence: 'Quarry the granite rock with razors or moor the vessel with a thread of silk; then you may hope with such keen and delicate instruments as human knowledge and human reason to contend against those giants, the passion and the pride of man.'[9] While this may have pleased his hierarchical audience and readership, the subtext is not an argument for the primacy of religion in the university, but the denial of such an expectation.

Meanwhile, Newman raises, although hardly settles, a problem with theology as a university discipline for his day, and for ours. His sadness on this point was registered in a letter to John Capes of the *Rambler* on the deplorable dearth of academic Catholic theology in Europe following the 'miserable state of the Church from 1780 to 1830':

At this moment, where are our schools of theology? a scattered and persecuted Jesuit School — one at Louvain – some ghosts of a short lived birth at Munich – hardly a theologian at Rome.[10]

NEW JERUSALEM ON EARTH

For Newman the ideal university is neither a set of vocational courses, nor a research institute; it is a community of scholars and students in pursuit of philosophy in its widest sense – 'a Knowledge that is capable of being its own end … liberal knowledge' through the 'intercommunion' of all the principal academic disciplines, including medicine and the natural sciences. All disciplines should be pursued without domination by any other since 'everything has its own perfection … and the perfection of one is not the perfection of another'. Education must not be 'merely a means to something beyond it'. Knowledge, or 'philosophy', is 'something intellectual, something which grasps what it perceives through the senses; something which takes a view of things; which sees more than the senses convey; which reasons upon what it sees, and while it sees; which invests it with an idea'.[11] Reminiscent of the Hellenistic academy at the origins of Western civilisation, Newman insists that the decisive attribute of a university is its disinterested intellectual creativity and enquiry: the opportunity and capacity to think *uselessly*. It is this notion of liberal philosophy, seen as 'the perfection of the intellect', that marks out the civilised and mature individual. He declares: 'not to know the relative disposition of things is the state of slaves or children; to have mapped out the Universe is the boast, or at least the ambition, of Philosophy.'[12]

What the university ideally creates, he writes in the sixth discourse, is

the clear, calm, accurate vision and comprehension of all things, as far as the finite mind can embrace them, each in its place, and with its own characteristics upon it. It is almost prophetic from its knowledge of history; it is almost heart-searching from its knowledge of human nature; it has almost supernatural charity from its freedom from littleness and prejudice; it has almost the repose of faith, because nothing can startle it; it has almost the beauty and harmony of heavenly contemplation.[13]

The peculiar feature of this remarkable passage, which brings the ideal university closer to a kind of New Jerusalem on earth, or Philosophical Religion, than Newman had ever previously dared articulate, is the employment of the word 'almost' no less than five times. If Newman had reaffirmed his conviction of fallen nature, the human tendency to idolatry and self-idolatry, in the 'quarry the granite rock with razors' passage, he comes close, nevertheless, to seeing the university as analogous to what the late Professor Adrian Hasting is termed 'the realm of grace'.[14] Although, again, only *almost*. To complete yet another layer of paradox, Newman, for all his insistence on knowledge for its own sake, urges that the university should indeed prepare students for practical life, 'training good members of society ... cultivating the public mind'. He writes: 'If a liberal education be good, it must necessarily be useful too.'[15] Yet he is unrelenting in his articulation of the crucial over-arching idea:

Educated men can do what illiterate cannot; and the man who has learned to think and to reason and to compare and to discriminate and to analyze, who has refined his taste, and formed his judgment, and sharpened his mental vision, will not indeed at once be a lawyer or a pleader, or an orator, or a statesman, or a physician, or a good landlord, or a man of business, or a soldier, or an engineer, or a chemist, or a geologist, or an antiquarian, but he will be placed in that state of intellect in which he can take up any one of the sciences or callings I have referred to, or any other for which he has a taste or special talent, with an ease, a grace, a versatility, and a success, to which another is a stranger.[16]

Given that Newman was attempting to establish a university under the auspices of a hierarchy that had determined ideas about control and ownership, his insistence is courageous:

The University ... has this object and this mission; it contemplates neither moral impression nor mechanical production; it professes to exercise the mind neither in art nor in duty; its function is intellectual culture; here it may leave its scholars, and it has done its work when it has done as much as this. It educates the intellect to reason well in all matters, to reach out towards truth, and to grasp it.[17]

The subtlety of the language is striking, emphasising the active engagement of the student, rather than the student as an object or recipient of instruction: educates, reaches out towards, *grasps*.

A token of the prophetic, timeless and universal nature of Newman's vision is its adoption by writers and thinkers generations on, and far removed, from the circumstances of nineteenth century tertiary education in Catholic Ireland. Universities 'will be modified in detail', he wrote in the *Catholic Gazette* for 17 August 1854, 'by the circumstances, and marked by the peculiarities, of the age to which they severally belong'.[18] A hundred and fifty years on, Edward Said, an agnostic of Palestinian origins, who strove to correct false Western impressions of 'Orientalism', would declare Newman's university discourses both true and 'incomparably eloquent':

The profound truth in what Newman says is, I believe, designed to undercut any partial or somehow narrow view of education whose aim might seem only to reaffirm one particularly attractive and dominant identity, that which is the resident power or authority of the moment.[19]

Said, moreover, grasps the dynamic nature of Newman's intellect and genius as a writer and thinker, his ability to create paradoxical echoes beyond the matter, time and context in hand. While placing the highest value on English, European, or Christian values, Newman expresses in his rhetoric 'another thought at odds' with what he is saying, 'and in effect criticizes it, delivers a different, and less assertive idea than on the surface he might have intended'. Reading Newman, Said declares,

we realize that although he is obviously extolling what is an overridingly Western conception of the world, with little allowance made for what was African or Latin American or Indian, his words let slip the notion that even an English or Western identity wasn't enough, wasn't at bottom or at best what education and freedom were all about.[20]

Inherent in Said's appreciation of the *Idea* is his acknowledgment as a political scientist of Newman's robust plea for the university as a focus and exemplar of secular humanism and pluralism. Newman writes that the university should ideally express:

the power of viewing many things at once as one whole, of referring them severally to their true place in the universal system, of understanding their respective values, and determining their mutual dependence.[21]

This is a large, imaginative vision of the university as a community of unity in diversity, as opposed to an ill-assorted assembly of unrelated, segregated disciplines, or a meaningless set of relativisms, still less a constituency of conflicts and disparities. In his novel, *Loss and Gain*, Newman had expressed disapproval of the involvement of Oxford University in 'party' politics. It anticipates his view in *Idea* of the university as a place of ideological amnesty, in which cultural and political clashes, unequal power relationships, and national prejudices, are not so much set aside as reduced through understanding. It is arguable, moreover, that the vision establishes the principle whereby smaller, neglected, less popular disciplines or subjects should be assisted and succoured by the larger and more popular disciplines for the contribution the less popular make to the 'whole'.

Is it possible that the fostering of pluralism in Newman's *Idea* might yet contribute to the reduction of conflict, especially in those parts of the world, in the Middle East, for example, where perceptions of historic injured national identity dominate education? Said writes:

A single overmastering identity at the core of the academic enterprise, whether that identity be Western, African, or Asian, is a confinement, a deprivation. The world we live in is made up of numerous identities interacting, sometimes harmoniously, sometimes antithetically. Not to deal with that whole – which is in fact a contemporary version of the whole referred to by Newman as a true enlargement of the mind – is not to have academic freedom. We cannot make our claim as seekers after justice that we advocate knowledge only of and about ourselves. Our model for academic freedom should therefore be the migrant or traveler: for if, in the real world outside the academy, we must needs be ourselves and only ourselves, inside the academy we should be able to discover and travel among other selves, other identities, other varieties of the human adventure.[22]

THE GENTLEMAN

So how was religion to relate to the wholeness of 'knowledge' or 'philosophy' in Newman's university? As Newman sees it, a successful university, by enlargement of the mind, and 'illumination', encourages a goodness, not only comparable to religion, but rivalling it:

The educated mind may be said to be in a certain sense religious; that is, it has what may be considered a religion of its own, independent of Catholicism, partly cooperating with it, partly thwarting it; at once a defence yet a disturbance to the Church in Catholic countries, – and in countries beyond her pale, at one time in open warfare with her, at another in defensive alliance.[23]

Within this context Newman writes his famous description of a 'gentleman'. Apart from 'Lead Kindly Light', it is perhaps the most quoted passage of all his works, and possibly, taken out of context, the least understood:

Hence it is that it is almost a definition of a gentleman to say he is one who never inflicts pain. This description is both refined and, as far as it goes, accurate. He is mainly occupied in merely removing the obstacles which hinder the free and unembarrassed action of those about him; and he concurs with their movements rather than takes the initiative himself. His benefits may be considered as parallel to what are called comforts or conveniences in arrangements of a personal nature: like an easy chair or a good fire, which do their part in dispelling cold and fatigue, though nature provides both means of rest and animal heat without them. The true gentleman in like manner carefully avoids whatever may cause a jar or a jolt in the minds of those with whom he is cast; – all clashing of opinion, or collision of feeling, all restraint, or suspicion, or gloom, or resentment; his great concern being to make every one at their ease and at home.[24]

If this sounds like an active disposition to give others space in which to flourish, the positive theological underpinning of Christian *agape* (unconditional love) entirely absent. From the first sentence – 'It is almost a definition of a gentleman to say he is one who never inflicts pain' – Newman reveals in his choice of syntax and language the negative qualities of philosophy in the wider sense of the word. The gentleman *removes* objects, he *concurs*, he *avoids*, he *guards against*. And he has already anticipated the irony of the passage by the proposal that Julian the Apostate is the perfect exemplar of 'the pattern-man of philosophical virtue':

Weak points in his character he had, it is true, even in a merely poetical standard; but, take him all in all, and I cannot but recognize in him a specious beauty and nobleness of moral deportment, which combines in it the rude greatness of Fabricius or Regulus with the accomplishments of Pliny or Antoninus. His simplicity of manners, his frugality, his austerity of life, his singular disdain of sensual pleasure, his military heroism, his application to business, his literary diligence, his modesty, his clemency, his accomplishments, as I view them, go to make him one of the most eminent specimens of pagan virtue which the world has ever seen.[25]

Newman, however, goes on to lament Julian's 'insensibility of conscience', his ignorance 'of the very idea of sin' in the 'Religion of Reason', the 'serene self-possession, in the cold, self-satisfaction, we recognize the mere Philosopher'.[26] And yet, Newman has expended much eloquence suggesting that it is the business of the university to encourage a proliferation of graduates precisely in the mould of Julian – Apostate and 'Anti-Christ'. The striking paradox inherent in Newman's counsel here, aimed, after all, at an audience of presumably perplexed Irish Catholic bishops, was that the Church as educator, and the university as educator, are two different entities; capable of collaboration, yet not one and the same thing. The civilizing auspices of the university, he is saying, 'can bring one half way to Heaven',[27] *almost*, and in that sense should not be seen as an enemy of the Church. But the university should be left to perform its task without control, interference, or hindrance, from religion. Just as the university should not be a tool of the state, so it cannot be the tool of the Church; it is to be viewed 'in itself, and apart from the Catholic Church, or from the State, or from any other power which may use it'.[28] The 'other power' anticipates contemporary tensions between the university and the sorts of situations cited by Edward Said. In the 1850s, and subsequently, Newman was principally concerned with pleading for a proper university in Ireland free to conduct its civilizing influence in its own time and space.

He is nevertheless clear as to what the 'Religion of Philosophy' can do and what it can not do. Newman elsewhere[29] contrasts the civilised, Oxford-educated, non-religious philosopher with a scabrous, diseased and filthy Sicilian beggar-woman, such as he himself had encountered on his Mediterranean journey. What the gentleman humanist fails to grasp, for all his civilisation, is that she would be saved, and that he might be damned. Philosophy might well prepare a person to be 'good' in society; but it does not prepare one to seek the face of God. On the other hand, while the beggar woman might be favoured in the sight of God, she might be distinctly unfavourable in the eyes of society. The resolution of the paradoxical contrasts and comparisons Newman makes in the *Idea* is that, spiritually, he must extol the circumstance of the beggar-woman; yet he appears to be saying now, in the presence of the Irish bishops, that the choice, or dilemma, is not between one or the other. He is promoting humanism, but his preference is for a Christian humanism that calls for a perfection of nature that rises to an acknowledgment of God as the author of all.

It is arguable that he saw in this kind of perfection, or wholeness, a human fulfilment more apt for the coming age. In other words, the radical, wounding and self-wounding model of holiness (of a Saint Catherine of Genoa, or Saint Francis, or Saint Teresa of Avila), must give way to a different kind of saint. Not for nothing does Newman end the discourses with a veneration of St Philip Neri, the founder of the Oratorians. In his early life St Philip had been a courtier and a philosopher who became a student of theology. Philip was a saint of the age of the sixteenth-century, who had grown to maturity in Florence and Rome. 'He lived', wrote Newman, 'at a time when pride mounted high, and the senses held rule ... when medieval winter was receding, and the summer sun of civilization was bringing into leaf and flower a thousand forms of luxurious enjoyment; when a new world of thought and beauty had opened upon the human mind, in the discovery of the treasures of classic literature and art.' He goes on to observe: 'He preferred to yield to the stream, and direct the current, which he could not stop, of science, literature, art, and fashion, and to sweeten and sanctify what God had made very good and man had spoilt.'[30]

JAMES JOYCE'S UNIVERSITY

Newman was particularly optimistic about the faculty of medicine he had founded by 1856. 'Our principal success', he wrote in June of that year, 'is and will be our Medical School, which promises to be the first in Dublin.'[31] The faculty survived and thrived in conjunction with the founding of the new St Vincent's Hospital, built in 1857. While other faculties in the humanities were to lose the spirit of the founder, the survival of Newman's ideas in the field of the arts is to be found in some unusual contexts – not least his influence on one of the university's most illustrious students, James Joyce.

There is a passage in *Portrait of the Artist as a Young Man* where the hero, Stephen Dedalus, depicts himself as being drawn beyond the allure of the 'oils of ordination' towards a 'new adventure' – to 'forge in the smithy of my soul the uncreated conscience of my race', to reject his Irish Catholic identity for the life of the literary artist. He hears 'notes of fitful music leaping upwards a tone and downwards a diminished fourth, upwards a tone and downwards a major third, like triplebranching flames'. He seems to hear wild creatures 'racing, their feet pattering like rain upon the leaves ... until he heard them no more and remembered only a proud cadence from Newman: "*Whose feet are as the feet of harts and underneath the everlasting arms*".[32]

Attention to the wide-ranging influences of Newman's ideal of the university, and the dialogue between secular and religious knowledge expounded in the *Idea*, aids our understanding of its essential paradoxes and literary genius. One of the more remarkable examples is the frequent citation of Newman's writings in Joyce's autobiographical novels (*Stephen Hero* and *Portrait of the Artist as a Young Man*). Joyce arrived in 1898 as a student at Dublin's University College, the successor institution to Newman's Catholic University of Ireland which had effectively died in the 1870s.

As a result of mounting frustrations, including lack of funding, Newman had resigned his post in 1858 and returned to the Birmingham Oratory. The institution, situated in a large house on St Stephen's Green next to the church Newman built, languished until 1879 when a government Universities Act provided an injection of funding after it was agreed that the university's qualifications would be authorised by an outside body – the Royal University. The name was changed to University College and the Jesuits took over the teaching faculty in 1882 on the understanding that they would offer vocational courses preparing students for the civil service and the professions.

Newman's ideas, and indeed his form and style of writing, haunt Joyce's early novels, which bear striking parallels with *Loss and Gain*. The contexts are similar – the main actions consisting of conversations between students and between the heroes and their teachers as they walk gardens, streets and tutorial rooms of their separate university cities. Stephen's debates with the Jesuit 'embassy of nimble pleaders' points back to Charles Reding who encounters parallel tempters on the eve of his conversion. Reding's almost mystical apparition of a pilgrim kneeling before a roadside crucifix anticipates Stephen's visionary encounter with a girl on the seashore: 'Her image had passed into his soul for ever and no word had broken the holy silence of his ecstasy … A wild angel had appeared to him … to throw open before him … the gates of all the ways of error and glory.'[33] Despite the civilizing influence of Gerard Manley Hopkins, who spent four years of 'exalted misery' at the college in the 1880s, Joyce's Stephen Dedalus finds a university in which Newman's vision of students in pursuit of 'knowledge for its own sake and nothing else' has been abandoned for useful knowledge and for religious indoctrination:

I found a day school full of terrorized boys, banded together in a complicity of diffidence. They have eyes only for their future jobs: to secure their future jobs they will write themselves in and out of convictions, toil and labour to insinuate themselves into the good graces of the Jesuits.[34]

Stephen in both early novels reveals a subtle and wide-ranging grasp of Newman's *Idea of a University*, the *Apologia*, and key sermons; while the Jesuits pay mere lip-service to the Cardinal's writings, which they neither know nor understand. Like Charles Reding in *Loss and Gain*, Stephen sees the university as an opportunity for, and a process of, alteration, conversion, metanoia. In Stephen's case, the conversion is to literature; not in the manner of a Walter Pater or a Matthew Arnold – as 'art for art's sake', or in order to seek moral goods, but according to the deeper principles expounded in the *Idea of a University*.

In *A Portrait* Stephen debates the crucial contrast between art and religion with the Jesuit Dean of Studies who has been laying a fire – demonstrating, as it were, the 'useful' arts. Unlike Newman, the Dean has become atrophied by his failure to change and to grow: 'his very soul had waxed old in that service without growing towards light and beauty or spreading abroad a sweet odour of her sanctity.'[35] They talk. The Dean argues that the beautiful should be marked by its utility and ethical value; while Stephen, quoting Aquinas, the heart and soul of Catholic orthodoxy under the recent influence of Pope Leo XIII, challenges the notion: 'Aquinas, answered Stephen, says *Pulcra sunt quae visa placent*' [Those things are beautiful that please on being seen].[36] By the same token, Stephen is following Newman, who himself follows Aristotle, in declaring that art should be regarded as enjoyable for its own sake: 'All I have been now saying is summed up in a few characteristic words of the great Philosopher', writes Newman, ' "Of possessions", [Aristotle] says, "those rather are useful which bear fruit; those *liberal, which tend to enjoyment*. By fruitful, I mean, which yield revenue; by enjoyable, where *nothing accrues of consequence beyond the using*." '[37]

At a deeper level Joyce identifies himself with Newman as a hero of apostasy and rebellion in his abandonment of the established Church of his nation, as well as friends and family.[38] Like Newman, Joyce is rejecting patriotism, Ireland's Catholicism and family, in order to embrace exile on the continent of Europe. In a paradox worthy of Newman himself, Joyce's motives for rejecting Catholicism find parallels with Newman's path to Rome. Irish Catholicism means narrow xenophobia for Joyce, while literature signifies pluralism, universalism, a wide ranging civilization. When Stephen is accused by his friends of preferring the oppressors' language of English to the study of Gaelic, he retorts that English literature and language are Aryan rather than merely English. It is reminiscent of Newman's criticism of the Church of England: 'You do not communicate with any one Church besides your own', whereas the Church of Rome 'has flourished through so many ages, among so many nations ... in such contrary classes and conditions of men.'[39]

The gulf between the Jesuit Dean and Stephen is exemplified by their unequal capacity to employ multidimensional language and dynamic metaphors. Stephen attempts to demonstrate this gulf by citing a sermon of Newman's:

– One difficulty, said Stephen, in esthetic discussion is to know whether words are being used according to the literary tradition or according to the tradition of the marketplace.

I remember a sentence of Newman's in which he says of the Blessed Virgin that she was detained in the full company of the saints. The use of the word in the marketplace is quite different. *I hope I am not detaining you.*
– Not in the least, said the dean politely.
– No, no, said Stephen, smiling, I mean …
– Yes, yes: I see, said the dean quickly, I quite catch the point: *detain.*[40]

Again, Stephen shows himself to be a disciple of Newman in his conviction that religious faith is a question of individual conversion and conviction, 'real assent', as opposed to mere group membership, or 'notional assent', according to Newman's discussion in the *Essay in Aid of a Grammar of Assent.* While Newman points out, in chapter four of the *Grammar,* that the distinction between 'notional' and 'real' assent is not concerned primarily with 'assent in the matters of Religion', Stephen fears that his own peculiar hell would consist in giving 'comfortable assent to propositions without in the least ordering one's life in accordance with them'.[41] Stephen's process of 'conversion', moreover, runs parallel to Newman's in his tendency to follow 'intuition', a sense of 'strange unrest', the exercise of imagination, and conscience in the form of private judgment.

For Newman and Stephen metanoia is akin to rebellion, apostasy, acting against the tide (small wonder Newman has an ironic admiration for Julian the Apostate). Stephen finds it harder to 'merge his life with the common tide of other lives … than any fasting or prayer'.[42] Both sacrifice family and community identity in order to follow private judgment and conscience. Newman writes: 'The resolution I speak of has been taken with reference to myself alone … without reference to success or failure other than personal.'[43]

Newman's influence on the young Joyce is theoretical, and even, by analogy, theological in structure. Above all it is stylistic in the deeper sense of style expounded in the *Idea*, anticipating the high modern in literature. For Newman style is not a superficial gloss on writing; it is the deepest expression of personality. The style of the literary genius, Newman writes, is:

the faithful expression of his intense personality, attending on his own inward world of thought as its very shadow: so that we might as well say that one man's shadow is another's as that the style of a really gifted mind can belong to any but himself. It follows him about *as* a shadow. His thought and feeling are personal, and so his language is personal.[44]

THE *IDEA* AND DISSENT

Newman characterised Anglo-Catholicism as a paper Church, as we have seen; and there is a sense in which his idea of a university is a paper university: an ideal rather than a reality. The structures, funding, and expansion of major universities in the West have become ever more remote from the possibility of the ideal university Newman had in mind. Not only are universities today heavily biased towards research rather than teaching, but the smorgasbord of vocational courses offered at undergraduate level could never have been envisaged in the mid-nineteenth century: degrees in sports technology, hospitality, shoe-craft, business studies, journalism, etc. At the same time, academics are now governed by monetarist business models – the application of the market to the curriculum and research 'outcomes'; the survival of disciplines based on 'client' choice. Distance learning expansion, moreover, takes universities ever further from the kind of ideal face-to-face 'college' communities of Newman's day.

Given the changing times, the sheer size of such universities, and the enormous contrast in backgrounds of students, it is difficult to see how Newman's vision could be anything but a remote overview, such as Edward Said invokes. In his preface to Allan Bloom's *The Closing of the American Mind* (a book that contains many echoes of Newman's *Idea*), Saul Bellow confirms, at least negatively, the central need Newman predicts and anticipates for our time. Bellow's strongly autobiographical fictional character, Charlie Citrine in *Humboldt's Gift*, attends Chicago University. He tells us: 'I meant that novel to show how little strength "higher education" had to offer a troubled man.'[45] Published in 1973, the novel describes the period of the Vietnam War, student protests, dissent in academe. Where do literature, poetry, the university, stand in the era of the industrial-military complex?

The country is proud of its dead poets. It takes terrific satisfaction in the poets' testimony that the USA is too tough, too big, too much, too rugged, that American reality is overpowering. And to be a poet is a school thing, a skirt thing, a church thing.... Orpheus moved stones and trees. But a poet can't perform a hysterectomy or send a vehicle out of the solar system.[46]

But the channel is always there, Bellow argues, in the kind of university which enables students to 'make final judgments and put everything together'. Bellow refers to this as 'that part of us which is conscious of a higher consciousness.... The independence of this consciousness, which has the strength to be immune ... from the distractions of our immediate surroundings, is what the life struggle is all about.' He concludes:

The soul has to find and hold its ground against hostile forces, sometimes embodied in ideas which frequently deny its very existence, and which indeed often seem to be trying to annul it altogether.[47]

Would Newman have deplored the sacking of Berkeley academics during the McCarthy era? Or applauded the student protests in the 1960s against the Vietnam War? Newman sets the scene of an academic community with passion, commitment, and potential for activism as a place in which the intellect may safely range and speculate, sure to find its equal in some antagonist activity, and its judge in the tribunal of truth ... where the professor becomes eloquent and is missionary and a preacher, displaying his science in its most complete and most winning form, pouring it forth with the zeal of enthusiasm, and lighting up his own love of it in the breasts of his hearers.[48]

Zeal gives rise to radicalism, or dissent, where members of the community feel 'a disgust and abhorrence, towards excesses and enormities of evil, which are often or ordinarily reached at length by those who are not careful from the first to set themselves against what is vicious and criminal'.[49]

CHAPTER 12

Tribulations, heresy, and the faithful

'What is the province of the laity? To hunt, to shoot, to entertain. These matters
they understand, but to meddle with ecclesiastical matters they have no right
at all ... Dr Newman is the most dangerous man in England ...'
LETTER FROM MONSIGNOR GEORGE TALBOT TO MONSIGNOR HENRY MANNING

'I listen, and I hear the sound of voices, grave and musical, renewing the old chant, with which Augustine greeted Ethelbert in the free air upon the Kentish strand.' Newman preached these words at Oscott College on 13 July 1852.[1] The occasion was the first synod of the newly restored Catholic hierarchy; the sermon was entitled 'The Second Spring'. 'Something strange is passing over this land, by the very surprise, by the very commotion, which it excites', he went on. 'It is the Coming in of a Second Spring; it is a restoration in the moral world.'[2] The college chapel, recently furnished by Pugin, was filled to capacity with bishops, clergy, and representatives of the religious orders. He spoke of the magnificence of Oscott's buildings, and the procession through its cloisters of vested, chanting clergy in due precedence. He pulled out all the rhetorical stops as he reflected on the dark days of persecution when Catholics in England had survived, like the persecuted early Christians, 'in corners, and alleys, and cellars, and the housetops, or in the recesses of the country; cut off from the populous world around them, and simply seen, as if through a mist or in twilight, as ghosts flitting to and fro ...'[3] A Second Spring had come, but he offered a warning, exploiting the vernal conceit with a characteristically paradoxical flourish. This Spring, he reflected, might 'turn out to be an English spring, an uncertain, anxious time of hope and fear, of joy and suffering, – of bright promise and budding hopes, yet withal, of keen blasts, and cold showers, and sudden storms.'[4] It was not among the best of his sermons, but there was a touch of the old magic in his words and the delivery; many in the congregation wept openly, including Cardinal Wiseman. They crowded around him affectionately in the college cloisters, offering their congratulations. Yet it would not be long before Newman himself would experience 'cold showers' of that spring time.

Through the 1840s and into the 1850s the Catholic Church in England had expanded and prospered numerically. Two significant events had given impetus to the self-confidence of the Catholic community – the Emancipation Act of 1829, which effectively ended social and political constraints on Catholics, and the restoration of the Catholic hierarchy in 1850. But the numerical increase was due to demographic realities, in particular the new converts from Anglicanism, and the influx of immigrants escaping the consequences of unemployment, poverty, and famine in Ireland. The ever growing visible presence of the Catholic Church could be seen up and down the country with the erection of schools, chapels, churches, and presbyteries, many of them designed by the indefatigable Pugin and courtesy the generosity of John Talbot, the Earl of Shrewsbury. The 1840s had seen the completion of two fine metropolitan cathedrals: St Chad's in Birmingham and St George's in Southwark; and the great stone monastery of Mount Saint Bernard's in Charnwood Forest, Leicestershire. The rapid growth had brought understandable tensions, between 'old' versus 'new' Catholics, clergy versus the laity, and contrasting styles of devotion. The old Catholics with their minimalist devotions preserved in Richard Challoner's *Garden of the Soul* felt at odds with the lush pieties and missionary enthusiasms of such as Father Faber. A significant division, for example, was growing between those who looked to the Pope in Rome as the arbiter of all: the so-called ultramontanes or Romanists, as opposed to those who were more inclined to favour local discretion.

Newman would find himself increasingly at odds with both Cardinal Wiseman and Father Faber, tensions which, as biographer Ian Ker has put it, were to do with 'the nature of the Church itself': what it meant to be a Catholic in England.[5] Newman's 'very great anxiety' was first occasioned by a dispute with Faber at the London Oratory. The matter, at this distance, appears trivial. Cardinal Wiseman had asked Faber's help in providing spiritual direction for an order of nuns in London. As it happened, St Philip Neri had banned his Oratorians from hearing the confessions of nuns. Faber, however, took it upon himself to write to the Vatican for permission to suspend St Philip's rule in the matter. The powers that be in Rome assumed that Newman, still officially overall head of both Oratories, had approved the application. He had done no such thing. Since it was not a question of obliging the Birmingham Oratorians to hear nuns' confessions, Newman's anxiety hardly seems merited in retrospect. But he was exasperated by Faber's appeal to higher Roman authority without consultation at home: a classically ultramontane act of obeisance to central authority.

Newman wrote a firm, but reasonable letter from Dublin reproving him:

We learn from accidental information, confirmed by our Bishop, that he has received, or is to receive, in our behalf a relaxation or suspension, which we neither desire in itself, nor desire should come to us without our asking for it.

It is desirable for your sake, as well as ours, that such misconceptions should not recur; for, as your House has unintentionally involved us, so we unintentionally might involve you.

Suppose we were to petition Propaganda, (to take a parallel case) that the Birmingham Oratory might claim the private property of each of its subjects, and your Bishop received a letter empowering the Oratory at Brompton to exercise a similar power over its own subjects, and you were suddenly informed of this by an accidental channel, after the transaction had been going on for months over and around you, I think you would consider our act at Edgbaston a great inconvenience to you.[6]

Faber chose not to reply. In fact, he would remain silent until the following May.

Meanwhile Newman got wind that the Vatican had consulted three English bishops on the matter, including Cardinal Wiseman. It seemed likely that Rome was preparing documents to allow a relaxation of the rule which forbade hearing nuns' confessions for both England's Oratories. Newman wrote to Propaganda asking that it be understood that the two English Oratorian houses should be regarded 'entirely independent of each other, and what one does is not the act of the other'.[7] Newman further insisted that the request for relaxation should come through him in Birmingham and not London.

Although still embroiled with the Achilli libel trial, and the practical tasks of establishing the university in Ireland – with frequent commutes between Dublin, Birmingham and London – Newman decided to hurry out to Rome to resolve matters. The journey, made in the company of Ambrose St John late in December 1856, had its hazards: 'In the afternoon', Newman writes, after a stay in Verona, we 'had got to the Station and were setting off for Padua, when we found the Engine of the train had burst on the way from Brescia, and we were detained at the Station. The day before Fr Ambrose had observed in the train with some anxiety how near we were to the Engine …'[8] They transferred to a diligence. 'In the midst of the journey too we heard that the brigands were every where in the Pope's territories – that there had been a rising in the streets of Bologna in day time a fortnight before, and a diligence robbed … a Frenchman had been killed and in the way to Imola a Cardinal had been kept prisoner till his ransom was sent.'[9] Travelling down through Italy and staying at various Oratorian houses, it had become clear to Newman that a circular letter had preceded him from the London Oratory, accusing him of ambition and of being an excessive controller. They finally entered the Eternal City in early January.

Their confrere, William Neville, would write a note about their remarkable act of asceticism on arrival near the Spanish Steps: 'on alighting from the diligence [Newman] went with Father St John to make a visit of devotion to the shrine of St. Peter, going there the whole way barefoot … the streets were very empty, and thus, and screened by his large Roman cloak, he was able to do so unrecognized and unnoticed.'[10] The journey was about three miles there and back.

On 25 January Newman was finally received by Pius IX, an audience he found 'long and most satisfactory'. Newman wrote to his confrere Father Edward

Caswall: 'He knew all about *us*.' Newman saw a letter from the London Oratory lying on the Pope's table. But the Pope was kindly and 'began by saying', wrote Newman, 'I was thin, and had done much penance – and that Fr Ambrose had got older'.[11]

Newman finally got from the Pope what he had set out to achieve 'that nothing done by the Holy See by one Oratory might affect another.'[12] He also received confirmation from Cardinal Alessandro Barnabò, Prefect of Propaganda, that his authority extended to sanctioning or vetoing the formation of any new Oratorian community in England. The significance of this understanding arose from Newman's wish to found a second Oratory in London in a poor district of the East End, quite independent of the Brompton Oratory in its well-heeled West London district. With this, Newman made the return journey to London in just four days.

His satisfaction was short lived. Faber now sent two of his London Oratory acolytes to Rome to undo everything Newman had accomplished. In direct contradiction to Newman's hopes, Faber received the backing of the Vatican in prohibiting the establishment of a second Oratory in London.

Letters of the period now show mounting antagonism between London and Birmingham. Faber wrote of the Birmingham Oratorians being 'extremely united in condemning us, in real spirits, not regretting the row and considering themselves a very successful house, and all that they could wish'.[13] He had evidence, he wrote, of their 'feeling against us' being 'something awful'. Father Dalgairns, who had become something of a stirrer and trouble-maker, after moving backwards and forwards between London and Birmingham, reported a Birmingham Oratorian as saying that the London Oratory's 'professions of religion are simply "humbug"'.[14,15]

One of the chief instigators of tensions between Newman and Faber had been Monsignor Talbot, the Papal Chamberlain, who had begun to loathe Newman. The feelings were mutual. Cardinal Wiseman had also done his bit to upset Newman, although the occasion was minor on the face of it. Wiseman had included Newman with Faber in the dedication of a book he had published on St Philip Neri. Newman, for whom dedications were a sign of profound affection, felt that this was done deliberately to annoy him. He did not wish his name to appear on the same page of a book as Faber, albeit a book devoted to their common saintly patron.

At the same time Newman had run into problems with the Irish bishops. John McHale, Archbishop of Tuam in Galway, and Paul Cullen, Archbishop of Dublin, were in a power struggle for control of the Catholic Church in Ireland and its future. Cullen, who was anti-Fenian, had been made Cardinal in 1850 and had been chairing a synod to reform the hierarchy and relations with the laity of which the foundation of the Catholic university was an important feature. While Wiseman was a confirmed ultramontane, McHale was a nationalist who hated all things English (he had translated the Pentateuch into Gaelic). He deplored Newman's appointment as Rector and attempted to thwart Cullen at every opportunity.[16] Newman's rectorship of the university was becoming untenable. Newman, back in Dublin, uttered a wail of frustration to Ambrose: 'I go to Rome to be snubbed. I come to Dublin to be repelled by Dr McHale and worn away by Dr Cullen. The cardinal taunts me with his Dedications, and Fr Faber insults me with his letters.'[17]

The letters between Faber and Newman were now crackling with mutual animosity. Faber wrote to Newman on 8 May complaining 'of a long series of jealousies, doubts and misconstructions', in Newman's mind. There followed an example of Faber's barbed religiosity:

At the beginning of the year I took St John the Evangelist for my year Saint, because of his being your patron, and in the hope of his bringing us together again, and so, what I am going to ask of you, I ask in his name. I know you well enough to know how you must yourself have suffered all this time. Now, is it quite impossible for you to forgive us, to be a father to us again, to destroy the scandal of unvisiting houses? What exactly is it in our conduct that has angered you so greatly …? Surely we are your sons, fathers must suffer for their children, must bear much from them.[18]

Newman, who had received no word from Faber for six months on the original quarrel between them, replied with his own brand of acidulously pious reproof:

My dear Father Wilfrid, It is a very great satisfaction to me to see your handwriting, and tho' this is May and I wrote you in November your writing now is more than compensation for your utter silence then. I put it down to your continued indisposition, which has grieved me very much, and which I have been for a long time in practice of remembering at Mass and before the Blessed Sacrament … I am startled to find you talk of scandal having occurred; if I, or any of my Congregation, is in fault, I am sorry for it. Talking freely is the common source of scandal. I do not think we have done so.[19]

Faber wrote back, complaining of the 'pain the perusal of your letter has caused. Why! my dear Father, almost every word of it seems full of alienation. But I must not be discouraged … If you leave it as your letter to me today leaves it, it will be refusing us peace.'[20] And so it went on.

CLERICALISM AND THE LAITY

No sooner had the coldness between Cardinal Wiseman and Newman over the trifling matter of the book dedication subsided than there was cause for a much more serious and lasting antagonism between Newman and Catholic authority on the score of the status and role of the Catholic laity.

In 1859 Newman wrote an article in which he remarked on 'the endemic perennial fidget which possesses us about giving scandal; facts are omitted in great histories, or glosses are put upon memorable acts, because they are thought not edifying, whereas of all scandals such omissions, such glosses, are the greatest'.[21] He was referring specifically to a row that had broken out over his links with a prominent Catholic periodical run by laymen. In the previous year, Sir John Acton, aristocrat and scholar, had become involved in the literary magazine, the *Rambler*, founded in 1848 for an educated Catholic readership. Acton, who had been a pupil of the German Church historian, Johann Joseph Ignaz Döllinger, insisted that lay Catholic scholars had an important part to play in the intellectual life of the Church. Newman agreed.

While Acton bound himself strictly to unquestioning belief in Church dogma, he was convinced that creative theology should be underpinned by historicity and that such scholarship should be conducted by laymen as well as clerics. Acton and Richard Simpson, a convert friend of Newman, took over the ownership of the *Rambler* in 1858, with Simpson as editor. The magazine straightaway began to concern itself with theological issues and became outspoken and irreverent about the shortcomings of Catholic clerical authority, past and present. Not only had Simpson run an article in which Döllinger argued that Augustine was the originator of Jansenism, but he revealed a mischievous streak by running pieces exposing past papal scandals. More pertinent for the papacy of his day, he allowed space for commentary that opposed the Pope's temporal sovereignty – a burning issue at the time as Pio Nono attempted to resist the unification of Italy and the loss of the Papal States. The ultramontane faction in England supported the Pope's temporal power enthusiastically, seeing it as tantamount to an article of faith. Cardinal Wiseman, who in any case saw the *Rambler* as a rival to the *Dublin Review* of which he was the proprietor, was furious.

Things came to a head over an article on Catholic education. The hierarchy had declined to cooperate with a Royal Commission on elementary schools. The bishops refused to appoint a Catholic representative on the committee since they were adamant that questions about religious teaching methods in Catholic schools were none of the government's business. In January 1859 the *Rambler* ran a forthright piece on the issue by Scott Nasmyth Stokes, a government Catholic Schools Inspector and elementary education expert. Stokes declared that the Church had nothing to fear from the Commission and that it was self-defeating to refuse cooperation since State funding might be withdrawn to the advantage of non-Catholic schools.

The *Rambler*'s other rival periodical, *The Tablet*, hastened to defend the bishops, accusing Stokes of disloyalty and impugning his Catholic credentials. Stokes replied in the correspondence pages of the *Rambler* that his Catholicism had nothing to do it; he implied that the problem was one of ignorance and prejudice on the part of the bishops as well as their failure to consult qualified lay Catholics. He opined that he would be surprised if the bishops should be 'displeased by the loyal expression of the opinions entertained by many Catholics, and supported by arguments that cannot be met'.[22] Emboldened by the *Tablet's* attack, and infuriated by Stokes's reply, several bishops decided that unless Simpson resigned his editorship forthwith, with consequent drastic changes of editorial policy, they would destroy the periodical by condemning it in their pastoral letters. So it was that Newman, at the direct request of Wiseman and his own Bishop, Ullathorne, agreed to become editor after persuading Simpson to withdraw.

Newman's first editorial as editor proclaimed the periodical's new mission statement: to promote 'the refinement, enlargement, and elevation of the intellect in the educated classes'. He declared, moreover, that the magazine would 'discountenance what is untenable and unreal, without forgetting the tenderness due to the weak and the reverence rightly claimed for what is sacred; and to encourage a manly investigation of subjects of public interest under a deep sense of the prerogatives of ecclesiastical authority'.[23] 'Manly investigation' was a curious note, but it seems that it was code for unflinching and courageous criticism of ecclesiastical matters where due.

There were instant complaints that Newman had not sufficiently censured Simpson (years later Newman wrote that he 'thought it unfair, ungenerous, impertinent and cowardly to make in their behalf acts of confession and contrition, and to make a display of change of editorship').[24] Newman had in fact been more than fair to the bishops in his adjudication of the schools' question, quoting their pastoral letters at length. But he then enlarged on his own views about the role of the laity in the Church. 'Acknowledging then most fully the prerogatives of the episcopate', he wrote, 'we do unfeignedly believe ... that their Lordships really desire to know the opinion of the laity on subjects in which the laity are especially concerned.' He went on to cite the case of the infallible definition of the dogma of the Immaculate Conception ten years earlier. 'If even in the preparation of a dogmatic definition the faithful are consulted ... it is at least as natural to anticipate such an act of kind feeling and sympathy in great practical questions ...'[25]

The tone was irenic, the proposal modest. But Dr Gillow, professor of theology at Ushaw College, seminary for the North East of England, accused Newman of heresy: the laity had no right to be consulted on doctrinal issues. Instead of addressing Dr Gillow directly, Newman decided to ask Ullathorne, his bishop, to appoint a theological censor for the magazine's copy, as would be the case with any Catholic book of theology published within the diocese. Ullathorne hurried over to Edgbaston for a conference. He complained that the new *Rambler* had not altered its ways, and something drastic must be done: but what? Newman kept a waspish note of the meeting dated 22 May:

The Bishop … thought there were remains of the old spirit [in the new *Rambler*]. It was irritating. Our laity were a *peaceable* set, the Church was *peace*. They had a deep faith – they did not like to hear that any one doubted … I said in answer that he saw one side, I another – that the Bishops etc did not see that state of the Laity, e.g. in Ireland, how unsettled, yet how docile. He said something like 'who are the Laity', I answered that the Church would look foolish without them – *not* those words.[26]

Ullathorne was deaf to Newman's insistence that the laity deserved encouragement, and to be heard. It ended with Ullathorne telling Newman to resign the editorship. Newman instantly acquiesced. Strangely, Ullathorne urged that Simpson should be allowed to take back the magazine. Evidently Ullathorne, Wiseman, and the other bishops, were now far less afraid of a lay editor than they were of Newman. 'Perhaps', Newman wrote in a memorandum, 'it was the Cardinal etc, were seized with a panic lest they had got out of the frying pan into the fire'.[27] Newman wrote to his friend Henry Wilberforce: .

If you attempt at a *wrong* time what in *itself* is *right*, you perhaps become a heretic or schismatic … When I am gone it will be seen perhaps that persons stopped me from doing a *work* which I *might* have done. God over-rules all things. Of course it is discouraging to be out of joint with the time, and to be snubbed and stopped as soon as I begin to act.[28]

His initiative might well have been untimely in the mid-nineteenth century, but his thoughts and writings on the matter would have reverberations down to the First Vatican Council of 1870 and beyond.

Newman had one more edition of the magazine to bring out and he used the opportunity to expound his views not so much on the laity as the 'faithful', for they were not necessarily synonymous in his view, the faithful including both clergy and laity.[29] The article has come down to us as the text of the essay *On Consulting the Faithful in Matters of Doctrine*.

A crucial test of Revelation, Newman maintained, consisted in the scrutiny of the beliefs of the faithful:

the tradition of the Apostles, committed to the whole Church … manifests itself variously at various times: sometimes by the mouth of the episcopacy, sometimes by the doctors, sometimes by the people, sometimes by liturgies, rites, ceremonies, and customs, by events, disputes, movements, and all those phenomena which are comprised under the name of history. It follows that none of these channels of tradition may be treated with disrespect.[30]

Invoking the case of the Arians, he argued how in the fourth century, 'the divine tradition committed to the infallible Church was proclaimed and maintained far more by the faithful than by the Episcopate'.[31] Indeed, 'the body of the Episcopate was unfaithful to its commission, while the body of the laity was faithful to its baptism'. The Church flourishes, he wrote, when at one with the faithful, but not 'when she cuts off the faithful from the study of her divine doctrines and the sympathy of her divine contemplations, and requires from them a *fides implicita* [implicit faith] in her word, which in the educated classes will terminate in indifference, and in the poorer in superstition'.[32] Resorting to the Early Fathers, Newman was expounding a powerful vision of the Church as a single, organic communion with a common conscience. In 1859, however, the Catholic ecclesiastical authorities in England were aghast. Dr Gillow of Ushaw now wrote to Bishop Brown of Newport who 'delated' the article to Rome; in other words, he found a bishop who would officially report Newman as a heretic. The process involved writing to the Congregation of Propaganda in Latin; alas Bishop Brown's Latin was not quite up to it and it was mistranslated, making Newman's proposal far more unorthodox than it originally sounded in English.

Realising what was afoot, Newman wrote to Wiseman, who happened to be in Rome at the time, making it clear that he would submit to the Church's teaching whatever that might be, at the same time attempting to explain himself as clearly as he could. Meanwhile, Propaganda had drawn up a list of their objections to the article and passed them to Wiseman who either forgot, or declined, to send them on to Newman for an answer. In the event Newman received a letter from Henry Manning, now Monsignor Manning, who was acquiring stature and influence as an administrator and Rome-England papal go-between. Manning indicated that Wiseman would settle everything in a manner that Newman would find acceptable on his return to London. And that was the last Newman was to hear of the affair.

Alas, in Rome, the orthodoxy watchdogs were still waiting for Newman's reply to their list of objections, and his failure to oblige them was taken as insolence and obduracy. Newman's reputation was sinking fast and a principal antagonist in his undoing was Monsignor Talbot. We gain an impression of Talbot's poisonous character, ecclesial attitudes, and animosity towards Newman, in a letter he later wrote to Manning about the *Rambler* article:

It is perfectly true that a cloud has been hanging over Dr. Newman in Rome ever since the Bishop of Newport delated him to Rome for heresy in his article in the *Rambler* ... [the laity] are beginning to show the cloven foot ... putting into practice the doctrine taught by Dr. Newman ... What is the province of the laity? To hunt, to shoot, to entertain. These matters they understand, but to meddle with ecclesiastical matters they have no right at all ... Dr. Newman is the most dangerous man in England.[33]

Three years after he wrote this letter, and with ample capacity to do more mischief in the meantime, Monsignor Talbot would be committed to a lunatic an asylum at Passy outside Paris; hence it is possible that he was suffering from mental illness during this period. But had Manning betrayed Newman, whom he professed to admire and love? In time, it would become apparent that Manning would sacrifice anything and anyone in defence of the papacy, a loyalty that coincided with his own rise to power. Samuel Wilberforce remembered a conversation with Odo Russell, ten years on from the *Rambler* debacle, who said:

Manning's influence at Rome absolutely a personal influence with the Pope. The Pope, a man of strong will, though of intense vanity, cannot bear the slightest contradiction, but very fond of all who take his absolute dicta as law. This Manning has played upon, and got on. He is more Papal than the Pope ... repeats to the Pope all his own ideas, which pleases him exceedingly ... Manning's appointment [as Archbishop of Westminster] protested against by all the old Roman families in England, but the Pope would not listen. Manning most obsequious: creeps on hands and knees to kiss his toe, and, even when bidden to get up, remains prostrate in awe. This delights Pio Nono.[34]

DEPRESSION

Reflecting on the five years following his resignation from the *Rambler*, Newman wrote: 'The cause of my not writing from 1859 to 1864 was my failure with the *Rambler*. I thought I had got into a scrape, and it became me to be silent. So they thought at Rome, if Mgr. Talbot is to be their spokesman....'[35] There had been a host of other, minor irritations and frustrations, including criticisms from old adversaries in the Church of England: 'little and ridiculous things taken separately', he wrote, 'but they form an atmosphere of *flies* – one can't enjoy a walk without this fidget on the nerves of the mind. They are nothing in the eye of reason, but they weary.'[36] Nor was he in good health. He complained of losing weight: 'I am an old man, and cannot get accustomed to the look of my fingers.'[37]

After the exertions of Dublin and the problems with Faber and Rome, Newman appears to have suffered a form of depression marked by insomnia and dark moods. He confided in his journal: 'Old men are in soul as stiff, as lean, as bloodless as their bodies, except so far as grace penetrates and softens them. And it requires a flooding of grace to do this.' Again, he notes, 'the deadness of my soul.'[38] He felt he was like 'a grey grasshopper or evaporating mist of the morning'.[39] He felt abandoned as well as persecuted: 'I am nobody. I have no friend at Rome, I have laboured in England, to be misrepresented, backbitten, and scorned. I have laboured in Ireland, with a door ever shut in my face. I seem to have had many failures, and what I did well was not understood. I do not think I am saying this in any bitterness.'[40] Despite his many attainments, he could say of himself: 'everything seems to crumble under my hands, as if one were making ropes of sand'.[41] He provides a vivid description of his sense of misery; although it was clear, even in the act of recording his feelings, that his literary talent was intact as was his sense of empathy for the sufferings of others, past and present. 'The wounds which one bears speechlessly', he wrote, 'the dreadful secrets which are severed from the sympathy of others, the destruction of confidences, the sense of hollowness all around one, the expectation of calamity or scandal, this was a portion of St Paul's trial, and all Bishops, as it is of all, in their degree, who have to work for God in this world. It is as real a penance as a hair shirt.'[42]

He goes on to reflect on his own 'hair shirt'. 'For myself, now I am deeply deficient in that higher life which lasts and grows in spite of the ills of mortality – but had I ever so much of supernatural love and devotion, I could not be in any different state from the Apostle, who in the most beautiful of his inspired epistles speaks with such touching and consoling vividness of those troubles, in the midst of which these earthen vessels of ours hold the treasures of grace and truth.'[43] Was it possible that he was regretting becoming a Catholic? In time there would be rumours to this effect, which he would emphatically deny. But in the absence of Catholic appreciation of his worth, he could confide to his journal an intriguing temptation: 'of looking out for, if not courting, Protestant praise.'[44]

During this 'real purifying "dark night"',[45] as Stephen Dessain put it, Newman had busied himself with the founding of a second educational establishment – a school in Birmingham for the sons of Catholic professional and upper class families. It would be a palpable achievement, but there would be swarms of flies and cold showers in plenty. Newman, in common with other Anglican converts, believed that there was a gap to be filled in Catholic secondary education in England. The public schools were unsuitable, closed, even, to the children of Catholics, and alternative Catholic institutions, like Oscott, St Edmund's, and Sedgley Park, which mixed 'church' and 'lay' students, and the monastic schools, were too much like seminaries. Newman believed strongly that women, or 'dames' (matrons in later parlance), banned from these institutions, should have charge of pupils' health and physical welfare.

Again, he saw the involvement of the laity as crucial. He turned to friends such as Edward Bellassis (a barrister who handled the legislation in the expansion of the railways), James Hope-Scott (who had defended him in the Achilli trial) and Acton. He was determined, moreover, to involve parents in every aspect of the school's formation and life. He wanted his school to offer a liberal education, carefully balanced with instruction in Catholic beliefs and practice.

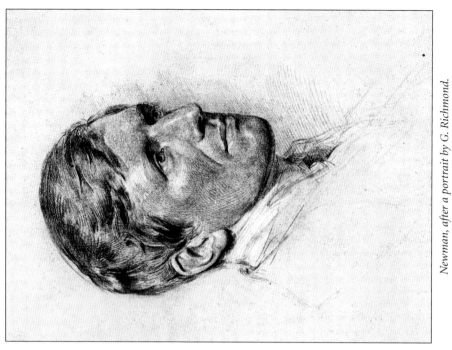

Newman, after a portrait by G. Richmond.

Newman preaching at St Mary's.

Punch cartoon of Wiseman (Wiseboy) and Newman (Newboy) after the restoration of the Catholic hierarchy in 1850.

Newman among his confreres at the Birmingham Oratory. Reproduced by kind permission of the Fathers of the Birmingham Oratory.

Cardinal Newman by John Everett Millais.
Reproduced by kind permission of the National Portrait Gallery.

Cardinal Newman in old age.   *Ambrose and John Henry.*
Both photographs above reproduced by kind permission of the Fathers of the Birmingham Oratory.

Newman's Catholic University, Dublin.

Newman on receiving the 'red hat' in Rome, 1879, with
Father William Neville at his right shoulder.
Reproduced by kind permission of the Fathers of the Birmingham Oratory.

Lead, kindly Light, amid the encircling gloom,
    Lead Thou me on!
The night is dark, and I am far from home;
    Lead Thou me on!
Keep Thou my feet — I do not ask to see
The distant scene; one step enough for me.

I was not ever thus, nor prayed that Thou
    Shouldst lead me on;
I loved to choose and see my path; — but now
    Lead Thou me on; —
I loved the garish day, and, spite of fears,
Pride ruled my will; — remember not past ... on.

So long Thy power has blest me, sure it still
    Will lead me on;
O'er moor + fen, o'er crag + torrent, till
    The night is gone;
And with the morn those angel faces smile
Which I have loved long since, + ... awhile.

at sea . on board   June 16. 1833
the Conte Ruggiero

MS of 'Lead Kindly Light'.

Portrait of John Henry and Ambrose at Propaganda College by Maria Giberne.

Ambrose St John in old age.

Both photographs above reproduced by kind permission of the Fathers of the Birmingham Oratory.

He believed that boys should be trusted and he was against harsh discipline.[46] He started with just seven pupils, all sons of converts, and delegated much of the day-to-day running of the school to competent staff. The school was owned by the Oratorian Congregation with Newman as its President. The Oratorian Father, Nicholas Darnell, who had been with Newman since 1848, was appointed headmaster and the school quickly began to prosper, expanding to seventy boys by 1861. Newman was soon to discover, however, that delegation, especially in the case of a boarding school, has its problems. Under Darnell's headship the school was moving more in the direction of a regular public school and away from Newman's vision of a civilised, homely Catholic community. Darnell refused to listen or to accept counsel, a circumstance that served, it seems, to exacerbate Newman's depression and ill-health. As Newman would write the following year to Henry Wilberforce: 'I have been more and more elbowed out of the school – till I knew nothing about any thing. This state of things was one of the trials which hung so heavily upon me in the summer. There seemed no way of righting matters. My rule has ever been to give a generous liberty to those I put in trust with any work – and, having put power out of my hands, there was no way of getting it back.'[47] The catastrophe, as he put it, came unexpectedly, after he had absented himself from Birmingham for several months.

TROUBLE AT THE ORATORY SCHOOL

In 1861 Newman turned sixty. He later wrote of his feelings that year:

I, when I was 60, was seized with an all overishness, which I could not analyze. I could not sleep – I could do nothing. This was my condition for several years and for a time I thought any thing might happen. My spirits were unaccountably low ...[48]

His doctor had prescribed a break to shake off depression and insomnia, so in July he took himself off on holiday with William Neville, who had joined the Oratory ten years earlier and whom Newman described as 'a sort of Guardian Angel or Homeric god'.[49] He had a desire to visit the scenes of his childhood, and their journey took them first to London, then to Ham in Wiltshire, scene of childhood holidays, before going on to Brighton where his sister Mary was buried. It was a thoroughly modern, high-speed journey. They travelled by rail to Waterloo Station and crossed the town to King's Cross where they took a train to Cambridge. While sight-seeing they were stalked by 'a little man', who 'fastened his eyes on us'. Neville, wrote Newman, 'instantly enveloped me in darkness, rustling with his wings, and flapping about with a vigor which for the time was very successful'.[50] Returning to Birmingham, Newman spent most of the summer at Rednal in the Lickey Hills followed by a week at Ventnor in the Isle of Wight, where he had not been since 1825. By November he was still on his break, for he was back in London on a month's stay with Henry Bowden, younger brother of his old deceased student friend, John Bowden. Here he received a letter from Faber, who had absented himself on many occasions over the years from the London Oratory on account of debilitating illness. Newman wrote mischievously to Ambrose St John back in Birmingham:

> Fr Faber, having been in his own belief given over, and in immediate prospect of death, suddenly got up, shaved himself, and announces his intention of coming to town next Monday ... Bowden gave us a sort of hagiographical account of it, said that the doctor pronounced that there had been an organic or structural change suddenly effected, and gave the Brompton judgment that it was a grazia.
>
> Father Faber has dictated a letter to me to beg pardon for any wilfulnesses of his in his – noviceship! and any disedification he gave any of our Fathers when he was a novice.[51]

Newman was still in London when he received news of an upset at the school, comical in itself but with serious implications in the long run for all concerned. There was a boy in the first year called Chomely, whose mother was anxious about his health. Chomely had developed chilblains and the Oratory's dame, Mrs Wootten (she who had fended off four kisses to the face and one to the hand by Brother Brendan), decided to take him out of classes and games until they healed. Mrs Wootten, considering it important that the boy should consolidate his convalescence with pleasurable outings, took him to a dog show in Birmingham. While at the show the pair ran into a group of Oratory boys led by the young Duke of Norfolk who said to them: 'Won't Father Darnell be in a wax?' On returning to school the noble youth evidently peached on Chomely and Mrs Wootten, whereupon Father Darnell did indeed get into a wax. He pinned up a notice proclaiming: *1. No boy to go to the Dame's rooms without permission of his tutor. 2. No boy on the sick-list to leave the premises without permission of the Headmaster.*

Mrs Wootten now offered her resignation to Newman who immediately became involved in a power struggle with Darnell over who was to be judged the ultimate authority at the school. From Darnell's point of view Mrs Wootten was mollycoddling the boys and she needed to be kept more firmly in check. He was furious that she had appealed to Newman, and he was even more angry at Newman for interfering. Questions arose as to whether Newman was ultimately responsible for the school or the collective body of the Birmingham Oratory Fathers. Newman made it clear where authority lay: Darnell was attempting to thwart 'the right of the appeal on the part of a subordinate in the school to me as President – and this I cannot for an instant allow'.[52] Newman nevertheless offered a compromise involving a separation of spheres of duty. Meanwhile

Darnell informed friends in London that he and the staff were determined to resign if he did not get his way: namely the dismissal of Mrs Wootten.

Newman refused to give way and found himself at New Year without any teaching staff to continue the school; but he still had Mrs Wootten. He solved the immediate problems by offering himself as a teacher, and getting Thomas Arnold, who had been a professor in Dublin, to join the school. The trusty Ambrose St John stepped in as headmaster. A letter to his old friend Henry Wilberforce about the affair reveals Newman's fairness and compassion as an employer:

Tho' [Darnell] had never urged a formal complaint against her before, and now had nothing definite to say except one act of hers, which she fairly explained, he insisted as the alternative of his and the Under-masters' immediately leaving, that she, in the depth of winter, should instanter be sent out of all our houses, she, who had lately been spitting blood and been confined to her room, she who had done us so many services, and had been our great benefactress. I should not have been a man, if I had consented to so cowardly an act. And, since I would not, (never, observe, refusing that she might *ultimately* go,) he would not to stay even till Easter, tho' I pressed him again and again ... And now I can't get him to say one single syllable in the way of sorrow for what he has done.[53]

Newman would call it 'family trouble ... for the faults of children are thrown back rightly upon their Fathers', but he could confide to Wilberforce that the local 'Protestants' were saying that Darnell had run away with Miss French, an assistant matron, who had also resigned. 'I am malicious enough', Newman jested in a PS, 'to wish this to get to her ears.' He goes on: 'They say "You don't mean to tell me that there is nothing more at bottom etc etc".'[54]

Under St John's headship the school began to flourish. Several years on, in 1865, we get an impression of the settled contentment of the place under Newman's benign presidency. On St Philip's Feast Day that year the boys acted in a Latin comedy by Terence. Newman had put enormous energy and enthusiasm into the casting and rehearsing. His friend and frequent correspondent Emily Bowles, who would fill in as matron after Mrs Wootten's death in 1876, left a record of the day. The play was performed in the morning, followed by High Mass at which a pupils' orchestra played. Then the entire school went out to Rednal in carriages and omnibuses where lunch awaited in a marquee. 'Everything was bright, gay with flowers, and festive with delightful conversation', wrote Bowles. 'The Father himself attending to the guests and providing for their accommodation and comfort until absolutely forced by Fr Ambrose, with playful violence, to keep his seat and take his own food.'[55] Lunch was followed by a cricket match and croquet, and at the end of the day the boys took walks with their parents. Emily Bowles walked with Newman up the hill behind the Rednal house. 'I remember his stopping with finger upraised at an opening as the breeze brought the sound of far off bells, and as we looked over what seemed a boundless stretch of blue distance, he spoke of the necessity of human life and its claims and interests coming in to make up the whole beauty of the picture or the poem, whichever you choose to call it, that a wide outlook creates.'[56]

NEWMAN THE 'CLERICAL PERVERT'

While the rumour circulated, quite inaccurately, among the Birmingham Protestants that the Oratorian Father Darnell had absconded with the assistant Matron, Newman himself became the victim of misinformation. A correspondent to a Linconsire paper claimed that Newman, the 'clerical pervert', had left the Oratorians and the Catholic faith and run off to Paris. Newman wrote to the editor bringing him up to date on the truth of his predicament: ('I have had the spiritual charge of various large districts, called missions, in Birmingham and its neighbourhood ...'[57]).

Meanwhile, Newman learnt from J. Spencer Northcote that it was put about by Catholics that he, Newman, had attempted to dissuade an Anglican clergyman from converting. Newman wrote back: 'I dare say I have said to *many* Protestants that they would be disappointed in the Catholic body, if they knew it experimentally; and I have said so, in order by that *anticipation*, to hinder them from being disappointed in *fact*. Protestants not unfrequently view us in an imaginative way, and are in consequence likely to suffer a reaction of mind.'[58] He goes on to draw up a catalogue of Catholic shortcomings. Catholics are not a 'powerful *organization*', but more often act in a 'second best way in a worldly aspect'. They do not possess 'deep, subtle, powerful intellects'; they lack education. They are not rich, but 'commonly live from hand to mouth'. As for spirituality, 'first rate direction is rare', and 'theological schools are sparse'.[59] Their advantages were not 'natural excellence, but supernatural'.

In June of 1862, he decided to scotch the rumour that he was on the way out of the Catholic Church with a letter to the *Globe*. First he denied that he was about to leave the Oratorians, then he asserted that he had never 'had one moment's wavering of trust in the Catholic Church'. His one hope was that Protestants could be 'partakers of my happiness'. Finally came his view of the Church he had left:

Therefore, in order to give them full satisfaction, if I can, I do hereby profess *ex animo*, with an absolute internal assent and consent, that Protestantism is the dreariest of possible religions; that the thought of the Anglican service makes me shiver, and the thought of the Thirty-nine Articles makes me shudder. Return to the Church of England! No; 'the net is broken, and we are delivered'. I should be a consummate fool (to use a mild term) if in my old age I left 'the land flowing with milk and honey' for the city of confusion and the house of bondage.[60]

Yet Newman's attitude towards the Church of England and his former co-religionists was complex, as was his attitude toward the Catholic Church. Newman told Manning that while he had referred to the Catholic Church as a land of milk and honey, in fact 'looking at it in a temporal earthly point of view, it was just the contrary. I had found very little but desert and desolateness ever since I had been in it – that I had nothing pleasant to look back on – that all my human affections were with those whom I had left.' Newman would regret that confidence. Some years later, writing to his friend Maria Giberne, who had just received a visit from Manning, he ventured:

He is quite violent sometimes in his effort to gain secrets. He does not fish, but extorts by force … I was always frank with him when he called here, till the Autumn of 1863. He saw *at once* the change, tho' my manner was quite free and easy; *because* he did not get what he came for.[61]

From 1863 onwards Newman was inclined to maintain a diplomatic silence, generally in public, on the shortcomings of the Curia and the Holy See. Writing in May to his friend Emily Bowles, he confessed: 'The only reason why I do not *enjoy* the happiness of being out of conflict is, because I feel to myself I could do much in it. But in fact I could not do much in it. I should come into collision with everyone I met – I should be treading on everyone's toes.'[62] He added: 'I never wrote such a letter to any one yet, and I shall think twice before I send you the whole of it.' It is indeed the most frank and devastating criticism of Roman authority he ever penned.

The Holy See, he wrote, was once the 'court of ultimate appeal' and not the 'extreme centralization which now is in use'. But, '*Now*, if I, as a private priest, put any thing into print, *Propaganda* answers me at once. How can I fight with such a chain on my arm? It is like the Persians driven to fight *under the lash*.'[63]

CHAPTER 13

Apologia

'... what I want to trace and study is the real, hidden but human life, or the *interior*, as it is called, of such glorious creations of God ...'

J. H. NEWMAN, *HISTORICAL SKETCHES*

Towards the end of 1863 Newman received through the post an advance copy of *Macmillan's Magazine* for January 1864, sent by an anonymous correspondent. There were pencil marks against a review article which charged that he along with the Catholic priesthood taught that lying is morally legitimate.

Macmillan's was one of a number of literary periodicals that started up at the end of the 1850s, employing new high-speed, steam-driven methods of print production. By 1863 the magazine was in its fifth year, priced one shilling with a sale of 15,000 and rising. Its founders saw themselves as men of social conscience; they included Alexander Macmillan (bookseller, publisher, and son of a Scottish crofter), Thomas Hughes (author of *Tom Brown's Schooldays*), and F. D. Maurice, moral philosopher, socialist, founder of the Working Men's College in London. One of its frequent contributors was the popular author and Cambridge historian the Reverend Charles Kingsley, famous for his promotion of Christianity as a 'manly', tough, honest, no-nonsense avocation, a living promotion of the ideals and qualities of Victorian patriarchy. These men had been involved since 1848 in furthering the cause of the poor in the wake of the failure of the Chartists' movement, invoking what they deemed a robust Christian socialism.

Newman's anonymous correspondent, a Catholic priest, had drawn attention to a review of J. A. Froude's *History of England*. The review was anti-Catholic in tone and content as was the book, which was initialled 'CK'. The offending passage read as follows:

Truth, for its own sake, had never been a virtue with the Roman clergy. Father Newman informs us that it need not, and on the whole ought not to be; that cunning is the weapon which Heaven has given to the saints wherewith to withstand the brute male force of the wicked world which marries and is given in marriage. Whether this notion be doctrinally correct or not, it is at least historically so.[1]

Here were three allegations: that Catholic priests did not believe lying wrong; that there was a link between clerical cunning and celibacy; and that John Henry Newman was guilty of both propositions. The reviewer's remarks, offensive as they were to Newman personally, reflected a familiar Protestant prejudice – that the Catholic clergy were equivocators; that their religious celibacy was a sham deriving not from the early Christian Church but from the reforming Council of Trent in the sixteenth century.

Newman wrote with lofty indignation to Messrs Macmillan and Co.:

Gentlemen,

I do not write to you with any controversial purpose, which would be preposterous; but I address you simply because of your special interest in a Magazine which bears your name.

That highly respected name you have associated with a Magazine, of which the January number has been sent to me by this morning's post ...

I should not dream of expostulating [he goes on] with the writer of such a passage, nor with the editor who could insert it without appending evidence in proof of its allegations. Nor do I want any reparation from either of them. I neither complain of them for their act, nor should I thank them if they reversed it. Nor do I even write to you with any desire of troubling you to send me an answer. I do but wish to draw the attention of yourselves, as gentlemen, to a grave and gratuitous slander, with which I feel confident you will be sorry to find associated a name so eminent as yours.[2]

Newman might well have assumed that this letter of superb condescension would reach not only the author and the editor but the book's author, J. A. Froude. It gainsaid the intention of virtually every sentence. Despite the disclaimers, Newman was spoiling for a fight. On 6 January, from his rectory at Eversley, Charles Kingsley wrote to Newman owning authorship of the review.

By 1863 Charles Kingsley, aged 44, was riding high. He had published *Westwood Ho!* and in the previous year his best selling *The Water-Babies* – a moral fable for children which had originally appeared in serial form in *Macmillan's* through 1862–63. Extrapolating a social conscience from the gospels, and a 'Do-as-you-would-be-done-by' ethic, Kingsley, from the late 1840s to the early 1860s, had agitated for amelioration of the poor, the abolition of child labour, and the institution of sanitary legislation. He had contributed as 'Parson Lot' to numbers of the *Politics for the People* and to the *Christian Socialist*. On questions of the relationship between social responsibility and the Gospel, Kingsley would have seen himself as morally superior to Newman. But his animus towards Newman, as we have seen in the first chapter, went further back. In the late 1830s, Kingsley had fallen under Newman's spell, only to spurn it. Writing in 1851 of Newman and his group's influence, Kingsley, as we have seen, had cast aspersions on their 'foppery' and their 'maundering die-away effeminacy, which is mistaken for purity and refinement'. He believed he had purged himself of Newman's unmanly influence by marriage, although his subsequent extrovert, 'muscular' Christianity concealed some strange proclivities. His hymn in celebration of the martyrdom of Saint Maura luridly depicts the woman saint blinded and crowned with thorns; and he had drafted a sketch of himself and his wife crucified.

Alexander Macmillan now wrote to Newman: 'Your letter convinces me that there was injustice, in Mr Kingsley's charge against you personally.' He conceded that because of his limited 'intercourse with members of the Church that holds us heretics', he had endorsed Kingsley's view, and he regretted that 'I may have allowed the heats of controversy to blind myself'.[3] He could assure Newman that Kingsley would write an apology in the next issue. Yet Macmillan had come down privately at least on Kingsley's side in the matter. Writing to J. A. Froude in February, he declared:

The old Saying attributed to Tallyrand [*sic*] that the use of words is to conceal thought might be extended in certain cases to intellects which would then be described as the power of perplexing truth. In this art apparently Newman is a master, and thank God C.K. is not even a learner.[4]

In the meantime Kingsley had sent Newman a draft apology that only served to exacerbate the original injury:

No man knows the use of words better than Dr Newman. No man, therefore, has a better right to define what he does, or does not, mean by them.

It only remains, therefore, for me to express my hearty regret at having so seriously mistaken him; and my hearty pleasure at finding him on the side of Truth, in this, or any other matter.[5]

The correspondence continued, with Newman paraphrasing Kingsley's apology back to him in withering parody. The elegant 'silver-veined' cadences give way to spontaneous, colloquial, speech rhythms: like a bar-room advocate, dramatising both sides of the argument, you can almost hear the voice – witty, biting, sarcastic:

Mr Kingsley begins then by exclaiming, 'O the chicanery, the wholesale fraud, the vile hypocrisy, the conscience-killing tyranny of Rome! We have not far to seek for an evidence of it. There's Father Newman to wit: one living specimen is worth a hundred dead ones. He, a Priest writing of Priests, tells us that lying is never any harm.'

I interpose: 'You are taking a most extraordinary liberty with my name. If I have said this, tell me when and where.'

Mr Kingsley replies: 'You said it, Reverend Sir, in a Sermon which you preached, when a Protestant, as Vicar of St Mary's, and published in 1844; and I could read you a very salutary lecture on the effects which that Sermon had at the time on my own opinion of you ...'

I make answer: 'Oh ... *Not*, it seems, as a Priest speaking of Priests; – but let us have the passage.'

Mr Kingsley relaxes: 'Do you know, I like your *tone*. From your *tone* I rejoice, greatly rejoice, to be able to believe that you did not mean what you said.'

I rejoin: '*Mean* it! I maintain I never *said* it, whether as a Protestant or as a Catholic.' Mr Kingsley replies: 'I waive that point.'

I object: 'Is it possible! What? waive the main question! I either said it or I didn't. You have made a monstrous charge against me; direct, distinct, public. You are bound to prove it as directly, as distinctly, as publicly; – or to own you can't.'

'Well', says Mr. Kingsley, 'if you are quite sure you did not say it, I'll take your word for it; I really will.'

My *word*! I am dumb. Somehow I thought that it was my *word* that happened to be on trial ...[6]

A shortened form of Kingsley's draft apology was published in the February edition of *Macmillan's*, which led to Newman's decision to go public. He told Macmillan: 'Any letter addressed to me by Mr. Kingsley, I account public property.'[7] In a pamphlet entitled *Mr Kingsley and Mr Newman* he now published the correspondence to date, including the imaginary dialogue above. It was eagerly purchased and circulated, especially in the London gentlemen's clubs. The reading public had a taste for such literary spats, and Newman was on superb form. The critic Richard Holt Hutton would write that he was 'not only one of the greatest of English writers, but, perhaps, the very greatest master of ... sarcasm in the English language'.[8] Writing later to Alexander Macmillan , Kingsley would betray how thoroughly chastised he was by the exchange. He compared Newman to 'a treacherous ape' who 'lifts to you meek and suppliant eyes, till he thinks he has you within his reach, and then springs, gibbering and biting, at your face'.[9]

Kingsley now responded with *What then does Dr Newman Mean?* – a 48-page pamphlet in which he cites passages from Newman's works as evidence that Newman indeed held that truth, for its own sake, had never been a virtue among the Catholic clergy. From *Sermon on Wisdom and Innocence* [1844] he argued that Newman endorsed cunning among Christians, and that Newman implied that monks and nuns were the only authentic Bible Christians. From *Sermon on the Apostolical Christian* [1844] Kingsley concluded that Newman was teaching Catholic doctrines while still nominally an Anglican, indicating his dishonesty. From *Sermon on Developments in Religious Doctrine* [1843] Kingsley alleged that Newman played fast and loose with truth in order to encourage credulity, while excusing economy of truth. He further charged that Newman's lectures on saints and miracles advocated credulity, and that his *Lectures on Anglican Difficulties* [1850] contained scandalous passages about the social backwardness of Catholic countries. He complained that Newman's imaginary dialogue, quoted above, misrepresented both what he, Kingsley, had written, and what Newman himself had written. Finally he asserted that on becoming a Catholic Newman had aligned himself with the views of 'St Alfonso da Liguori [*sic*]' and other Catholic casuists, well-known masters of equivocation.

Up to a point, Kingsley had a case; but the men were now arguing about the gulf between intentions and impressions: about words written or said, and what the speaker or author had originally meant by those words. Kingsley had attempted to make his exit from the quarrel by conceding that if Newman's intentions were innocent of the meaning that could be inferred from his words then he was satisfied. But he now made a graver charge, suggesting that Newman had pretended to be an Anglican while being a Catholic in secret. Here was the insupportable allegation that tipped the scales. Newman wrote to W. J. Copeland on 31 March that the salient point in the popular mind 'lies in the antecedent prejudice that *I was a Papist while I was an Anglican.* Mr K *implies this.* The only way in which I can destroy this, is to give my history, and the history of my mind, from 1822 or earlier, down to 1845. I wish I had my papers properly about me.'[10]

The *Apologia Pro Vita Sua*, however, would develop into a work of much greater consequence than his response to Kingsley's charges. For the question as to whether there is a gulf between intentions and the words and expressions of the tongue and face had provided Newman's literary genius with potential for a highly original autobiography. Thus, on 10 April 1864, he embarked on the 'hard work' of the *Apologia*.

For years Newman had been sifting and reorganising his vast correspondence. Just a year earlier he had written to his sister Jemima: 'When I have a little leisure, I recur to my pigeon-hole of letters, where they stand year by year from 1836 down to this date. I have digested them up to the former year. Thus from time to time I do a little work in the way of sifting, sorting, preserving, or burning.'[11] While exploiting his own letters, journals, and memoranda, he wrote to old friends requesting that they should return letters, or check certain facts.

According to the fashion of the time, the publisher wanted advance sections of the book to appear week by week in serial form. The first appeared on Thursday 21 April, just ten days after he plunged into the task, followed by an issue every Thursday for the next seven weeks, with a final appendix after a gap of two weeks. The entire work, 'one of the most terrible trials that I have had',[12] came to five hundred published pages, which he completed in under eleven weeks. He wrote from early morning to late at night while standing up. On one occasion he wrote non-stop for 22 hours. He wept over the pages, 'I wrote the greater part of it, *crying* all the time', he told a friend.[13] He barely found time to eat, and the labour was all the more intense as he frequently drafted and redrafted in order to compress. He was obliged, he recorded, to reject ruthlessly whole swathes of his manuscript with the next deadline 'yawning close upon me'. He describes in vivid metaphors how he had to cope with the current manuscript for the printer while correcting the proofs of the last so that 'manuscript and proof got jammed together, as in a stoppage in the streets of London – and the proof almost got ahead of the manuscript, if that can be'.[14] He felt as if he was 'ploughing in a very stiff clay', it was as if he was 'moving on at the rate of a mile an hour, when I had to write and print and correct a hundred miles by the next day's post'.[15] He was like a man, 'who had fallen overboard and had to swim to land'.[16]

WHAT KIND OF A BOOK?

Unlike the confessional accounts of his post-Reformation predecessors, John Bunyan and George Fox, Newman was not writing an allegory or a memoir of spiritual trials and tribulations. The *Apologia* is no *Grace Abounding*, nor an inspirational work in the manner of Fox's *Autobiography*. It has more in common with Augustine's *Confessions*, proceeding as it does from meditations on the inwardness of consciousness, and the outwardness of the world. Augustine writes that his 'wishes were inside, and they [the people in the world] were outside, and powerless to get inside my mind by any of their senses'. Newman, as we have seen, starts by asserting that he was isolated 'from the objects that surrounded me ...' leading to that conviction of 'two and two only absolute and luminously self-evident beings, myself and my Creator'.[17] And while Newman resorts in part to Augustinian images, of illness and health, signalling influences from the Church of the Early Fathers rather than the Old and New Testaments, his story is in no sense an Augustinian conversion to Christian belief, nor to holiness after a life of sin.

The *Apologia*, on the face of it, tells the story of a deeply learned and devout Christian's mounting anxieties about the rival claims for authenticity of the Church of England and the Church of Rome. The Church of England, as Newman saw it, could claim continuity with the primitive Church of the Apostles, but was no longer universal, or catholic; the Roman Church could claim universality but was subject to corruptions – not least 'Popery'. Newman's anxieties, as we have seen, reached crisis point as he attempted to combine the best of both Churches in a *Via Media*: the fruit of the Oxford Movement. But the bid to have his ecclesiastical cake and eat it did not work: the Anglican bishops rose up against him, and he finally became convinced that his *Via Media* existed only on paper. The denouement of the *Apologia* finds him making a final choice between the two Churches.

At the time that Newman embarked on the *Apologia*, it was nearly twenty years since he had been received into the Roman Catholic Church. His aim was to explain to the reading public of England the tortuous path that led to that momentous step, including the many misunderstandings of both friends and enemies. But it seemed evident to him that the book's significance and scope had the potential to go well beyond his initial purpose. His decision to write a kind of autobiography, rather than a logical and factual self-defence, was critical. 'Logic', as he wrote in the Tamworth Reading Room debate in 1841, 'makes but a sorry rhetoric with the multitude; first shoot round corners, and you may not despair of converting by a syllogism.'[18] In the same text, as we have seen, he argued that 'the heart is commonly reached, not through the reason, but through the imagination'. A literary narrative of his journey was the only feasible way of explaining himself. And yet he was daunted by the task. He unburdened himself of both the labour and the huge difficulty of autobiography. 'I feel overcome with the difficulty of satisfying myself in my account of it, and have recoiled from the attempt.' He goes on:

For who can know himself, and the multitude of subtle influences which act upon him? And who can recollect, at the distance of twenty-five years, all that he once knew about his thoughts and his deeds, and that, during a portion of his life, when, even at the time, his observation, whether of himself or of the external world, was less than before or after, by every reason of the perplexity and dismay which weighed upon him ...[19]

The *Apologia*, as autobiography, stands in its own right as a remarkable work of literary and religious imagination. The nub of Newman's story is continuity and discontinuity, and he would express this central tension in the structure. To what extent, Newman is asking, am I a consistent, abiding self while subject to change, growth, and multiple versions of identity? And how can the Church of Rome claim continuity with the authentic apostolic Church when it has undergone so many apparent novelties and alterations since Christian antiquity? Newman gives the impression, false as it turns out, that he is refraining from creative recollection. He is to tell his story, he assures his readers, through painstaking contemporaneous documentation. There are repeated expository signposts to this effect: 'To illustrate my feelings during this trial, I will make extracts from my letters ...'; 'I have the first sketch or draft of a letter, which I wrote to ...'; 'I have turned up two letters of this period, which in a measure illustrate what I have been saying ...' Newman lets us in on his literary craft, as if we are looking over his shoulder observing his handling of source materials. He gives the impression, moreover, of proceeding prospectively rather than retrospectively. Readers are invited to collaborate in the narrative by tracking the unfolding evidence. Yet, as he admits, the sense of tight, authorial control of the record is every where evident: 'It is the concrete being that reasons; pass a number of years, and I find my mind in a new place; how? the whole man moves; paper logic is but the record of it.'[20] Pondering, earlier, the art of saints' lives he had written: '... By "Life". I mean a narrative which impresses the reader with the idea of moral unity, identity, growth, continuity, personality.'[21] Hence the *Apologia* becomes not just a history of his opinions, but a dramatised psychology of philosophy of mind, fraught with intellectual, historical, and spiritual anxiety. It is the tale of a personal bid to be both right and righteous; a sustained struggle with doubt and doubt of doubt; a quest for certitude:

Certitude of course is a point, but doubt is a progress, I was not near certitude yet. Certitude is a reflex action; it is to know that one knows. Of that I believe I was not possessed, till close upon my reception into the Catholic Church. Again, a practical, effective doubt is a point too, but who can easily ascertain it for himself? Who can determine when it is, that the scales in the balance of opinion begin to turn, and what was a greater probability in behalf of a belief becomes a positive doubt against it?[22]

The *Apologia* thus embarks on the ambitious task of reporting the functions of conscience, belief, and conviction, as they occur: not by recollection alone, nor by archival retrieval, but by both. How could anybody judge his private motivation, he is saying, his innermost thoughts and feelings, objectively, accurately, when even he himself remained frustrated, uncertain, assailed by intellectual and religious scruples? And how can one report the action of God in the equation? In one of the most remarkable passages of the *Apologia* Newman reveals how he sees the relationship between his conscience and God's promptings. Religious inquiry, he begins, is not like mathematics – which proceeds to certitude by rigid demonstration; it progresses by 'probabilities of a special kind, a cumulative, a transcendent probability but still probability':

[God] has willed, I say, that we should so act, and, as willing it, He co-operates with us in our acting, and thereby enables us to do that which He wills us to do, and carries us on, if our will does but cooperate with His, to a certitude which rises higher than the logical force of our conclusions.[23]

The *Apologia* contrasts and parallels a complex inner story with two overarching outer narratives – the history no less of Christianity from antiquity to Newman's present, and the story of the Church of England from the sixteenth to the first half of the nineteenth century. And if the *Apologia* parallels both personal and ecclesiastical permanence and change, it is also a study of the tensions between Church authority and the primacy of individual conscience.

In Chapter III of the *Apologia* Newman impresses upon his reader what is at stake: emotionally, personally. The imagery evokes the trauma of a family or domestic break-up; of a man perhaps who is about to abandon a cherished wife and children for the bosom of another: what caused him 'to leave my own home, to which I was bound by so many strong and tender ties'.[24] The crisis is depicted, at first, as a conflict between refined English tradition and scruffy Roman superstition. Newman's conservatism, the ties of home and vocation, ran deep. Oxford especially represented permanence, entitlement, heritage. Clerical, patriarchal, bound by privilege, Oxford was loveable even in its torpor. Newman was at home within its cloisters and enjoyed its preferments. Comfortable in the protection of its auspices, his attachment to the snap-dragon on the walls of Trinity College, signalled, as he tells us, the permanence to which he was wedded as a member of an Oxford college. He saw himself as that clinging, perennially flowering creeper. As he had written, at the age of 28, to his sister: 'I am more than ever imprest too with the importance of staying in Oxford ... "I am rooted ..."' [25]

Rome, however, towards which he was increasingly, often reluctantly, drawn in fits and starts, with a pause in the 'paper Church' of his *Via Media*, had been characterised in his upbringing as the great whore, the Anti-Christ. None of it was natural to him: the Counter-Reformation architecture, the dog-Latin, the dreary Plain Chant, scholasticism, casuistry, the turbulent Irish, the treacherous Spanish. Then there were the miracles, indulgences, plaster saints, idolisation of the Virgin Mary, and papal demagoguery. Rome was unstable, unreliable, corrupt. Rome had severed its links with the authentic Church of the past. Rome was fickle, corrupt, *foreign*.

Yet as he plunged into the Early Fathers, he tells us, Rome began to appear, in the course of the years, not decaying but protean, *dynamic*, all-embracing, while preserving its essential unbroken connection to its origins and extending its authority and welcome universally. It was not a 'local' church, but universal, and yet composed of so many unique individuals: a 'vast assemblage of human beings with wilful intellects and wild passions, brought together into one by the beauty and the Majesty of a Superhuman Power, – into what may be called a large reformatory or training-school, not as if into a hospital or into a prison, not in order to be sent to bed, not to be buried alive ...',[26] images designed to contrast with both the sterility of England's Benthamite institutions, as well as the Protestant fantasies of *Maria Monk* and live burial of nuns! Through his reading in Christian antiquity, and Augustine's phrase '*securus judicat orbis terrarum*' (the world's judgment is secure) in that essay by Cardinal Wiseman, he realises that the Church of England is in heresy. Thus the 'theory of the *Via Media* was absolutely pulverised',[27] he writes. The image of being ground to dust, absolutely, leaves nothing. The yearning for permanence and development would be finally satisfied in the Church of Rome.

THE ART OF THE *APOLOGIA*

The episodes of realisation and resolution are narrated in the course of several, isolated set pieces. While he writes in the main with austere objectivity, citing his horde of documents, he expands during these episodes of transformation, into retrospective dramatisation, his creative imagination fully engaged. These moments include his suspenseful return from the Mediterranean to England in 1833; the shock in 1839 of seeing connections between early Christian heresies and the circumstances of the Anglican Church; the aggressive reception of his *Tract 90* in 1841 and final reception into the Catholic Church in 1845.

His discovery of the *Via Media's* heretical position in 1839, for example, starts with the promise that he will now relate the 'course of that great revolution of mind'. But he repeatedly delays the promised delivery for eight thousand words as he teases the reader with stratagems of suspense. He asks how he is to 'gird' himself for the tale he has volunteered ('gird' suggesting the Israelites preparing for their great wilderness journey) while deprived of 'calm leisure', 'calm contemplation'. Yet these irenic references only serve to emphasise the anticipation of the 'extreme trial' to come. It is, he tells us, the *'infandum dolorem'* (unutterable suffering) – a phrase plucked without explanation or citation from Virgil's *Aeneid* Book Two.

It is no mere flourish of a classicist. Aeneas is speaking to Queen Dido in Carthage. She has asked him to tell the story of the fall of Troy, and he declares that the obligation to relive the terrible events would be unbearable. The original line in Virgil – *'Infandum, regina, jubes renovare dolorem'* – might be translated: 'Beyond all words, O Queen, is the grief you ask me to recount.' The allusion might not have been at all obscure to a literate Victorian readership. The phrase is often repeated by the Sancho Panza figure, Partridge, in Fielding's *Tom Jones*, a best-seller in the 1860s. It also featured in a popular anecdote told in *Punch* in April 1860, about Good Queen Bess asking a schoolboy to give an account of being flogged: upon which the clever lad responded with that famous line '*Infandum* …' The phrase suggests the Church of England, as Troy, sacrificed in the interests of the flourishing of Rome. Between the lines, moreover, one detects the calm before the tragic break between Aeneas and Dido, followed by Dido's suicide, and her haunting ghostly presence. (The '*infandum*' phrase is also employed by Dante as he meets Dido's ghost in the *Inferno*). And Newman is about to make skilful use of the ghostly images.

The terrible, 'unutterable', trial ahead is Newman's recognition of the Church of England as a heretical Church, and the row that would follow. The trial, Newman tells us, was akin to a 'cruel operation', involving the 'ripping up of old griefs', images that anticipate two subsequent mutilation and death anecdotes. While arguing in the post-1841 section that attack is the best form of defence (he means the battles he had over *Tract 90*), he proclaims: 'We all know the story of the convict who on the scaffold bit off his mother's ear.'[28] He rams the point home by confessing that he had been in a 'humour, certainly to bite off the ears [of Anglican divines]'. Then, a page on, he makes manifest the 'cruel operation', with the story of an injured sailor persuaded to have his leg amputated at sea:

Then, they broke it to him that he must have the other off too. The poor fellow said, 'You should have told me that, gentlemen', and deliberately unscrewed the instrument and bled to death.[29]

The gruesome story, told in the final stage of his conversion, illustrates a degree of mordant humour in his sympathy for Anglican friends who had followed him into the *Via Media*, cutting themselves off from their many ties and associations, only to be devastated by the news of a further severance: his reception into the Catholic Church. 'How could I ever hope to make them believe in a second theology, when I had cheated them in the first?'[30] The word 'cheat' is, again, disturbingly ironic: for cheating is the accusation levelled by Dido against Aeneas, and by Kingsley against Newman. Severed love, executions, ear-bitings, amputations, blood letting, suicides, connect with the arresting image of Newman on his 'death bed'. He found himself, he writes, on his 'death bed' as far as the Anglican Church was concerned, an image that recalls the death bed scenes of his father, his sister Mary, his mother, and his beloved Hurrell Froude.

The critical moment of his shift towards Catholicism had occurred in the long vacation of 1839 when, as we have seen, he read the history of the Monophysite heresy, recognising that the Church of England was similarly heretical. 'The shadow of the fifth century was on the sixteenth', he writes: in other words the early Christian heresy anticipated the heresy of the Reformation Church. The 'shadow', however, now becomes 'a spirit rising from the troubled waters of the old world, with the shape and lineaments of the new',[31] culminating in the recognition of a second parallel heresy, that of the Donatists. Then there came the 'shadow of a hand upon the wall'. The shadow is a precursor to the shadow as 'shade' or ghost. 'He who has seen a ghost, cannot be as if he had never seen it',[32] he writes. The ghost points back to his original introduction, and his intention to dismiss the 'ghost that gibbers' instead of the real 'me'. The shadow as mirror image, moreover, connects with two further moments in Newman's story: 'I saw my face in that mirror and I was a Monophysite', and the stunning line that follows his reception into the Catholic Church: 'If I looked into a mirror, and did not see my face, I should have the sort of feeling which actually comes upon me, when I look into this living busy world, and see no reflection of its Creator.'[33]

The significance is far from Freud's 'blindness of the seeing eye' or D. W. Winnicott's patient: 'Wouldn't it be awful if the child looked into the mirror and saw nothing.'[34] But the image captures dynamically, and with a hint even of gothic horror (vampires traditionally do not reflect in mirrors), the potent shock of the image shared by psychoanalysts a century on. Certain of the personal presence of a Creator in the inner depths of conscience, the darkness of the world – already alluded to in the '*infandum*', is an extension to another Virgilian reference: that 'the stars of the heaven were one by one going out' – the sense that God has withdrawn from his creation: and that nature is 'out of joint with the purposes of its Creator'. Hence were it not for the voice of God 'speaking so clearly in my conscience and my heart, I should be an atheist, or a pantheist, or a polytheist when I looked into the world'.[35] Towards the climax of this summation of the annihilation which 'fills me with unspeakable distress', he comes to an impression of the wholesale suffering, evil and darkness of the world:

the defeat of good, the success of evil, physical pain, mental anguish, the prevalence and intensity of sin, the pervading idolatries, the corruptions, the dreary hopeless irreligion, that condition of the whole race, so fearfully yet exactly described in the Apostle's words, 'having no hope and without God in the world', all this is a vision to dizzy and appal; and inflicts upon the mind the sense of a profound mystery, which is absolutely beyond human solution.[36]

FREEDOM AND AUTHORITY

Such is his conviction of the absence of God that standard rational arguments and proofs for His existence, through nature and history, leave him cold. He sees humanity as a tree in winter waiting for spring time. Attempts to find God through the exercise of reason, such as the presence of design in the world, he writes, 'do not warm me or enlighten me; they do not take away the winter of my desolation, or make the buds unfold and the leaves grow within me, and my moral being rejoice'.[37] His sense of the world's futility, vanity, evil and darkness, matches and exceeds the vision of many of the great poets of the age: Wordsworth's 'still, sad music of humanity', Matthew Arnold's 'turbid ebb and flow of human misery', Thomas Hardy's procession following the dead God, as 'darkling and languid-lipped, we creep and grope'. With chilling foresight Newman proceeds to declare that 'things are tending, – with far greater rapidity than in that old time from the circumstance of the age, – to atheism in one shape or other ... not only Europe, but every government and every civilization through the world, which is under the influence of the European mind!'[38] For Newman 'the sight of the world is nothing else than the prophet's scroll, full of "lamentations, and mourning, and woe"'.[39]

Like an orphan child, 'of good make and mind', and a 'refined nature', thrown into the world without provision, family connexions, or birth-place, the human race appears, writes Newman, a 'heart-piercing, reason-bewildering fact'. Hence: 'Either there is no Creator, or this living society of men is in a true sense discarded from His presence.'

And so I argue about the world, *if* there be a God, *since* there is a God, the human race is implicated in some terrible aboriginal calamity. It is out of joint with the purposes of its Creator. This is a fact, a fact as true as the fact of its existence; and thus the doctrine of what is theologically called original sin becomes to me almost as certain as that the world exists, and as the existence of God.[40]

From original sin, Newman moves rapidly, not by proof, but by imaginative intuition, to a conviction of a divine 'interposition' that is both extraordinary and necessary. Given that reason moves 'towards a simple unbelief in matters of religion', he 'supposes' it to be 'the Will of the Creator to interfere in human affairs, and to make provisions for retaining in the world a knowledge of himself, so definite and distinct as to be proof against the energy of human scepticism'. In other words, 'there is nothing to surprise the mind, if He should think fit to introduce a power into the world invested with the prerogative of infallibility in religious matters'.

Such a provision would be a direct, immediate, active, and prompt means of withstanding the difficulty; it would be an instrument suited to the need; and, when I find that this is the very claim of the Catholic Church, not only do I feel no difficulty in admitting the idea, but there is a fitness in it, which recommends it to my mind. And thus I am brought to speak of the Church's infallibility, as a provision, adapted by the mercy of the Creator, to preserve religion in the world, and to restrain that freedom of thought, which of course in itself is one of the greatest of our natural gifts, and to rescue it from its own suicidal excesses.[41]

But is the individual to submit to the Church's version of redemption uncritically and unthinkingly? Individual liberty of conscience and reason, he insists in the final section of the *Apologia*, is protected by the infallibility of the Catholic Church, for it saves them from those inevitable self-destructive tendencies. The 'energy of the human intellect ... thrives and is joyous, with a tough elastic strength, under the terrible blows of the divinely-fashioned weapon, and is never so much itself as when it has lately been overthrown.' In Newman's view the tension between the Church's authority and private judgment creates a dynamic, imaginative energy in which dogma and freedom of intellect are mutually kept in check.

... it is the vast Catholic body itself, and it only, which affords an arena for both combatants in that awful, never-dying duel. It is necessary for the very life of religion, viewed in its large operations and its history, that the warfare should be incessantly carried on. Every exercise of Infallibility is brought out into act by an intense and varied operation of the Reason, both as its ally and as its opponent, and provokes again, when it has done its work, a re-action of Reason against it; and, as in a civil polity the State exists and endures by means of the rivalry and collision, the encroachments and defeats of its constituent parts, so in like manner Catholic Christendom is no simple exhibition of religious absolutism but presents a continuous picture of Authority and Private Judgment alternately advancing and retreating as the ebb and flow of the tide ...[42]

THE RECEPTION

The *Apologia* was enthusiastically reviewed, and Kingsley was widely deemed to have been trounced. Among the book's many keen admirers was Newman's old friend, now Bishop of Winchester, who wrote in the *Quarterly Review* that Kingsley would go down in history as 'the embedded fly in the clear amber of his antagonist's Apology'.[43] Dean Church wrote in the *Guardian*:

Those who know Dr Newman's powers and are acquainted with his career, and know to what it led him, and yet persist in the charge of insincerity and dishonesty against one who probably has made the greatest sacrifice of our generation to his convictions of truth, will be able to pick up from his own narrative much that they would not otherwise have now, to confirm and point the old familiar view cherished by dislike and narrowness.[44]

The novelist George Eliot was deeply affected by the *Apologia*. She saw it as the 'revelation of a life – how different from one's own, yet with how close a fellowship in its needs and burthens – I mean spiritual needs and burthens'.[45] Later she wrote that it 'breathed much life into me'.

The publication of the *Apologia* and its generally enthusiastic reception marked yet another turning point in Newman's life. After many years of suspicion and even hatred on the part of Anglicans he emerged once again as a figure of respect, his reputation as a great churchman and spiritual writer restored. As for Kingsley, who died ten years later, Newman claimed to harbour no bitterness against him. Writing to Edmund Sheridan Purcell in 1881, he declared that Kingsley 'by his passionate attack on me became one of my best friends, whom I always wished to shake hands with when living, and towards whose memory I have much tenderness'.[46]

The book would not, however, enjoy unalloyed praise down the years. Benjamin Jowett wrote: 'In speculation [Newman] was habitually untruthful, and not much better in practice. His conscience had been taken out and the Church put in its place.'[47] As late as 1969 a critique entitled, *Apologia Pro Charles Kingsley*, was published by the late P. J. FitzPatrick under the pseudonym G. Egner. FitzPatrick professed to be concerned because he thought the accusations levelled by Kingsley 'were far more substantial than Newman allowed, and that Newman's reply, taken as a reply, is inadequate'. FitzPatrick claimed that Kingsley raised genuine questions which Newman did not and could not answer. 'What is more, his objections, for all their incompleteness and at times incoherence, do touch aspects of Newman's thought that must be borne in mind if we are to pass an adequate judgment on him a century later.'[48]

FitzPatrick's book has had a favourable if restricted following over the past forty years. He himself, however, admitted that his reading of Newman, outside of the Kingsley polemic, was slight, a point emphasised by those Newman scholars who nevertheless recommend it as a token of balance.

Meanwhile, writing to the ultramontane W. G. Ward of Newman's views in the *Apologia*, Herbert Vaughan declared: 'There are views put forward which I abhor, and which fill me with pain and suspicion.'[49] He was referring to Newman's resistance to Roman devotional practice, his general sense of moderation, his recent reconciliation with old Anglican friends, his refusal to emphasise papal dogma over conscience, his lukewarm attitude to the embattled papal temporal power. Manning, without mentioning the *Apologia* by name, criticized its advocacy of reason in tension with dogma. In a pamphlet against Pusey, he went on to take issue with Newman's scepticism about logical proofs for God's existence.

The publication of the *Apologia* identified Newman as an opponent of the ultramontane party within the Catholic Church in England. Newman consequently became increasingly guarded with Manning, who was to succeed Wiseman as Archbishop of Westminster in 1865, and dismissive of Monsignor George Talbot, Manning's champion in Rome. Not long after the publication of the *Apologia* Talbot called unannounced and uninvited at the Oratory in Birmingham. Newman was not at home, and most of the other Fathers kept to their rooms. Talbot, ludicrously, asked a junior member of the community whether Newman read books. The young man replied that he knew that Newman took books from the library, but he could not say whether he actually read them. A brief correspondence followed, demonstrating Newman's new determination to resist Talbot's machinations.

The day after his visit, Talbot wrote to Newman inviting him to preach a series of sermons in Rome. He attempted to persuade Newman by noting that 'you would have a more educated Audience of Protestants than could ever be the case in England, and where they are more open to Catholic influences'. Talbot went on to argue that he would 'derive great benefit' from showing himself to the 'Ecclesiastical Authorities' in Rome. The clincher, however, was the implication that it was a request by His Holiness in person. 'When I told the Holy Father that I intended to invite you, he highly approved of my intention … it would be a great consolation to be able to tell the Holy Father that you have accepted my invitation, and I am sure that the Blessing of the Vicar of Christ will amply repay you for going so far.'[50]

While such soft bullying, with its sanctimonious undertones and pontifical overtones, routinely worked wonders among the clerical courtiers, Newman was having none of it. He evidently felt doubly insulted, knowing only too well that Talbot had been maligning him, spreading rumours that he supported Garibaldi 'and other bad things', and implying that he needed to 'rub up' his Catholicism. Newman responded curtly: 'I have received your letter, inviting me to preach next Lent in your Church at Rome, to "an audience of Protestants more educated than could ever be the case in England". However, Birmingham people have souls; and I have neither taste nor talent for the sort of work, which you cut out for me: and I beg to decline your offer.' As for the Pope's endorsement of the scheme, writing to a friend the following year, Newman had evidently rumbled the truth: the invitation 'was suggested by Manning – the Pope had nothing to do with it – When Talbot left for England, he said among other things to the Pope, "I think of asking Dr Newman to give a set of lectures in my Church –" and the Pope of course said, "a very good thought", as he would have said, if Mgr.T. had said "I wish to bring your Holiness some English razors".' [51]

A RETURN TO OXFORD?

In the midst of the excitement occasioned by the *Apologia*, Newman was offered a five-acre site in North Oxford. At the same time, Bishop Ullathorne suggested that Newman should found a Catholic parish in Oxford to meet the needs of Catholics within the University. Newman thus set about raising the money to build a church and an oratory with the additional possibility of founding a hall of residence under his supervision for Catholic undergraduates.

The scheme, which might one day have given Oxford a fully fledged Catholic college (although that was not Newman's original intention), was instantly opposed in Rome and Westminster. Cardinal Wiseman, who was dying (and listened to the plan 'half querulously'), accused Newman of 'insolence'. Manning wrote to the Vatican claiming that the Cardinal was 'entirely opposed to any contact between the faithful in England and the heretical intellectual culture of the country'. [52] The view coincided with his own, and betrayed his ill-concealed distrust of the Catholic laity and Newman. Newman wrote to Thomas Allies, that the opposition even to a university church for Catholics in Oxford, illustrated 'the same dreadful jealousy of the laity, which has ruined things in Dublin, is now at the bottom of this unwillingness to let our youths go to Oxford … Propaganda and our leading Bishops fear the natural influence of the laity: which would be their greatest, or (humanly speaking) is rather their only, defence against the world.' [53]

A meeting of the English Catholic bishops under the ailing and distant supervision of Wiseman was inconclusive about the scheme, so the case was passed back to the Vatican and Cardinal Barnabò in Rome. Newman was in despair both on account of the timidity of the bishops and the Roman clique. 'We are certainly under a tyranny', he wrote to a friend 'one or two persons such as Manning seem to do everything.' [54]

Newman was not prepared to countenance a situation where he might have to abandon a project halfway through. On Pusey's instigation he sold the plot to the university in January 1865. Three months later the bishops expressed their final opposition to the building of a Catholic college at Oxford, or at Cambridge; although that had not been Newman's intention. Newman, moreover, thought he had reasons to believe that the Pope himself was behind the veto constituting a stumbling block.

Then Wiseman died and Manning succeeded him, a triumph for which Talbot claimed a large measure of responsibility. Newman was crestfallen. As he remarked to Allies, 'If you write to inspire me with confidence in the Archbishop, *laterem lavas*'.[55] In other words, you might just as well wash a brick. Writing to a woman friend, Newman confided that Manning 'has a great power of winning men, when he chooses'.[56] To another he declared Manning 'so mysterious, that I don't know how one can ever have confidence in him'.[57] Newman nevertheless attended the consecration on the understanding that he was present as a friend and not as a clerical dignitary. He also wanted Manning to understand that he would refuse a bishopric if one were proffered. Newman had got wind of Manning's plan to have him made a bishop in order to muzzle him.

NEWMAN 'MOST DANGEROUS MAN IN ENGLAND'

The extent of the antagonism towards Newman now became manifest following the publication of an essay of Pusey's aimed at defining what separated Catholicism and Anglicanism. Pusey entitled it the *Eirenicon*, the gesture of peace. According to Pusey, what kept the Churches apart was the ultramontane surge of Manning and Ward, and the Mariolatry of Faber. Newman published his response in *A Letter to the Rev E. B. Pusey, D.D., on his recent Eirenicon*. 'You discharge your olive branch', he wrote, 'as if from a catapult.'[58] He vigorously defended Catholic devotion to the Virgin Mary, then went on to insist that Ward and Faber were not representative of Catholicism. On the question of Manning, he declared that it was hardly his place to defend a bishop of the Church.

He nevertheless took a decided position against the saccharine Italianate devotions that so many Anglicans, and Old Catholics, despised. He himself had felt a sense of 'grief and almost anger' at the excesses quoted by Pusey. Such devotions were not suited to the English tradition, he argued, and were likely to alienate potential converts. Newman's *Letter* drew support from a wide constituency of Catholics in England, including Bishop Ullathorne. Ward, however, author of the notorious quip that he would relish a new papal Bull every morning with his *Times* at breakfast, was furious, more on account of Newman's reticence on papal authority and temporal power than anything he actually said against it. Monsignor Talbot delivered a poisonous attack on Newman, assuring Manning that 'every Englishman is naturally anti-Roman ... to be Roman is to an Englishman an effort. Dr Newman is more English than the English. His spirit must be crushed.'[59]

In response, and as if to endorse Ward's resentment at Newman's reticence on the score of the papacy, Manning replied that Newman had become a leader of those who 'hold low views about the Holy See', and who are

cold and silent, to say no more, about the Temporal Power, national, English, critical of Catholic devotions, and always on the lower side. I see no danger of a Cisalpine Club rising again, but I see much danger of an English Catholicism, of which Newman is the highest type. It is the old Anglican, patristic, literary, Oxford tone transplanted into the Church. It takes the line of deprecating exaggerations, foreign devotions, Ultramontanism, anti-national sympathies. In one word, it is worldly Catholicism, and it will have the worldly on its side, and will deceive many.[60]

While the idea for a Catholic college had been finally quashed, the arguments about the suitability of a Catholic 'mission' to serve the members of Oxford University under the direction of the Birmingham Oratory dragged on for three years. Ullathorne, in whose diocese Oxford lay, wrote to the Vatican urging the case for an Oratorian community in the university. Manning warned Talbot: 'I think Propaganda can hardly know the effects of Dr Newman's going to Oxford. The English national spirit is spreading among Catholics and we shall have dangers.'[61] At about this time Newman received the poet and Oxford scholar Gerard Manley Hopkins into the Church; precisely the sort of young man who might have benefited from Newman's presence, or at least the auspices of the Oratory, in Oxford. But it appeared to Manning that the drawbacks were infinitely more dangerous than the advantages. Newman wrote to his friend Emily Bowles:

At present things are in appearance as effete, though in a different way, (thank God) as they were in the tenth century. We are sinking into Novatianism, the heresy which the early Popes so strenuously resisted. Instead of aiming at being a world-wide power, we are shrinking into ourselves, narrowing the lines of communion, trembling at freedom of thought, and using the language of dismay and despair at the prospect before us, instead of, with the high spirit of the warrior, going out conquering and to conquer.[62]

Eventually Rome gave permission for an Oratorian mission in Oxford, but there was a qualification that Ullathorne initially kept from Newman: that should he show a wish to reside in the city he should be *'blande suaviterique'*,[63] blandly and smoothly, dissuaded. When the information about the ban on Newman residing in Oxford was leaked to the Catholic press, Newman was appalled. Surely, this was Manning once more: 'who wanted to gain me over; now, he will break me, if he can.'[64] Next came a letter from Barnabò at Propaganda, mentioning that the Pope had been 'deeply saddened' by the 'recent unhappy perversion of a number of Catholic youths'[65] at Oxford. In the end, it was made abundantly clear that Newman would not be allowed to take up residence in Oxford. Now Newman himself put his foot down: 'If I am a missioner at Oxford, I claim to be there, as much or as little as I please.' Writing to St John, who was on his way to Rome, he expostulated that the Roman 'blandness and sweetness are hollow'.[66]

Newman had been treated badly and to his aid came a distinguished representation of great and good Catholics led by the Duke of Norfolk's guardian, Lord Edward Fitzalan Howard:

We the undersigned, have been deeply pained at some anonymous attacks which have been made upon you ... we feel that every blow that touches you inflicts a wound upon the Catholic Church in this country. We hope, therefore, that you will not think it presumptuous in us to express our gratitude for all we owe you, and to assure you how heartily we appreciate the services which, under God, you have been the means of rendering to our Holy Religion.[67]

Manning remarked that the address of the Catholic lay group showed 'the absence of Catholic instinct', and was 'directed and sustained by those who wish young Catholics to go to Oxford'. Monsignor Talbot was apoplectic, declaring it a 'most offensive production'.[68]

Talbot went on to warn Manning that if he did not 'fight the battle of the Holy See against the detestable spirit growing up in England, [Pio Nono] will begin to regret Cardinal Wiseman, who knew how to keep the laity in order'.[69] It was the same tactic that he had employed against Newman earlier, based on the assumption that the mere mention of the approval or displeasure of the Pope, whose ear he had, would galvanise the victim of his machinations.

In Newman's view, Talbot, Manning and Barnabò had formed a toxic cabal to run the Church. 'Such tyranny and terrorism as they exercise, please God, shall have no power over me, nor will I think myself disobedient to the Church because I utterly ignore them.'[70] Yet Newman realised that Manning was as much a victim of Romanism as a perpetrator. He wrote to Pusey in 1865: 'Manning is under the lash as well as others. There are men who would remonstrate with him and complain of him at Rome, if he did not go to all lengths – and in his position he can't afford to get into hot water, even tho' he were sure to get out of it.'[71]

In June of 1868, Newman and St John took a train from Birmingham to Abingdon, then went by fly to Littlemore, his old Oxford parish. There were tears, and meetings with old friends, twenty years on from his departure. It struck him as a 'most strange vision – I could hardly believe it real'. Writing to friends, he declared: 'I wanted to see it once before I died.'[72] Yet he had more than twenty years to live; and he would be back.

CHAPTER 14

The Dream of Gerontius

'Heart speaks unto heart.'
NEWMAN'S MOTTO AS CARDINAL

In the early 1860s Newman had been working on a poem about death and the after-life, entitled *The Dream of Gerontius*. He said that he had no idea why he composed it, but 'I wrote on till it was finished, on small bits of paper'.[1] Published in 1865, it was well received and he was encouraged to collect and publish all his verse to date. To have written in the same year and in his prime an autobiography of endur-ing literary merit in a matter of weeks, as well as a substantial poem that would be set to music by Edward Elgar, reveals a formidable imaginative range and stamina.

Supremely literary among English theologians of the nineteenth century, Newman had no aptitude for the abstractions of metaphysics, the severe disci-plines of syllogistic logic, the arid prose of stock theological manuals. His pref-erence across the entire corpus of his writing is for feeling, concrete language, irony, satire, the dynamism of metaphor. He belongs, to an extent, within a Romantic tradition that paid tribute to imagination as the source of human creativity and the means of aspiring to the sublime. Yet Newman had found it difficult over the years to capture imagination in the round. In 1868 he wrote in a notebook: 'I have not defined quite what imagination is. I began by saying "making images".'[2] And there he stops abruptly.

Like his early seventeenth century predecessors he would have found no dif-ficulty in associating prayer with religious imagination, of which George Herbert's beautiful poem *Prayer* is the outstanding exemplar:

Heaven in ordinarie, man well drest,
The milkie way, the bird of Paradise,
    Church-bels beyond the stares heard, the souls bloud,
    The land of spices; something understood.

But Newman belonged to a generation of writers influenced, directly or in-directly, by Bishop Robert Lowth's famous 1740s 'Lectures on Hebrew Poetry'. Lowth had subjected the Psalms and other biblical prophecies to detailed prac-tical criticism, drawing attention to the underlying literary mechanisms, thereby revealing what Scripture shared with poetry of every genre. Lowth identified a special kind of metaphor or symbol, which, rather than being arbitrary, partakes in that which it renders intelligible (bread is the staff of life). He showed how repetitions, and verse parallelisms, and the context of metaphors (natural forms – mountains, woods, plants, animals, simple rural communities and crafts), give rise to sublime poetry and thereby a literary sense of the prophetic. Lowth's legacy influenced among many the work of Blake, Wordsworth, Coleridge, and Shelley, who came to regard imagination as the principal faculty of the mind, and poetry as a source of prophecy and transcendence. Lowth's Latin lectures, moreover, would be translated and read by German poets and philosophers in the late eighteenth and early nineteenth century, creating a seminal influence on continental literature and aesthetics for generations to come. Ironically, in drawing an equivalence between literary and religious imagination, Lowth may well have encouraged theologians to eschew the siren call of imagination, resulting in what Professor Stephen Prickett has called 'theology's missing limb'.

Inseparable from this tribute to imagination's primacy, was Romanticism's emphasis on individual subjectivity: the self, the 'egotistical sublime'. Not for nothing has Newman been compared with Wordsworth. Both had an early scepticism about the visible world, and a consequent sense of awe for interiority, the *self*. Both made it their life's work to tell the story of the growth of their individual minds. Yet the contrasts between the two are instructive. In an early sermon on 'The Individuality of the Soul' Newman claims that the inner world of each human being is 'an unfathomable, an infinite abyss of existence; and the scene in which he bears part for the moment is but like a gleam of sunshine on the surface'.[3] How different from Wordsworth's sense of a reciprocal equivalence between inner and outer depths, the spiritual and the material, expressed in the description of the boy by the lake in 'The Prelude':

Then sometimes, in that silence, while he hung
Listening, a gentle shock of mild surprise
Has carried far into his heart the voice
Of mountain torrents; or the visible scene
Would unawares enter into his mind
With all its solemn imagery, its rocks,
Its woods, and that uncertain heaven, receiv'd
Into the bosom of the steady lake.[4]

Not only does Wordsworth claim a parallel, rooted, equivalence between the inward domain of the mind and the outward world of nature, but he skilfully demonstrates the interaction poetically. Newman, however, merely asserts the infinite scope of the soul, with a rhetorical, unmediated gesture towards its surface sublimity. In another sermon, 'the Invisible World', preached in the 1830s, Newman reveals the distance between himself and Wordsworth when he claims nature's sublimity as symptomatic of God's presence beyond the veil of appearances. The beauties of nature are merely catalogued in a series of surprisingly feeble epithets for such a painstakingly original writer, as if thereby reducing the status of natural beauty:

Bright as is the sun, and the sky, and the clouds; green as are the leaves and the fields; sweet as is the singing of the birds; we know that they are not all, and we will not take up with a part for the whole. They proceed from a centre of love and goodness, which is God himself; but they are not his fullness; they speak of heaven, but they are not heaven; they are but as stray beams and dim reflections of His Image; they are but crumbs from the table.[5]

From early adulthood Newman's appeal to natural forms is didactic rather than, as Wordsworth would put it – 'felt in the blood, and felt along the heart'. When Newman invokes a wild landscape in 'Lead Kindly Light', it is to suggest, allegorically, a place of trial and moral danger: 'Oe'r moor and fen, oe'r crag and torrent …' The resolution is the arrival home, earthly or celestial, where he is greeted by those lost 'angel faces', suggestive of a Victorian familial fireside, or a Christianized-Platonic ambiance of unborn souls. When an old acquaintance enquired in 1879 what he meant by those angel faces, Newman retorted:

it would be quite a tyranny, if, in an art which is the expression, not of truth, but of imagination and sentiment, one were obliged to be ready for examination on the transient states of mind which come upon one when homesick or sea sick, or in any other way sensitive or excited.[6]

Newman, of course, emphatically did not believe that imagination and truth are mutually exclusive. He was more likely expressing a grumpy version of Wordsworth's salutary warning: 'We murder to dissect.' Yet, much as he had a poet's sensibility, frequently manifested in his letters and diaries, his priorities and preoccupations as a religious writer inhabited a different dimension of the mind and heart. When he was walking one summer with the poet Aubrey de Vere in the Wicklow Mountains, he refused to visit a nearby lake, despite its legendary beauty, because, he told de Vere, life is 'full of work more important than the enjoyment of mountains and lakes'.[7] De Vere, in defence of Newman, went on to comment that while the poem 'Tintern Abbey' celebrates the beauty of the scene, the poet fails to ponder the history and the spirituality of the ruined monastery itself. The comment of course tells us more about Newman and de Vere than about Wordsworth.

'Obstinate questioning/Of sense and outward things' in his youth, had drawn Wordsworth towards a visionary apprehension of 'the still, sad music of humanity', a panentheistic 'spirit that rolls through all things', and his peculiar version of Platonic pre-existence – increasingly lost as the 'shades of the prison house' gather with age. Wordsworth would be troubled only in late middle age by what he came to see as his earlier departures from Christian doctrinal orthodoxy. Newman from his very childhood enjoyed a similar interiority, a similar interplay of dream and reality; but his imagination was essentially, constitutionally, wedded to a passion for human virtue as a prelude to the quest for the God of Revelation; as if virtue and religion were somehow in competition with nature. He made this plain in his famous Second Spring sermon:

… Fair as may be the bodily form, fairer far, in its green foliage and bright blossoms, is natural virtue. It blooms in the young, like some rich flower, so delicate, so fragrant, and so dazzling. Generosity, and lightness of heart and amiableness, the confiding spirit, the gentle temper, the elastic cheerfulness, the open hand, the pure, affection, the noble aspiration, the heroic resolve, the romantic pursuit, the love in which self has no part, – are these not beautiful? [8]

Newman's imagination is constantly in play as an explanatory tool. The dominant imagery is of light and luminosity; the total, subtle effect chiaroscuro. In contrast to the light, he resorts to shades, shadows, ghostly images. If he appeals to natural forms it is to elucidate an argument, as when he explicates the development of doctrine with the image of a stream broadening to a river, becoming ever purer and truer to itself : a paradoxical conceit worth an entire chapter of abstract exposition. He favours simple illustrative objects, contrasting for example two paths to religious certitude, by comparing an iron bar (as a single, linear logical proof) with the many-stranded strength of a rope (as the multitudinous experience that leads to assent to faith). He employs a variety of metaphors to grasp the journey to faith: the action of a mountain climber, the relationship of a proliferating polygon to a circle, the dynamic accumulation of arches supporting a gothic vault each separately inadequate to the task, yet together dynamically strong. His elastic imagination appropriates imagery across the widest range of exemplars, from mathematics to astronomy, from music to architecture, from steam engines to the industrial landscapes of his day. He likens Catholic Christendom to 'some moral factory, for the melting, refining, and moulding, by an incessant, noisy process, of the raw material of human nature, so excellent, so dangerous, so capable of divine purposes'. [9] What ecclesiologist before or since has described the Church as a resounding, smelting, clashing factory or foundry?

Newman's stated, as opposed to exemplified, view of the central importance of imagination waxed and waned throughout his writing life, but Samuel Taylor Coleridge exerted the strongest influence from 1835 onwards. Newman, long suspicious of Coleridge's thought (he deplored his defence of the Established Church, and even more the fact that Mr Coleridge was not in residence with Mrs Coleridge) confessed himself 'surprised how much I thought was mine, is to be found there'. Imagination, in Coleridge's view, was essentially vital, it 'dissolves, diffuses, dissipates, in order to recreate; or where this process is rendered impossible, yet still at all events it struggles to idealize and to unify. It is essentially *vital*.'

Newman appears to have maintained both a Lockean view of the mind, as a blank sheet or receptacle, while adopting, alternately and even at times in striking parallel, a Coleridgean image of imagination as a living organ of digestion, which assimilates, grows and develops by what it feeds on. Coleridge favoured the word 'coadunation', a biological term that would now be close to our understanding of symbiosis. Newman at times brought the images of the capacity of a receptacle and digestive organs together as if to combine the contrasts in creative tension. The broadening of the mind, he wrote on one occasion, is 'a digestion of what we receive, into the substance of our previous state of thought; and without this no enlargement is said to follow.' [10] The duality confirms Newman's tendency to combine empirical and Romantic perspectives, as if attempting to reconcile intellectual and aesthetic tensions that tended to subvert each other in the first half of the nineteenth century. Artistic truth, through authentic imagination, is living, organic, possessed of a truth potentially sublime and unsusceptible to analysis ('We murder to dissect'). Scientific, empirical truth is machine-like, driven by direct sense impressions and logic.

Newman's early tendency to understand Christianity in imaginative terms was evident in his mid-twenties when he wrote the essay for Blanco White on Aristotle and the art of poetry, concluding that every Christian is essentially a poet. At the time of the Tamworth Reading Room dispute, we saw the importance he placed on imagination in apprehension of religious truth. Again: 'The heart is commonly reached not through the reason, but through the *imagination* [my italics] …' It is a thought that anticipates his chosen motto, on becoming a Cardinal, 'Heart speaks unto Heart'. In his *Essay on Development* (1845), he had endorsed not only the idea of the Christian as poet, but Christianity itself, the person even of Christ through history, as analogous to a living ever expanding poem, or fugue. And he repeats the notion in his essay on Keble published the following year: 'The Church herself is the most sacred and august of poets …' [11]

Newman had used this notion of living imagination to devastating, almost callous, effect in his *Lectures on Certain Difficulties felt by Anglicans* (1850), suggesting that the Church of England lacked a life of its own, being 'no body politic of any kind', but a 'department of government'. [12] In Newman's view, moreover, the Anglican Church lacked conscious, intelligent life: 'Nor can it in consequence be said to have any antecedents, or any future; or to live, except in the passing moment. As a thing without a soul, it does not contemplate itself, define its intrinsic constitution, or ascertain its position.' [13] The latter thought combines with an extraordinary conceit that exploits imagination itself as metaphor:

Thus it is that students of the Fathers, antiquarians, and poets, begin by assuming that the body to which they belong is that of which they read in time past, and then proceed to decorate it with that majesty and beauty of which history tells, or which their genius creates ... but at length, either the force of circumstances of some unexpected accident dissipates it; and, as in fairy tales, the magic castle vanishes when the spell is broken and nothing is seen but the wild heath, the barren rock, and the forlorn sheep-walk: so it is with us as regards the church of England, when we look in amazement of that which we thought so unearthly, and find so common-place or worthless.[14]

Newman appeared convinced in a guarded and frequently qualified fashion that imagination has primacy not only in our apprehension of religion, but in the Church's living knowledge of itself – themes that will be picked up in the next chapter on the *Grammar of Assent*. In the meantime, writing for no reason but to please himself, and with no combative purpose, he embarked on a poem about the moment of death and the soul's journey into eternity. 'The Dream of Gerontius' provides yet another glimpse into the imagination of John Henry Newman.

GERONTIUS

The narrative is composed of soliloquies and dialogues spoken by a dying Catholic, Gerontius (the 'Old Man'), and his Guardian Angel, punctuated by interventions from death-bed attendants, angelic hosts, demons, and the Angel of the Agony. Gerontius is destined for Purgatory since he has led a good life yet is not sufficiently perfect to go straight to Heaven: he is no Blessed, no Saint. We are allowed no information about his background, or profession, although it seems likely that it was Newman's sustained meditation on his own death, a fantasy indulged perhaps with some frequency.

While the idea of the poem has resonances of other journeys to the underworld, the ambiance is distinctly, religiously, Roman Catholic. We meet no known personalities in the poem, in this life or the next. There are doctrinal expositions in the form of prayers, hymns, and the Creeds; the poem is preoccupied with the nature and function of angels. A segment of the poem, 'Praise to the Holiest in the Height' (sung by the 'Fifth Choir of Angelicals'), is popular among Catholic and Anglican congregations to this day, as are the verses that begin 'Firmly I believe and truly'. There are two high points of drama, demonstrating the difficulty of even a venial sinner encountering the face of God without purgation.

The quality of verse in the opening section hardly lives up to the drama of the soul approaching death: there is, says Gerontius, 'a visitant ... knocking his dire summons at my door. The like of whom ... Has never, never come to me before ...' It is an idealised, sanitized death-bed scene; an absence of pain and fear, neither sorrow for those he leaves behind nor regrets at departing this world; no illness, no pain. He refers in passing to 'O loving friends' – indicating not those *he* loves, so much as those who love *him*, and whose main purpose is to pray for him 'who have not strength to pray'. The friends embark on the rituals for the dying, beginning with a Litany that includes 'holy Hermits', and 'all holy Virgins', giving the poem a Medieval tone. There is no thought in the poem for the corruption of the body in the grave, or morbid funereal accompaniments familiar to the Victorian culture of death. In fact, strictly speaking, the point of the poem is that Gerontius does *not* die. His Cartesian-like soul continues to live on a different plane, his presence surviving, according to Newman's ingenious speculation, in the way that phantom-limb sufferers experience sensation in their absent members.

The verse at last bursts into life with a recasting of the De Profundis and a rendering of the Psalm 90 sung by all the Souls in Purgatory: 'A thousand years before Thine eyes are but as yesterday' (a rewording of 'For a thousand years in thy sight are but as yesterday'), in which the poetry is carried on the original Hebrew parallelisms. The dying man's soliloquies are peppered with adjectival epithets – 'dizzy brink', 'vast abyss', 'loathsome curse', 'hideous wings' ... mounting to his plaint that he feels 'wild with horror and dismay'. At the moment of death, however, the verse begins to attain imaginative power:

This silence pours a solitariness
Into the very essence of my soul;
And the deep rest, so soothing and so sweet,
Hath something too of sternness and of pain.

His Guardian Angel appears, announcing that his 'work is done', his 'task is o'er', and Gerontius, now called 'Soul', is accompanied to the 'Judgement House'. On the way they are verbally abused by a horde of demons, who hurl 'uncouth and sour' insults. Jeering at human holiness, they describe a saint as 'a bundle of bones,/Which fools adore, Ha! Ha!'

There are interesting speculations about time and space beyond the material universe:

Divide a moment, as men measure time,
Into its million-million-millionth part,
Yet even less than that the interval
Since thou didst leave the body ...

A note on eternal punishment, added to the *Grammar of Assent*, ponders the 'temporary absence of the lost soul of the consciousness of its continuity or duration'. He goes on to relate the story of a monk for whom three hundred years passed as if no more than an hour while in an ecstasy. 'Now pain as well as joy, may be an ecstasy, and destroy for the time the sense of succession.'[15] While he rejects the idea that he is attempting to 'explain away' the severity of eternal punishment by the abolition of time, it is clear that he has problems with an eternity without pain as much as eternal suffering. 'Mere Eternity, though, without suffering, if realized in the soul's consciousness, is formidable enough; it would be insupportable even to the good, except for, and as involved in the Beatific Vision; it would be perpetual solitary confinement. It is this which makes the prospect of a future life so dismal to our present agnostics, who have no God to give them "mansions" in the unseen world.'[16]

Meanwhile the suffering of Purgatory, as manifested in the *Dream*, consists of the briefest of glimpses of the face of Jesus, and the painful realization of the Soul's unworthiness, reminiscent of the wounds of mystical love experienced by Saint Teresa of Avila. The Angel says:

There is a pleading in His pensive eyes
Will pierce thee to the quick, and trouble thee.
And thou will hate and loathe thyself; for, though
Now sinless, thou wilt feel that thou hast sinn'd,
As never thou didst feel; and wilt desire
To slink away, and hide thee from His sight …

Newman's Purgatory is not a place of physical suffering (although the phantom-limb speculation leaves the question open). The temporary suffering of Purgatory, and hence the eternal suffering of Hell, is the mental agony of shame and frustrated longing for the absent Lord. Not since the expression of his love for Hurrell Froude had Newman written of love in such anguished terms. In the 'Presence Chamber', mediated by the Angel of the Agony (the angel that attended Christ in the Garden of Gethsemane), Newman is finally granted, or is afflicted with, that briefest vision of the beloved Lord. The Soul cries out:

I go before my Judge. Ah! …

If the reader feels let down by this abrupt exclamation, the line is more strikingly expressed in Elgar's oratorio as a thrilling, climactic cry. The Angel explains:

… the keen sanctity,
Which with its effluence, like a glory, clothes
And circles round the Crucified, has seized,
And scorch'd, and shrivell'd it; and now it lies
Passive and still before the awful Throne.

The conclusion of the poem sees the Soul accepting his departure into Purgatory, where he will 'throb, and pine, and languish', singing of his 'absent Lord and love'. The Angel then delivers these arresting lines:

Softly and gently, dearly-ransom'd soul,
   In my most loving arms I now enfold thee,
And, o'er the penal waters, as they roll,
   I poise thee, and I lower thee, and hold thee.

And carefully I dip thee in the lake,
   And thou, without a sob or a resistance,
Dost through the flood thy rapid passage take
   Sinking deep, deeper, into the dim distance.

Gerontius acquiesces without 'resistance' in the intensely physical, controlling affection of the angel, the entire fantasy expressed as a combination of dominance and submission. The Angel enfolds, lowers, and dips him – 'softly … gently …' in those 'most loving arms'. There is no indication in Newman's writings, despite the huge artistic and intellectual energies expended through his life, that he somehow displaced his sexual libido through the practice of 'sublimation' – the mental discipline whereby sexual desires are elevated imaginatively to a spiritual plane. It appears rather, as argued earlier, that he had a lifelong aversion to what he called sensuality. The *Dream* confirms this aversion when the Angel characterises sexual generation as a form of seminal contamination through Original Sin:

O Man, strange composite of heaven and earth!
   Majesty dwarf'd to baseness! fragrant flower
Running to poisonous seed! and seeming worth
   Cloking corruption!

The closing lines express abandonment with ambivalent echoes of Eros and Thanatos – consummation as death. Accustomed as a child to creating fantasies of a world peopled by angels, it is as if he sees himself as a passive human love-object, enveloped by a dominant angelic lover as he sinks with pleasurable pain into a Lethe-like Purgatory. Newman, again, seems imaginatively engaged both as the Angel and Gerontius. That final easeful abandonment, anticipated through the poem – 'innermost abandonment … deepest abyss … infinite descent … falling … solemn consummation …' – is experienced both actively and passively.

Does the *Dream* suggest an authentically mystical meditation? The poem certainly expresses, albeit unevenly, resonances of the three classic stages of the 'mystic way', purgation, illumination, and union, which would have been familiar to Newman in Christian writings influenced by the Neoplatonists. While Gerontius gives the impression of being detached from the world, there is very little indication of his penitence, remorse, sense of sinfulness. The momentary purgation experienced briefly before the face of Christ, 'scorch'd and shrivel'd', is reported by the Angel rather than confessed by Gerontius. Yet the poem confidently proclaims the second step of 'illumination', repose in the certitude of God's reality, as does so much of Newman's writing throughout his life. Finally, the third step of 'union', described by Evelyn Underhill as that 'perfect and self-forgetting harmony of the unregenerate will with God' [17], is promised rather than portrayed. As Gerontius's soul is launched into the deeps of Purgatory, the oceanic impression familiar in so much mystical writing is unmistakeable.

CHAPTER 15

The Grammar of Assent

'... the human mind is made for truth ...'

J. H. NEWMAN, *THE GRAMMAR OF ASSENT*

'In these latter days', Newman had written in the *Apologia*, '... things are tending ... to atheism in one shape or another.'[1] The spread of atheism, he warned, was happening 'with far greater rapidity' than at any time in history. What had begun during the days of the Paris Enlightenment of Rousseau and Voltaire as salon scepticism was by the mid-nineteenth century a rising floodtide of religious scepticism across Europe. As science and technology expanded, so inductive perspectives on human nature flourished. In the second half of the eighteenth century in England, David Hartley's best-selling *Observations on Man*, a materialist, determinist theory of 'everything', found popular appeal among radicals and Unitarian dissenters alike for its promotion of a Christianity free of dogma, not least Original Sin. The perfectibility of man and society was now a prospect achievable by social and political change, and the Utilitarianism of Bentham and John Stewart Mill – the greatest happiness for the greatest number – offered practical social solutions. In the decade before the publication of the *Apologia*, Marx's *Communist Manifesto* and Darwin's *On the Origin of Species* had been published with further potential for materialist explanations of history, society and human nature. Meanwhile, throughout Europe the formation of nation states continued to drive the pace of secularism. England's poets – Blake, Wordsworth, Coleridge, Shelley – had signalled their troubled despondency ahead of the religious disillusionment of Matthew Arnold, Arthur Clough, and Tennyson. More than twenty years before Nietzsche's 'God is dead', and forty years ahead of Thomas Hardy's 'God's Funeral', Newman had predicted 'what a scene, what a prospect, does the whole of Europe present at this day ... and every civilization through the world, which is under the influence of the European mind!'[2] What was to be done?

DRAFTING THE GRAMMAR

After returning from Rome as a Catholic priest, Newman began to draft notes towards a detailed argument to justify belief in God and Christianity. This was a book, he thought, that could turn the tide of unbelief. He wrote of it: 'I had felt it on my conscience for years, that it would not do to quit the world without doing it.' [3] But as time passed, he complained of the difficulties. He was 'too old', he wrote, 'too weary, too weak, and too busy'. [4] He found it a sheer slog, like 'tunnelling through the Alps'. [5] In 1866, the year before Matthew Arnold published *Dover Beach*, echoing what had now become a general sense of spiritual crisis – 'Nor certitude … we are here as on a darkling plain', Newman was convinced at last that he had found the key. And yet, 'the work was not less like tunnelling than before'. Then, on 3 February 1870, he could write to a friend: 'for twenty years I have begun and left off an inquiry again and again, which yesterday I finished … Now at last I have done all that I can do according to my measure.' [6]

As with other books, the *Grammar* was given shape by a personal correspondence, in this case a discussion, starting in 1859, with the distinguished scientist William Froude, brother of Newman's long-dead friend Hurrell. The nub was the attainment of certitude of knowledge, and the status of scepticism. Newman could see the relationship between 'scientific' method in both secular and theological matters, but he wanted to clarify a distinction which showed that 'the scientific proof of Christianity is not the popular, practical, personal evidence on which a given individual believes in it'. [7]

As we accompany Newman through a series of beautifully written reflections, and meditations, he explores how Christian believers arrive at certitude in faith. We do not reach that certitude, he is saying, by employing logical arguments or proofs – like following the clues to solve a crime, or conducting a complicated experiment to prove a scientific hypothesis. It is an 'assent', a kind of 'eureka moment', literally a 'feeling towards', or a 'yes', not as a result of a *leap* of faith, or a blind act of the will, but in consequence of encountering the Christian religion, its people, its objects, and its practices over time. That acquaintance with religion involves imaginative apprehension of its prayers and sacraments, its rituals and Scriptures, its Creed, and all the tangible, visual and concrete expressions of the Christian faith. Above all it involves the presence of Jesus Christ in our imaginations, in the Eucharist, and in the community of the Church.

If one is already aware, naturally, from childhood of the presence of God in the voice of conscience, Newman argues, then the moment of *assent* to revealed religion is the moment when one recognizes that primal inner voice to be the selfsame voice of the Lord discovered in Christianity. Hence it is a *moral* assent, and a personal assent.

FROM GOD'S EXISTENCE IN NATURE TO GOD'S REVELATION

For all its impressive beauty as a work of prose, the *Grammar* is a difficult book to follow. It is easy to be discouraged because of its discursive style and lack of signposting. Most commentators, moreover, seek to elucidate the *Grammar* by offering explanatory 'hints' and 'clues' to its meaning outside of the text itself, reinforcing one's conclusion that the book fails to deliver Newman's intended argument.

I began reading the *Grammar*, aged nineteen, when the Catholic theologian, the late Doctor 'Ikey' Davis, then parish priest in Bearwood, Birmingham, placed it in my hands, intending that we should study it together over tea on Thursday afternoons during the winter of 1960. After a month of increasing confusion, I said to him: 'It would help if I had just a brief general idea of where Newman is trying to take us.' Ikey explained that it was not appropriate to produce a brief summary, precisely because Newman's arguments about assent to faith are so subtle, mysterious, complex and resistant to analysis. Nevertheless, for better or worse, he threw me a lifeline. It went something like this: 'Newman is saying that certitude in the truth of Christianity occurs when one finds it to be a perfect fit with one's heart.' Religion, he went on, like loving someone, is a matter of total engagement – emotions, intellect, experience, imagination. One does not assent to science in this fashion. So one does not approach the truth or otherwise of religion as one would attempt to prove or disprove a scientific hypothesis. After that we did not always follow Newman's precise sequence of arguments, but maintained priorities that Ikey thought might help. We started with Newman's discussion of the early discovery of God, from childhood.

It had been common for theologians from the eighteenth century to attempt to 'prove' the existence of God through philosophical arguments about the design of the universe and arguments about causation. Newman was not happy with such 'proofs'. He wrote in the *Grammar*: 'I do not want to be converted by a smart syllogism; if I am asked to convert others by it, I say plainly I do not care to overcome their reason without touching their hearts.'[8] The theists' notion of God, he maintains in the *Grammar*, 'requires but a cold and ineffective acceptance, though it be held ever so unconditionally'.[9]

Newman declares that the natural encounter with God, which he found in his youth through the voice of conscience, is comparable to our possession of reason, memory, and the perception of the beautiful. It requires no 'proof'. He goes on to explain that he is not referring to conscience as a set of specific judgments of right and wrong, but an underlying conviction that we ought to *do* what is right and *avoid* what is wrong. He adds that this does not depend on an impersonal abstract idea, but comes with a sense of emotion. There is an awareness of a voice that is personal. As the heroine of his novel *Callista* says:

You may tell me that this dictate is a mere law of my nature, as is to joy or to grieve. I cannot understand this. No, it is the echo of a person speaking to me. Nothing shall persuade me that it does not ultimately proceed from a person external to me. It carries with it its proof of its divine origin.[10]

The mind is conscious of 'one to whom he is amenable, whom he does not see, who sees him'. One hears echoes of 'a Moral governor, sovereign and just'. At other times he wrote of the 'echo of the living Word', and 'the echo of a person speaking to me', and 'our great internal teacher …' This, for Newman, is God's echo in nature, and, consciously or unconsciously, we are seeking the ultimate source of His voice, from very childhood, in the God of Revelation:

To a mind thus carefully formed upon the basis of its natural conscience, the world, both of nature and of man, does but give back a reflection of those truths about the One Living God, which have been familiar to it from childhood.[11]

Looking forward to the book's conclusion, Newman is saying that Christianity makes a perfect fit with the human heart when varied experience of revealed religion finds unity with the God of nature experienced in the depths of one's conscience. As he would write, feelingly, prayerfully, in his *Meditations and Devotions*[12]: 'By nature and by grace Thou art in me. I see Thee not in the material world except dimly, but I recognize Thy voice in my own intimate consciousness. I turn round and say Rabboni. O be ever thus with me.'

REAL AND NOTIONAL ASSENT

The *Grammar* is a book about different ways of knowing, rather than different ways of thinking. How do we *know* the faith? Newman makes an important distinction between 'notional' knowledge, by which he means knowledge of abstract ideas or concepts in science and philosophy, for example, and 'real' knowledge, by which he means knowledge that is encountered holistically with all one's faculties engaged: senses, emotions, intellect, imagination. This real knowledge of the faith can include a broad span of encounters: prayer, lives of the saints, the sacraments, religious art, Scripture, the Eucharist, the living communities of the Church and awareness of its history.

He then describes two ways in which we 'assent', or come to accept what we know: '*notional* assent' and '*real* assent'. 'Notional assent' involves acceptance of the truth of abstract ideas attained through linear, logical inferences. He classes this kind of knowledge as second-hand. 'Real assent' involves acceptance of truth through first-hand evidence, the 'real knowledge' of religion across a broad span of experience encountered with the whole of one's being. Notional assent is a consequence of a prospective process of reasoning moving logically forward with a proposed goal in mind; real assent is retrospective, a realisation that follows a variety of parallel evidences and experiences. Real knowledge of religion, he argues, is supported by the strength of many strands (he calls them 'accumulations of probabilities'), a complexity of encounters 'too fine to avail separately, too subtle and circuitous to be convertible into syllogisms, too numerous and various for conversion, even were they convertible'.[13] Religion, he goes on, defies 'the rude operation of syllogistic treatment', just as a portrait is different from a sketch in 'having, not merely a continuous outline, but all its details filled in, and shades and colours laid on and harmonized together'.

Taking the doctrine of the Holy Trinity as an example, Newman argues that the mystery ('which is addressed far more to the imagination and the affections than to the intellect') is apprehended by the faithful through devotions rather than by theological study. In the Creeds, moreover, it is encountered in prayer. 'For myself', Newman writes, 'I have ever felt [the Creed] as the most simple and sublime, the most devotional formulary to which Christianity has given birth, more so even than the *Veni Creator* or the *Te Deum*'.[14]

This leads him to a point where he employs a striking metaphor to illustrate his claim that it is possible to believe without understanding:

Break a ray of light into its constituent colours, each is beautiful, each may be enjoyed; attempt to unite them, and perhaps you produce only a dirty white. The pure and indivisible Light is seen only by the blessed inhabitants of heaven; here we have but such faint reflections of it as its diffraction supplies; but they are sufficient for faith and devotion. Attempt to combine them into one, and you gain nothing but a mystery, which you can describe as a notion, but cannot depict as an imagination.[15]

Hence members of the faithful address the Father, Son and Holy Spirit, imaginatively as individual, separate realities. Whereas 'theology has to do with the Dogma of the Holy Trinity as a whole made up of many propositions, religion has to do with each of those separate propositions which compose it, and lives and thrives in the contemplation of them'.[16]

'ILLATIVE SENSE'

It is not possible to practise religion, Newman declares, without certitude. 'Without certitude in religious faith', he maintains, 'there may be much decency of profession and of observance, but there can be no habit of prayer, no directness of devotion, no intercourse with the unseen, no generosity of self-sacrifice.' Certitude, moreover, requires perseverance. It is 'essential for the Christian; and if he is to persevere to the end, his certitude must include in it a principle of persistence'.[17]

He goes on: 'If religion is to be devotion, and not a mere matter of sentiment, if this is to be made the ruling principle of our lives, if our actions, one by one, and our daily conduct, are to be consistently directed towards an Invisible Being, we need something higher than a mere balance of arguments to fix and control our minds.'[18] Or as he puts it succinctly in the *Apologia*: 'Who can really pray to a Being, about whose existence he is seriously in doubt?'[19]

As he explores the nature and necessity of arrival at certitude, real assent (or the eureka moment), he appeals to the term 'illative sense', which, in an earlier draft, he had called 'illative imagination'. Newman had expressed the thought behind this term in different ways down the years. Thirty years earlier he had employed the metaphor of a mountaineer:

The mind ranges to and fro, and spreads out, and advances forward with a quickness which has become a proverb, and a subtlety and versatility which baffle investigation. It passes on from point to point, gaining one by some indication; another on a probability; then availing itself of an association; then falling back on some received law; next seizing on testimony; then committing itself to some popular impression, or some inward instinct, or some obscure memory; and thus it makes progress not unlike a clamberer on a steep cliff, who, by quick eye, prompt hand, and firm foot, ascends how he knows not himself, by personal endowments and by practice, rather than by rule, leaving no track behind him, and unable to teach another.[20]

The climber has reached the summit through an accumulation of disciplined manoeuvres, chance discoveries, training, memories, physical fitness, ropes, grappling irons, courage. He knows that he has reached the summit through an accumulation of factors operating in parallel, but looking back he cannot tell you precisely how the summit was achieved.

Elsewhere Newman employs the alternative, telling metaphor of a 'cable'. Writing to a correspondent in 1864 he explains his reference to 'probability' in the *Apologia*. It was not that he was arguing that God is a probability rather than a certainty, but that he believes in God, in Christianity, in Catholicism, *on* a probability – 'a cumulative, a transcendent probability, but still probability; inasmuch as He who made us has so willed, that in mathematics indeed we arrive at certitude by rigid demonstration, but in religious inquiry we arrive at certitude by accumulated probabilities'.[21] Newman is not talking here about probability in the conventional sense, but a narrative of probabilities leading to certainty within the personal and moral domain: 'The best illustration of what I hold is that of a *cable* which is made up of a number of separate threads, each feeble, yet together as sufficient as an iron rod.'[22]

An iron rod represents logical, linear, mathematical demonstration; a cable represents an assemblage of probabilities, separately insufficient for certitude, irrefragable when put together. A man who said 'I cannot trust a cable, I must have an iron bar', would, in certain given cases, be irrational and unreasonable: – so too is a man who says I must have a rigid demonstration, not a moral demonstration, of religious truth.[23]

Invoking another metaphor, he writes:

I liken it to the mechanism of some triumph of skill, tower or spire, geometrical stair-case, or vaulted roof, where the '*Ars est celare artem*' where all display of strength is carefully avoided, and the weight is ingeniously thrown in a variety of directions, upon supports which are distinct from, or independent of each other.[24]

The unspoken assumption is that the imagination has a 'coadunating' capac-ity, as Coleridge called it, to create a whole that is greater than its parts. 'Such a living organon is a personal gift', Newman writes in the *Grammar*, 'and not mere method of calculus.'[25] Attainment of certitude, then, is 'an action more subtle and more comprehensive than the mere appreciation of syllogistic logic'. Reli-gious faith, religious certitude, is not a consequence of a blind leap into the dark, leaving reason behind. But unlike scientific knowledge religious knowledge is an assimilation of, and a participation in, the living, organic life of a community, involving its culture, language, symbols, and sacramentals, encountered and assented to with the heart.

OBJECTIONS, COMMUNITY AND GIFT

Although Newman's conviction of the presence of God in conscience is not intended as an unquestioned axiom, but a probability to be pondered, it never-theless raises objections. For example, it has failed to persuade the agnostic philosopher Anthony Kenny. Kenny objects that the feelings Newman describes of 'inward experience of the divine power', may be 'appropriate only if there is a Father in heaven', but cannot be taken as any kind of guarantee of their own appropriateness. He goes on: 'If the existence of God is intended simply as a hypothesis to explain the nature of such sentiments, then other hypotheses must also be taken into consideration. One such is that of Sigmund Freud …'[26]

Kenny has a second, parallel objection to Newman's central argument. He writes that the notion of cumulative probabilities on encountering Christianity 'may be equally available for what is true and what merely pretends to be true, for counterfeit revelation as well as a genuine one. They supply no intelligible rule to determine what is to be believed and what not.' Certitude is no guaran-tee, after all, of truth. Newman was aware of such difficulties. In chapter six of the *Grammar* he writes of 'the all important question, what is truth, and what apparent truth? what is genuine knowledge, and what is its counterfeit? What are the tests for discriminating certitude from mere persuasion or delusion?'[27]

Newman's answer lies within the realms of imagination rather than philos-ophy. In his *Essay on Development* Newman had applied the test of 'life' to distinguish between 'genuine development' and 'corruption'. The capacity to distinguish true revelation from counterfeit, Newman believed, is owed not alone to the 'gift' of individual imagination on the part of each member of the Church, but the 'gift' of imagination inherent and bestowed by the entire Catholic Church on the faithful and on those who approach her. The answer to the question, then – how does the Catholic church itself avoid error in its organic life? – is contained in the essay Newman wrote on Keble in 1846: 'The church herself is the most sacred and august of poets …' [28] That statement invokes the notion of the Church as a dynamic living idea or symbol, and the imaginative capacity of its members to apprehend its self-authenticating truth. The Church seen as poet and living work of art is the generator and guarantor of truths, recognised and endorsed by the religious imaginations of its members.

Yet even as figures such as Coleridge and Newman appealed to the power of imagination in their justification of belief, the marriage of poetry and religion, literature and theology, as exemplified by George Herbert, were shearing apart. Some scholars identify that fragmentation, as mentioned in the previous chapter, with the application of literary criticism to the Bible in the work of the Oxford Professor of Poetry, Robert Lowth, in the 1740s. Others argue that the Romantic imagination, with its egoism and neglect of social and political ills of the nineteenth century contained the seeds of its own downfall: the divine spark in Coleridge's definition of imagination could be appropriated as easily by those Promethean poets bound for self-idolatry.

The legacy of the *Grammar*, then, may well be its potential to restore, with necessary distinctions, the self-authenticating power of religious imagination. It may well be its potential to reverse the neglect and disillusionment with imagination which reached final eclipse in the so-called 'death of imagination' of Jacques Derrida. The challenge for contemporary theologians is to demonstrate how the *Grammar's* insights answer the charge that faith involves blind leaps and abandonment of reason. Equally important, the *Grammar* attempts to demonstrate the fallacy of drawing an equivalence between religion and artistic imagination. In his recent *History of Christianity* (2009), Oxford's Professor of Church History, Diarmaid MacCulloch, states that, for him, Christianity is true in the sense that *Hamlet* is true; in an essay in *Philosophers without God* (2007) the Cambridge Professor of Philosophy, Simon Blackburn, argues that 'onto-theology' (the idea that God is 'real') should give way to 'expressive theology' (the idea that God is a figment of 'uplifting fiction'). The popular apotheosis of religion as make-believe, however, is crudely summed up by Richard Dawkins's comment in *The God Delusion* that: 'the only difference between *The Da Vinci Code* and the gospels is that the gospels are ancient fiction while *The Da Vinci Code* is modern fiction.'

Newman's central idea in the Grammar of Assent is today subject to a daunting challenge within the Church, rather than outside it; not so much because of the weakness of his arguments, but its authenticity. He argues that real assent to the Catholic faith emerges, as we have seen, from the 'popular, practical, personal evidence on which a given individual believes in it'. The past two decades have witnessed an unrelenting series of images, stories, 'evidences', of the paedophile priest scandal. In the light of such 'evidences and contents', the 'accumulated probabilities' have been potentially destructive of the Catholic clergy's reputation for moral integrity despite the fact that the perpetrators were a small minority. The insidious irony is that Newman summoned all the brilliant satire at his command to dismiss fictitious claims of clerical abuse in the mid-nineteenth century, promoted in books such as *The Awful Disclosures of Maria Monk*. He successfully turned the allegations back against the accusers because they were untrue and prompted by malice. In view of the appalling truth of Catholic clerical abuse, Newman's insights into the power of religious imagination, as justifying faith, are all the more significant, since they demonstrate the profound and far reaching impact of the scandal and the difficult task of reversing it.

CHAPTER 16

Papal infallibility

'… I shall drink – to the Pope, if you please, – still, to
Conscience first, and to the Pope afterwards.'
J. H. NEWMAN, A LETTER TO THE DUKE OF NORFOLK

Through the 1850s, following Pio Nono's return from exile in Gaeta in the Kingdom of Naples, his papacy experienced a period of uneasy peace. The trauma
of being ousted from Rome at the risk of his life disabused Pio of any further
ideas of promoting a liberal regime within the Papal States. As the process of
secularization spread across Europe, and the unification of Italy continued apace,
his rule over the papal territories – from Terracina in the South West to Ravenna
in the North East – became increasingly shaky and repressive.

The impetus for a united Italy under the monarchical leadership of Vittorio
Emanuele II, King of Piedmont-Sardinia, found support throughout the peninsula in preference to the republican ambitions of Mazzini and Garibaldi, or the
federalist dreams of Balbo and Gioberti. Should not Pio for the sake of peace,
unity, and an end to foreign military occupations, negotiate with Vittorio and
surrender at last his temporal possessions which severed the peninsula in two?
Count Cavour, Vittorio's Prime Minister, devised a compromise. A devout
Catholic and related, it was said, through forebears to the family of St Francis
de Sales, Cavour pressed for a treaty that would free the remaining papal states
from papal rule, allowing Pio just the city of Rome – the best that could be
hoped for in the long run. By way of compensation the papacy would be given
the honorary title of president of the Italian Confederation, a theoretical entity
that did not, in the event, come to pass. Pio, however, was opposed not only to
surrendering an inch of papal soil, but even lived in hope of retrieving lands
and property already lost. His oft repeated view was that 'the States of the
Holy See belong to no royal dynasty, but to all Catholics … We cannot give up
what is not Ours.'[1] His intransigence earned him severe public criticism across
Europe. Within the Catholic Church opinion was sharply divided. Newman had
already declared himself to be against papal temporal power. He could see no
case for arguing that such authority was an authentic development of Christian
doctrine.

Manning, who appealed to no such theory of development, would come out
vehemently for the Pope in his *The Temporal Power of the Vicar of Christ* (1862).

He held that Pio's right to rule over his territories was comparable to his spiritual authority: it had a theological basis, he insisted, in that Christ's sway over heaven and earth had been inherited by the Holy Father as the Vicar of Christ. He cited the Archbishop of Canterbury as an enfeebled example of pretensions to authority lacking essential freedom from British rule. Indeed he urged the Pope to define the temporal authority as a dogma.

By the end of the 1850s Pio Nono, who had once so impressed all who met him for his angelic charisma, became a target of widespread hostility. The catalyst was a scandal that reverberates to this day. In 1858 a six-year-old Jewish child, Edgardo Mortara, was kidnapped by papal police in Bologna on the pretext that he had been baptized *in extremis* by a servant girl six years earlier.[2] Placed in the House of Catechumens (a Roman institution for converts, closed on Pio's accession, but now reopened), the child was forcibly instructed in the Catholic faith. Despite the pleas of Edgardo's parents, Pio adopted the child and liked to play with him, hiding him under his soutane and calling out, 'Where's the boy?' Pio kept Edgardo cloistered in a monastery, where he was eventually ordained priest. It is difficult to exonerate Pio entirely on the principle of anachronism, for his predecessor Benedict XIV had criticised such treatment of Jewish children and their parents. No less than twenty editorials on the subject were published in the *New York Times*, and both Emperor Franz Josef of Austria and Napoleon III of France begged the Pope to return the child to his rightful parents, to no avail. The affair had the effect of uniting Jews in America to lobby for Jewish rights and campaign against anti-Semitism at home and abroad; which became the principal aim of the Board of Delegates of American Israelites founded in New York in 1859. Newman remained silent on the Mortara affair, as did Manning, yet it is likely that Newman's view of Pio's papacy, characterised in 1870 as 'a climax of tyranny', had begun to take shape at the time of the scandal.

By 1870, Vittorio had managed to deprive the Pope of all his territories save Rome itself. The juggernaut of the new Italy brought in secular laws affecting education, marriage contracts, property ownership, press freedom, as well as modern communications, and popular franchise. Pio reacted with sadness and anger. In his *Syllabus of Errors*, published in 1864 as an adjunct to the new encyclical of that year, *Quanta Cura*, Pio denounced the unstoppable social and political realities all around him by denouncing eighty 'modern' propositions, including socialism and rationalism. In the eightieth proposition, a cover-all denunciation, he declared it a grave error to assert that the 'Roman Pontiff can and should reconcile himself with progress, liberalism, and modern civilisation'. Four years later he would attempt to ban Catholics from voting in elections.

As Pio, and those who sympathised with him, saw it, temporal and spiritual powers were now in a life and death struggle with aggressive man-centred ideologies that had been gathering impetus across Europe ever since the French Revolution. And the enemy was to be found even within the Church itself. Bishops, especially in France, had attempted to undermine papal authority with calls for more local discretion.

Pio now attempted to retrieve what had been lost in terms of temporal power by urging the notion of papal infallibility and the exercise of centralised power. Despite the bad press he continued to receive in the secular domain, there were many within the Church, ready to support and encourage him. As the historian the late H. Daniel-Rops has put it, Pius IX became the centre of an ultramontane cult. '[His] personality … was undeniably responsible for a great deal of the fervour he aroused. All were struck by his charm, his affability, the noble simplicity of his welcome and that sense of humour which seldom deserted him even in his darkest hour. The exaltation of the papacy was the triumph of a man as much as, if not more than, of a doctrine.'[3] The world would know where the Pope stood by the ratification of a dogma, a fiat, to be held by all Catholics under pain of excommunication. The setting for the deliberations that preceded the proclamation would be a great council of the Church, a meeting of all the bishops capable of making the journey to Rome: the Vatican Council of 1870.

Back in England, Archbishop Manning, along with W. G. Ward, now editor of the *Dublin Review*, had supported and encouraged Pio every step of the way. Indeed Manning may well have encouraged the Pope towards an extreme definition of a dogma of papal infallibility, to be applied to all of his official utterances. For Manning the question was now bigger than the issue of the pope's temporal power, there were bigger fish to be basted as the challenge of the new biological sciences sank in across Europe. In response to Darwin's theory of evolution, Manning asserted that 'an internecine conflict is at hand between the army of dogma and the united hosts of heresy, indifferentism and atheism'. Dogma must confront science, Manning declared, which traces 'mankind to a progenitor among the least graceful and most grotesque of creatures, and affirms that thought is phosphorous, the soul a name for the complex of nerves, and, if I rightly understand its mysteries, that our moral sense is a secretion of sugar'.[4] Papal dogma was the antidote that would confirm Catholics in their faith while withstanding the spread of atheism, secularism, and evolutionary science.

On the Feast of Saints Peter and Paul, 1867, Manning made a joint vow with Bishop Senestrey of Ratisbon (Regensburg) to lobby the bishops in the forthcoming Council to push through the proclamation of the Pope's infallibility. Those bishops who responded to Manning's and Senestrey's call were to be known as the infallibilists. Yet there was one Frenchman, Bishop Dupanloup of Orleans, who was vociferous for the 'inopportunists' – those who called not only for sensible limits to any dogmatic of papal infallibility, but for a delay.

Newman's view, already expounded in the *Apologia*, was that a dogma of papal infallibility could not involve new doctrine: it would only serve to clarify which areas of authority in the Church were protected from error. He suggested to the arch infallibilist W. G. Ward that a doctrine of papal infallibility was only 'likely to be true' rather than actually be true. Which was like telling Ward that the Pope was only 'likely' to be a Catholic. The Pope was infallible, Newman believed, in so far as he was head of a Church that was infallible. And he was on the side of the inopportunists in that he believed a dogma of papal infallibility would cause anxiety among Catholics and antagonism among non-Catholics. He also saw the campaign for a dogma as a further tendency towards Roman centralisation. He would write in June 1870, 'I certainly think this agitation of the Pope's Infallibility most unfortunate and ill-advised, and I shall think so even if the Council decrees it, unless I am obliged to believe that the Holy Ghost protects the Fathers from all inexpedient acts, (which I do not see is any where promised) as well as guides them into all the truth, as He certainly does. There are truths which are inexpedient.' [5]

Writing to a clerical friend, Canon Malcom MacColl, he summed up the problem of fideism:

To take up at once ... [a new] article [of faith] may be the act of a vigorous faith, but it may also be the act of a man who will believe anything because he believes nothing, and is ready to profess whatever his ecclesiastical, that is his political, party requires of him. There are too many high ecclesiastics in Italy and England, who think that to believe is as easy as to obey – that is, they talk as if they did not know what an act of faith is. A German who hesitates may have more of the real spirit of faith than an Italian who swallows. [6]

Writing to Richard Wegg-Prosser in 1851, Newman had expressed his understanding of the importance of papal infallibility as a gate to Catholic belief, and as a blank wall:

Suppose a man planted himself against the *walls* of Rome and declared he would not go round to one of the *gates* – for he had a fancy to enter the city at that particular point. Equally unreasonable is it, to attempt to become a Catholic *through* one particular doctrine ... There *are* persons who have found Papal Infallibility to be the gate; let them, if they will ... However, to you and to me, Papal Infallibility is *not* a proof. *I* say, Very well, go to that which *is* a proof ...

Newman goes on to 'bring out his meaning':

I conceive that the fundamental proof of Catholicism (i.e. the basis according to *my* conception of Catholicism) is the promise that the Primitive church shall continue to the end, the likeness of the (Roman) Catholic church to the Primitive, and the dissimilarity of every other body – the (Roman) Catholic church then, being proved to be the organ of revelation, or infallible in matters of faith, will *teach* the Pope's Infallibility, as far as it is doctrine, just as it teaches the Divinity of our Lord …[7]

In conclusion he declares that 'to *defend* the church's doctrines, when she is proved to be the divine *oracle*, is a very different thing from *proving* those doctrines nakedly by themselves'.

In advance of the Council, Newman was invited by Rome to become an official 'consultor' on one of the groups or commissions that prepare Conciliar sessions and debates. At the same time, Bishop Dupanloup asked him to be his *peritus*, or theological adviser. He declined both invitations, pleading ill-health. Yet he still attempted to influence events from afar. The Council opened on 8 December 1869, and Newman wrote on 28 January to Bishop Ullathorne, now in Rome, 'one of the most passionate and confidential letters' he had ever written in his life:

Rome [he pleaded] ought to be a name to lighten the heart at all times, and a Council's proper office is, when some great heresy or other evil impends, to inspire the faithful with hope and confidence; but now we have the greatest meeting which has ever been, and that at Rome, infusing into us by the accredited organs of Rome and its partizans (such as the Civiltà, the Armonia, the Univers, and the Tablet) little else than fear and dismay … What have we done to be treated, as the faithful never were treated before? When has definition of doctrine de fide been a luxury of devotion and not a stern painful necessity? Why should an aggressive insolent faction be allowed to make the heart of the just to mourn, whom the Lord hath not made sorrowful? [8]

The letter was private but Ullathorne passed it around, and it was accordingly copied and published in full in the *Standard* newspaper. It would do Newman no favours among Manning's faction, although it would remain a counsel of good sense for subsequent generations of Catholics.

At the outset, only one half of the bishops attending were disposed to support a dogma of papal infallibility. There was strong opposition from some of the bishops of the great Sees of the world. When Cardinal Guido of Bologna protested that only the assembled bishops of the Church could claim to be witnesses to the tradition of doctrine, the Pope replied: 'Witnesses of tradition? *I* am the tradition.' In the course of the debates the extremist position was forced to give way, and a carefully worded, substantially moderated document was eventually agreed.

The historic dogma was finally passed on 18 July 1870 by 433 bishops, with only two against. The definition reads:

The Roman Pontiff, when he speaks *ex cathedra*, that is, when, exercising the office of pastor and teacher of all Christians, he defines … a doctrine concerning faith or morals to be held by the whole Church, through the divine assistance promised to him in St Peter, is possessed of that infallibility with which the Divine Redeemer wished His church to be endowed … and therefore such definitions of the Roman Pontiff are irreformable of themselves, and not from the consent of the Church.[9]

During the hour of the great decision, a storm broke over St Peter's dome and a thunderclap, amplified within the basilica's cavernous interior, shattered a pane of glass in the tall windows. According to *The Times* (London), the anti-infallibilists saw in the event a portent of divine disapproval. Archbishop Manning responded disdainfully: 'They forgot Sinai and the Ten Commandments.' Manning also came close to what Newman would have deemed theological blasphemy by declaring the definition a 'triumph of dogma over history'.

With both the moderates and the extremists claiming victory, it was the turn of the secular world to react to this belated boost to papal authority. Before the Council could turn to other crucial matters, such as a doctrine of the Church, a universal catechism of Christian doctrine, and a code of Canon Law, the French troops protecting the Eternal City pulled out to defend Paris in the Franco-Prussian War. In came the soldiers of the Italian state, and Rome was lost to the papacy for a second time in twenty years, this time forever. All that remained to Pio and his Curia was the 108.7 acres of the present-day Vatican City, and that on the sufferance of the new Italian nation-state. Shutting himself inside the apostolic palace, Pio refused to come to an accord with the new Italy.

In the period that followed the First Vatican Council, many of Pio's worst fears were realised. In Italy, processions and outdoor services were banned, communities of religious dispersed, Church property confiscated, priests conscripted into the army. A catalogue of measures understandably deemed anti-Catholic by the Holy See, streamed from the new capital: divorce legislation, secularization of the schools, the banning of numerous holy days. In Germany, partly in response to the 'divisive' dogma of infallibility, Bismarck initiated the *Kulturkampf*, the culture struggle against Catholicism. Religious instruction came under state control and religious orders were forbidden to teach; the Jesuits were banished; seminaries subjected to state interference; Church property fell under the control of lay committees; civil marriage was introduced in Prussia. Bishops and clergy resisting *Kulturkampf* legislation were fined, imprisoned, exiled.

In England, the reaction was delayed, muted, and to an extent both literary as well as political. Four years after the great definition of papal infallibility, Prime Minister William Gladstone was defeated after his failure in 1873 to introduce an Irish University Bill into the House of Commons aimed at better provision of tertiary education in Ireland. The Bill was a repeat of the Queen's University scheme in the early 1850s, an attempt to secularise the Irish universities in order to make them more acceptable to Catholics. The Irish bishops were against it, and the Catholic members of Parliament voted accordingly. Gladstone blamed the failure of the Bill (which forced him out office) on the influence of the papal infallibility dogma which, he believed, bound politicians religiously to the Pope's orders irrespective of their secular policies.

In November 1874 Gladstone published a pamphlet entitled *The Vatican Decrees in their bearing on Civil Allegiance*. He accused the Catholic Church of betraying its claim to be *semper eadem*, ever the same, being unhistorical, and adopting principles that could only lead to violence; converts to Catholicism risked surrendering their moral and political freedoms to become slaves of papal whim. The pamphlet sold 150,000 copies in the first year. The allegations find an echo today in the objections levelled against religion as dividing the loyalties of believers from their duties towards the state, and their capacity to play a part in democratic societies.

LETTER TO THE DUKE OF NORFOLK

It fell to Newman to reply to Gladstone's attack, but instead of responding directly he wrote to the Duke of Norfolk, England's leading Catholic layman and something of a national figure. They knew each other well, for the duke had been a pupil at the Oratory School. Written towards the end of 1874, the text was published as *A Letter addressed to the Duke of Norfolk on account of Mr Gladstone's Recent Expostulation*. Newman took the opportunity to hit out at the infallibilist extremists – Manning and W. G. Ward. For it was their extremism that had provoked Gladstone, a reasonable and indeed religious man:

I own to a deep feeling, that Catholics may in good measure thank themselves, and no one else, for having alienated from them so religious a mind. There are those among us, as it must be confessed, who for years past have conducted themselves as if no responsibility attached to wild words and overbearing deeds; who have stated truths in the most paradoxical form, and stretched principles till they were close upon snapping; and who at length, having done their best to set the house on fire, leave to others the task of putting out the flame. [10]

Approaching his 74th birthday, Newman's polemical prose was in superb form. This was just the preface, and he would return to the theme in the letter's summation. The Catholic extremists were guilty of 'violence and cruelty' in print, and of 'rash language'. They had unsettled those who were 'weak in faith' and dissuaded 'inquirers' to the Catholic faith. They had shocked the 'Protestant mind'.

Having commented on the questions of the papacy and history, and the importance of understanding that there was to be no new doctrine, no new revelation, after the death of the last Apostle, Newman launched into the real stuff of Gladstone's allegations: divided loyalty between religion and the state. Both one's religion and one's nation-state have a claim on the individual, and both would attempt to curb an individual's liberty, he began. Yet the Pope had far less effective power over the citizens of England, and he interfered far less in practice than the state. Indeed it was not possible for either religion or state to impose itself upon, or interfere with, an individual's conscience.

This was now his central theme: the sovereignty of conscience, which 'is the voice of God, whereas it is fashionable on all hands now to consider it in one way or another a creation of man'. Conscience, he goes on, is not a recipe to behave as one is inclined – which is more like dispensing with conscience altogether. Conscience is 'the voice of God in the nature and heart of man … it is a messenger from Him, who, both in nature and in grace, speaks to us behind a veil, and teaches and rules us by His representatives. Conscience is the aboriginal Vicar of Christ, a prophet in its informations, a monarch in its peremptoriness, a priest in its blessings and anathemas.' [11] For a Catholic, however, conscience also involves the Pope's authority, which is founded on Revelation to make good the deficiencies of the conscience of nature: 'the championship of the Moral Law and of conscience is his [the Pope's] *raison d'être*.' [12]

Both Newman and Gladstone were conscious that Catholics might not discriminate between dogma and encyclicals like *Quanta Cura* and its notorious off-shoot, the *Syllabus of Errors*. Newman had a rather different point to make about the latter, however. In denouncing the 'sentiment that he ought to come to terms with "progress, liberalism, and the new civilization" ', the Pope, after all, was expressing a conservatism no less passionate than had Newman and Gladstone in their youth. But one had to understand the long-term historical background as well as the tendency of local officials to stir things up for the right audience:

Now, the Rock of St. Peter on its summit enjoys a pure and serene atmosphere, but there is a great deal of Roman *malaria* at the foot of it. While the Holy Father was in great earnestness and charity addressing the Catholic world by his Cardinal Minister, there were circles of light-minded men in his city who were laying bets with each other whether the Syllabus would 'make a row in Europe' or not … it was very easy to kindle a flame in the mass of English and other visitors at Rome which with a very little nursing was soon strong enough to take care of itself. [13]

The passage explodes with striking metaphors – the clean upper air, with the malarial swamps beneath; the 'light-headed' gamblers, and what we might call spin-doctors today, kindling and 'nursing' a conflagration.

But then, the question arises. What happens when there is a conflict between the Pope's utterances and one's individual conscience? The same question might well be asked today in the context of papal decrees on contraception. Newman is adamant that if, after prayer and due consultation, a Catholic believes that an order from the Pope is immoral, he or she is bound to disobey. Citing the Fourth Lateran Council, he quotes: 'He who acts against his conscience loses his soul.' Then he allowed himself this famous concluding remark:

Certainly, if I am obliged to bring religion into after-dinner toasts, (which indeed does not seem quite the thing) I shall drink – to the Pope, if you please, – still, to Conscience first, and to the Pope afterwards.[14]

Newman's *Letter* was received with enthusiasm in England by both Anglicans and Catholics, and especially by Archbishop Cullen, who was now a Cardinal in Ireland. Gladstone responded generously, mentioning its 'integrity', 'acuteness', and 'kindliness of tone'. Gladstone replied that he was not so much attacking Catholics, but 'Vaticanismus'. In Rome, however, the reception of the *Letter* was mixed. Cardinal Barnabò's successor at Propaganda, Cardinal Franchi, informed Manning that while the first half of the letter was a triumph, the second part contained ideas that could give scandal. Manning responded in a way that belies any assumption that he was constitutionally ill-disposed towards Newman. He counselled that it would be best to leave well alone; that no public action should be taken against him. 'The heart of the revered Fr Newman is as right and as Catholic as it is possible to be … [he] has never hitherto so openly defended the prerogatives and infallible magisterium of the Roman Pontiff, although he has always believed and proclaimed these truths …' In any case, any condemnation would prompt controversy, 'now by the grace of God extinguished'.[15]

PART THREE

CHAPTER 17

Death of Ambrose St John

'As far as this world was concerned I was his first and his last.
He has not intermitted this love for an hour up to his last …'
NEWMAN ON THE DEATH OF ST JOHN, 1875

While Newman was writing his letter to the Duke of Norfolk, a 100,000 word book on the dogma of infallibility was published in German by Bishop Joseph Fessler, Secretary General of the Vatican Council, entitled *The True and False Infallibility of the Popes*. Newman felt that he could not complete the letter without checking Fessler's views to ensure his own orthodoxy in the eyes of Rome. He was up against a deadline and had no German; so, according to his practice of many years, he asked his companion Ambrose to translate the text as a matter of urgency.

Ambrose worked day and night on the translation while juggling with other responsibilities at the Birmingham Oratory, its school, and beyond. That summer he was holding instruction classes in Catholicism, giving lectures around Birmingham, producing a school play. He was also in charge of the financial and domestic running of the Oratory and its community. Then there were his pastoral duties, Mass, prayer gatherings, and confessions. On a single day in the previous month, St John had spent six hours hearing confessions: a fact known to Newman.

That same month St John had purchased a property called Ravenhurst Farm where he was setting up a chapel in the house and organising the levelling of playing fields for the Oratory school boys. He was also attempting to help a number of relations who were dependent on him. St John got through this helter-skelter life by an ebullient and decisive nature. Yet Newman recollected only later, after it was too late, that St John had been behaving in a peculiar manner since the Spring, and had 'surprised and annoyed him' on occasion by interrupting his work, detaining him in conversation. St John had been suffering nightmares. He dreamt that Newman was being persecuted by the Vatican; that his books and writings had been put on the Index of forbidden books. The story of St John's illness provides an unusual insight into Newman's empathetic character and his devotion to his companion.

On an unusually hot day in May 1875, still burdened with the Fessler translation chore, St John drove Newman in the community's pony and trap to the

Oratorian summer house at Rednal to enjoy some cool air. The following morning, after Mass, Newman found St John strangely nervous. St John nevertheless drove Newman on to the Ravenhurst Farm, leaving him and the trap there, and setting off on foot for Harborne, a district of Birmingham where the Passionist order had established a new community and chapel. It was a five mile walk. 'The sun was scorching', wrote Newman later, 'and he was pressed for time … But, alas, he resolved to walk in spite of what I said. And he did walk; he hurried on a very hot day; and something occurred to frighten him.'[1] On a lonely stretch of road, at a point where a murder had recently been committed, St John encountered a man loitering suspiciously and was terrified into a state of shock, thinking him to be the murderer in wait.

Another Oratorian, William Neville, picks up the story. He joined St John on the road to Harborne and they attended the Mass together. St John, overweight, and out of breath with heavy smoking, arrived overheated, but was now obliged to don heavy vestments. The new chapel was in the conservatory of the house and stifling. As St John sat through a lengthy sermon with his back to the glass under the full intensity of the sun's rays, he felt a violent pain in his head and thought he was going to pass out. As he sat there, petrified, he heard, or thought he heard, the preacher speaking about Newman's difficulties with Rome, and referring to one of the community going mad. Was this himself? After Mass he hastily quaffed a glass of liquid he thought was lemonade. It was whisky.

Back at the Oratory, St John was convinced that his experiences were a premonition of Newman's persecution. On encountering Newman he cried out 'Let *me* suffer: *I* am ready to bear it.'[2] Despite feeling ill he continued his usual workload, translating, hearing confessions, teaching, making visits to the sick around the parish. One evening he came into Newman's room and drank brandy and orange juice. He complained of a 'weight, heat or pain at the back of his neck'.[3] He begged Newman to pray with him, just as they had done in Rome when they were younger. He could not concentrate on the prayers by himself.

St John was now persuaded to stay in the room next to Father William Neville, the infirmarian. When a doctor was called, St John became agitated, terrified that he was going to be sent to an insane asylum. He settled down for a day or so, and even took a walk with Newman. But again he acted strangely. He stopped to root up some wild flowers in the school yard, convinced that they were poisonous.

A specialist was called in the second week of May, as St John's mind and speech seemed to be rambling. The doctor suggested he be removed to Ravenhurst Farm, for better air and quiet. St John said accusingly to Newman: 'I knew you would expel me from the Oratory.'[4] Newman thought that St John was losing his mind. He went out to Ravenhurst with him, returned to the Oratory, felt anxious, and went back again.

The following Sunday Newman had to return to the Oratory to preach, but no sooner had he arrived back in Birmingham than the message came that St John was in distress, accusing the doctor of poisoning him. Newman returned once more to his friend. 'He threw his arms round my neck', Newman would write, 'and called me his best friend, and said I would be able to defend him against all evils.' [5]

As the days passed St John became violent by turns, and had to be tied to the bed. He shouted incoherently while Newman struggled to pacify him. 'I had to say to him', Newman wrote, ' "Don't you think you had better speak lower?" … he used to turn round and look hard at me with eyes like sapphires, not his usual eyes, but with a steady translucent gaze and answer: "Whisper, better whisper", with a child-like simple sweetness which I think and hope I shall never forget … [It] was very much beyond any thing I had ever seen in him – His face was so like a child's; so tender and beseeching.' [6]

For a period St John grew quieter, less violent, but kept speaking incoherently in a gentle, affectionate low voice. On 24 May Newman was writing letters in the room below when St John rose from his bed and was halfway through the door. Newman and William Neville struggled with him and got him back on the side of the bed. 'I sat by him and he threw his arm round my neck and hugged me close to him, so close that I laughed and said "he will give me a stiff neck". I did not understand he was taking leave of me.' Newman continued: 'So he kept me some time, and even in that position ate some bread and butter, folding it with great deliberation with the right hand still around my neck.' The doctor had apparently recommended that St John eat as much as possible. 'After a time I got free; then he took my hand, and clasped it so tight as to frighten me, for in one of his wild moments some days before he had seemed as if he could not help hurting me, by the violence of his grasp; so I called to those about him to loosen his hand, little thinking it was to be his last sign of love.' [7]

Newman left the house and returned to the Oratory, but he was woken at midnight with a message that St John was much worse. He went straight to Ravenhurst Farm. 'We found him dead', wrote Newman. [8] According to Newman's first biographer, Wilfrid Ward, who knew both men, and may have got the information from Newman himself: 'Newman threw himself on the bed by the corpse and spent the night there.' [9] This has been challenged by subsequent biographers. What is not in dispute is that, according to the reliable William Neville, Newman said the office for the dead that night, wrote telegrams and letters, and in the early hours celebrated Mass for his deceased friend. [10]

The Oratory church was packed for the funeral. Father Denis Sheil, who died in 1962, was a boy in the school in 1875. He told Newman's biographer, Meriol Trevor, that he watched the ceremony from the gallery at the back of the church.

'When Newman was giving the absolutions after the Mass, he broke down ... [there was] an extraordinary noise all over the church, and for an uncomfortable minute he thought everyone was laughing. But they were crying.'[11]

In the following weeks and months, Newman would write many letters to those who had sent condolences. His replies reveal the depth not so much of their mutual love as Newman's remorseful realisation of the love St John bestowed upon *him*. 'As far as this world was concerned I was his first and last. He has not intermitted this love for an hour up to his last ...'; 'From the very first he loved me with an intensity of love, which was unaccountable ...'; 'he has been to me Azarias the son of Ananias ... Raphael to my Tobit ... Ruth to my Naomi ...'; '... this sudden blow ... is a shock parallel to that of a railway accident ...'; '... since his death, I have been reproaching myself for not expressing to him how much I felt his love ...'; 'I am under the greatest affliction which has ever befallen me.'[12] What comes across is that Newman had taken St John's love for granted; that he had not understood his emotional dependence on him until after he had died. In the depths of his grief he wrote to a correspondent: 'I have ever thought no bereavement was equal to that of a husband's or a wife's, but I feel it difficult to believe that any can be greater, or any one's sorrow greater, than mine.'[13]

LATE LITERARY LABOURS

In the 1860s, Newman had undertaken the remarkable feat of editing his own complete works. His motive was to provide the Catholics of his country with a body of work that would edify. Writing to a religious sister, he noted: 'Catholics are so often raw. Many do not know their religion – many do not know the reasons for it ... If we are to convert souls savingly they must have the due preparation of heart.'[14] In 1863, he had commented in his journal that 'the Church must be prepared for converts, as well as converts prepared for the Church'.[15]

After St John's death, he settled into a working routine, doing ever more for the Oratory school, hearing the confessions of penitents who had been used to going to Ambrose, and preaching. Meanwhile, convinced that he had not long to live himself, he continued to sort his papers and prepare for republication a new edition of *Lectures on the Prophetical Office of the Church*. It was to be published as volume one of *The Via Media of the Anglican Church* with an eighty page preface written for Anglicans who were attracted to Catholicism but who held back. Here he wrote eloquently of Christ as Priest, Prophet and King; these roles, he argued, were reflected within the Church – the Christian community as the flock around its pastor, the Church's school of theologians, and the ecclesiastical government of papacy and Curia. All three, he pointed out, have their tendency to excess: some devotions can be overdone and even lead to superstition, theology can degenerate into abstract rationalism, and Church rule to bullying.

By 1877 Newman had republished the writings of his entire Anglican period, save for his treatises on Saint Athanasius. Many old friends had come back into his ambit after the publication of the *Apologia*, and now new correspondents emerged as people read him and turned to him for advice. Many of his correspondents were women. There were women of his family, and the families of his friends; but then there were nuns, like Maria Giberne, whom he had known since the 1830s, and members of religious congregations who would write to him without introduction, as well as an expanding constituency of converts, and intending converts. Among this circuit of women, were aristocrats, teachers, governesses, and such as Margaret Hallahan, who began her working life as a servant girl, and Jane Todd who was a seamstress. Some of his women sought to engage him in theological discussion, others simply asked him for money. Of the enormous range of topics broached in these letters, charitable work ranks very high. But even higher, are references to the literary works of these ladies, including poetry, hagiography, biography, and novels.

Then on 14 December 1877, at the age of 76, he received a letter from the President of Trinity College, Oxford:

My dear Sir,
I am requested to say that it is the desire of this College that you would be pleased to accept the position of an Honorary Fellow of the College.
   I may mention that if you should do so, you will be the first person in whose case the College will have exercised the power which was given to it in 1857, and that at present it is not contemplated to elect another Honorary Fellow.[16]

Newman wrote by return of post:

No compliment could I feel more intimately, or desire more eagerly at once to seize and appropriate than that which is the subject of your letter just received. Trinity College is ever, and ever has been, in my habitual thoughts. Views of its buildings are at my bed side and bring before me morning and evening my undergraduate days, and those good friends, nearly now all gone, whom I loved so much during them, and my love of whom has since their death ever kept me in affectionate loyalty to the college itself.[17]

Newman travelled to Oxford to receive his honorary fellowship in February, 1878. He stayed for two days, and while he felt it had been successful, he noted that 'it was a trial both to my host and to me'. He saw his old Tutor, Thomas Short, aged 87, in his rooms, so blind that he could not see his distinguished former pupil. As he approached Short's rooms on the staircase, Newman heard the old man crying out: 'Is that dear Newman?' He called on Pusey, and found him 'much older since I last saw him in 1865 – as I suppose he found me'.[18]

THE HAT

The final years of Pio Nono's reign were marked by stagnation. Even his firmest supporters were beginning to suspect that the great longevity of this papacy lay at the root of its torpor. Reflecting on the matter in 1876, Archbishop, now Cardinal, Manning, dwelt on the Holy See's 'darkness, confusion, depression ... inactivity and illness'.[19] As for the man himself, Pio admitted: 'Everything has changed; my system and my policies have had their day, but I am too old to change my course; that will be the task of my successor.'[20] After his death on 7 February 1878 his corpse was eventually taken from its provisional resting place in St Peter's to a permanent tomb at San Lorenzo. When the cortege approached the Tiber, a gang of anticlerical Romans threw mud, and threatened to throw the coffin into the river. Only the arrival of a contingent of militia saved his body from final insult.

Pio's successor, Leo XIII, was 68 years of age in the year in which he was elected and regarded a stop-gap. He was to reign for a quarter of a century. He has gone down in history as the Pope who expounded a modern approach to Catholic social teaching, writing many key encyclicals on matters such as employment and poverty in belated response to Karl Marx's *Communist Manifesto*. Trained in diplomacy, Leo believed that the papal diplomatic service had a crucial role to play in both the implementation of internal Church discipline and the conduct of Church-State relations. He was also a keen educationist and intellectual, encouraging the study of Thomas Aquinas in seminaries. He had developed over the years, it appears, a knowledge and appreciation of the works of Newman, although he had unavoidably gained the impression that Newman was somewhat 'liberal', a view shared, of course, by Cardinal Manning. The old tensions between Manning and Newman appeared to have been quietly laid to rest, especially as Newman seemed permanently and safely in harbour in Birmingham. Events, however, were to bring them into sharp antagonism once more.

On the election of Leo XIII a rumour did the rounds in England that the new Pope would most likely make Newman a Cardinal. Whether the Duke of Norfolk had prompted the idea or not, England's leading lay Catholic decided to make it a reality by getting support from other great and good Catholics of the time. According to Manning's first, and not always accurate biographer, Purcell, when the matter was broached the Cardinal bowed his head and appeared struck dumb for a while, before pulling himself together to acquiesce reluctantly in the idea of sending a petition to Rome.

Manning's letter to Rome is reserved, stressing that the request came from leading English lay men rather than the hierarchy; his own endorsement is polite rather than enthusiastic. Cardinal Edward Henry Howard, resident in Rome and charged with the care of Anglican converts to Catholicism, was to take the letter personally to Rome. He received it from Manning in August of 1878, but it still had not reached Cardinal Nina who dealt with such matters when the Duke of Norfolk turned up in Rome in December. When Norfolk raised the matter with Leo, it was the first the Pope had heard of it. So Norfolk asked Manning to write once again. He did not. In the meantime the original letter at last reached the Pope in the New Year. So Leo asked Cardinal Nina to write to Manning to 'enquire, with the necessary tact and discretion, of the Rev. Fr Newman, or better still of his Bishop or other trustworthy person, what are his dispositions in regard to accepting the sacred purple, should it be offered him by the Holy Father'.[21]

Manning now came off looking every bit as devious as Newman ever thought him to be. To Bishop Ullathorne, Newman's bishop, had been assigned the task of formally telling Newman that the Pope wished to honour him with a Cardinal's hat. Newman felt greatly honoured, but he was naturally anxious about the prospect of having to move to Rome rather than remaining in Birmingham. Cardinals who were not archbishops of dioceses normally took up residence in Rome. Ullathorne was conscious of this problem, so he suggested that Newman should write a letter of thanks to the Pope, pointing out how difficult it would be for him to leave Birmingham. At the same time, Ullathorne wrote a covering letter, explaining that Newman nevertheless accepted the honour of the Cardinalate, yet pleading with the Pope to allow Newman to stay put in Birmingham.

Manning forwarded Newman's letter to Cardinal Nina (and hence to Leo XIII), with its fears about living in Rome, and failed to send Ullathorne's accompanying letter confirming that Newman had accepted the Cardinalate. Furthermore, within a day or two it was published in the British newspapers that Newman had been offered the red hat, but had refused. As *The Times* reported on 18 February 1879: 'We are informed that Pope Leo XIII has intimated his desire to raise Dr Newman to the rank of Cardinal, and that with expressions of deep respect of the Holy See Dr Newman has excused himself from accepting the Sacred Purple.'[22]

Newman was devastated. Offers of the hat were conducted with the greatest discretion; nobody was supposed to know except the Duke of Norfolk, Manning, Ullathorne, and Newman himself. And now it looked as if a loose-tongued Newman had insulted the Pope by refusing the honour. By this time both Manning and Cardinal Howard were in Rome and after a bombardment from the lay Catholic great and good they went to see the Pope to explain and resolve matters. Whereas the very first letter had travelled with the tardy courier Howard the summer before, taking six months to arrive in Rome, Manning sent

Ullathorne a telegram saying that the Pope had sanctioned the Cardinalate and that Newman would be allowed to remain in Birmingham.

Newman travelled to Rome by rail with William Neville, who had taken the place of Ambrose St John as his companion and factotum. Father Thomas Pope, a late-vocation Oratorian, already in Rome, and staying at the English College, joined the party which finally met the Pope. Newman wrote to his friend Henry Bittleson from Via Sistina where he had taken rooms on 2 May:

The Holy Father received me most affectionately – keeping my hand in his. He asked me 'Do you intend to continue head of the Birmingham House?' I answered, 'That all depends on the Holy Father'. He then said 'Well then I wish you to continue head'; and he went on to speak of this at length, saying there [was] a precedent for it in one of Gregory xvi's cardinals.

He asked me various questions – was our house a good one? was our Church? how many were we? of what age? when I said, we had lost some, he put his hand on my head and said 'Don't cry'. He asked 'had we any lay brothers?' 'how then did we do for a cook?' I said we had a widow woman, and the kitchen was cut off from the house.[23]

Newman added this vivid description of Leo: 'I certainly did not think his mouth large till he smiled, and then the ends turned up, but not unpleasantly – he has a clear white complexion his eyes somewhat bloodshot – but this might have been the accident of the day. He speaks very slowly and clearly and with an Italian manner.' When it was time to go he took Newman's arm and led him to the outer door of the papal apartment. Then Cardinal Nina kissed him on both cheeks. As Newman was to say to Bishop Ullathorne, who reported it to Manning: 'The cloud is lifted from me for ever.'[24]

A reception took place on 12 May in Cardinal Howard's apartments, where Newman received the special *biglietto*, the summons to attend the conferring of his red biretta personally by the Pope, set for the following morning. On receiving the letter Newman made the address, known as the *biglietto* speech of acceptance. Father Pope observed that although Newman had a heavy cold 'he did not cough – and his delivery was very animated, and perfect, as the vehicle of his words … The Italian ladies behind me were unanimous that he was: "che bel vecchio! che figura! … pallido si, ma bellissimo" [What a beautiful old man! How elegant! … Pale, yes, but very handsome].'[25]

The next day, 13 May, he received the biretta from the Pope, and the day after took possession of the Cardinal robes at the English College along with his chosen motto: *Cor ad cor loquitur*: Heart speaks to heart, echoing the note written by Beethoven on the score of his Mass in D: 'From the heart – may it go to the heart again.'

BIGLIETTO SPEECH

In the *biglietto* speech, delivered on the eve of his investiture as Cardinal, Newman told a select audience of ecclesiastics and English lay persons gathered in Cardinal Howard's *salone* in Rome that his life's work, as an Anglican and as a Catholic, had been a struggle against 'liberalism in religion'. This liberalism, he went on, was a 'great mischief' and 'an error overspreading, as a snare, the whole earth'.

There followed an eloquent warning of the danger inherent in liberalism as religious toleration and religious relativism: the idea that one religion may be as good as any other, or indeed as no religion at all. Liberalism

teaches that all are to be tolerated, for all are matters of opinion. Revealed religion is not a truth, but a sentiment and a taste; not an objective fact, not miraculous; and it is the right of each individual to make it say just what strikes his fancy. Devotion is not necessarily founded on faith. Men may go to Protestant Churches and to Catholic, may get good from both and belong to neither. They may fraternise together in spiritual thoughts and feelings without having any views at all of doctrine in common, or seeing the need of them.[26]

He goes on to claim that in a liberal society, what we might call a pluralist, secular society today, the public promotion of religion becomes intrusive. The idea that religious opinions expressed publicly undermine the rights of others not so minded was prophetic. In these circumstances religion is a 'private luxury', he said, which one might have 'if he will; but ... which he must not obtrude upon others, or indulge in to their annoyance'.[27]

This liberalism, he asserts, began on the continent of Europe, where the great apostasy came about with the widespread abandonment of faith itself, by nation States and individuals. In his own country, however, the collapse of religion stems from the 'religious sects, which sprang up in England three centuries ago'. He is speaking, of course, of the variety of dissenters and Evangelical groups that have challenged the 'Union of Church and State, and would advocate the un-Christianising of the monarchy and all that belongs to it' since such a disestablishment would 'make Christianity much more pure and much more powerful'.[28] The stance is interesting, since forty years earlier he seemed to be urging the independence of the Church of England from the Government and Parliament, arguing that no secular political system (composed of dissenters and unbelievers) should have the authority to abolish Anglican dioceses in Ireland. In 1879, however, he is focusing on the Christian monarchy as representative of the unity of Church and State – although the monarchy had of course long been constitutional.

Then comes, nevertheless, a prediction that raises more questions than it answers, or could possibly answer.

Consider what follows from the very fact of these many sects. They constitute the religion, it is supposed, of half the population; and, recollect, our mode of government is popular. Every dozen men taken at random whom you meet in the streets have a share in political power, – when you inquire into their forms of belief, perhaps they represent one or other of as many as seven religions; how can they possibly act together in municipal or in national matters, if each insists on the recognition of his own religious denomination? All action would be at a deadlock unless the subject of religion was ignored. We cannot help ourselves. [29]

Thus Newman goes to the heart of the dilemma that faces not only the Catholic faith, but any of the Christian denominations and main non-Christian Faiths active in our complex societies today. He surely did not think that the sects could simply disappear, or be converted to Anglicanism or Catholicism. They were there to stay, and to increase and multiply. Hence he clearly accepts that, in England, the process of expanding secularisation was inevitable. He has no answers for this, other than dependence on God's providence. What he did not, and perhaps could not, envisage was the positive requirement of a secular government to protect the religious freedoms in a multi-Faith society. Nor could he have envisaged the development of Catholic principles of religious freedom that were only endorsed, and with difficulty, in 1965 at the very end of the Second Vatican Council.

It is arguable, however, that he had already foreseen the theological underpinning of individual religious freedom, by invoking the importance of conscience and 'private judgment'. He was also prepared, in the speech, to grant the 'liberalistic theory' much that is 'good and true; for example, not to say more, the precepts of justice, truthfulness, sobriety, self-command, benevolence, which, as I have already noted, are among its avowed principles, and the natural laws of society'. Yet he was of his age, and personal history, in seeing that these selfsame benefits of liberalism prove an enticement to deeper and total secularism: 'the device of the Enemy so cleverly framed and with such promise of success.' [30]

It would have dawned on many of his listeners that his bold anti-liberalism was paradoxical and ironic. Pope Leo would remark later of Newman's elevation: 'My Cardinal! it was not easy, it was not easy. They said he was too liberal.' [31] Despite that famous anti-liberal profession in Rome, Newman from his own day to this has been claimed by 'progressives' as one of them. The outspoken laymen Acton and Döllinger certainly thought of him as on their side and were disappointed when he refused to carp publicly about the shortcomings of the Holy See.

CHAPTER 18

Last years and death

'To be detached is to be loosened from every tie which
binds the soul to the earth ...'

J. H. NEWMAN, *HISTORICAL SKETCHES*

After he had received the Cardinal's hat, Newman had twelve more years to live. His work as an author was at an end, although his flow of correspondence continued unabated into his late eighties. There were old friends and young members of family to keep up with; and deaths. He would occasionally go into the school. Hilaire Belloc remembered him standing at the classroom door, weeping as he heard Virgil's *Aeneid* being read out (whether the tears were for the poetry or the brutal juvenile rendition, Belloc did not say).

An old friend, Charles Furse, visited the Oratory in the late 1870s and recorded: 'He looks well, and *so happy.*' Gone was the furrowed brow of the earlier days. 'There is not a line about him that is careful or severe – especially when he is going to say something about any one given *his* point of view, he has the gentlest apologetic smile.' Furse went on: 'He is less acute in look, and voice, and mind than he was, if acuteness means sharpness with a turn towards harshness; but he seems as facile, and quick, and fluent in thought and action, as ever.'[1]

Matthew Arnold, aged fifty-seven, met Newman at the Duke of Norfolk's house in St James's Square, a year after the bestowal of the hat. Arnold wrote of the encounter:

Newman stood in costume, in a reserved part of the drawing room, supported by a chaplain and by the D. of Norfolk. Devotees, chiefly women, kept pressing up to him; they were named to him, knelt, kissed his hand, got a word or two and passed on ...

Arnold made 'the most deferential of bows' when it came to his turn. He went on: '[Newman] took my hand in both of his and held it there during our interview.' Newman said to Arnold: 'I ventured to tell the Duchess I should like to see you.'[2]

Newman's charisma still had power impress; even to heal. A visitor at the Oratory reported how Newman healed his toothache: 'at the instant of touching his hand when he received me, my pains vanished, nor did they return while I was staying in the house. Newman's was a wonderful hand, soft, nervous, emotional, electric. I felt that a miracle had been wrought.'[3]

213

Writing on his knees one day, he wondered whether with the passing of time he had 'less sensible devotion and inward life'. He wondered whether it was age itself: 'Old men are in soul as stiff, as lean, as bloodless as their bodies except so far as grace penetrates and softens them.' He prayed to St Philip for a share of the fervour the saint evidently enjoyed in old age.[4]

In his *Meditations and Devotions* he penned a remarkable, original prayer for fervour:

In asking for fervour, I ask for all that I can need, and all that Thou canst give; for it is the crown of all gifts and all virtues. It cannot really and fully be, except where all are present. It is the beauty and the glory, as it is also the continued safeguard and purifier of them all ... In asking for fervour ... I am asking for the gift of prayer ...[5]

As he entered his eighties, Newman continued to model his spirituality, his habits of prayer and devotion on the example St Philip Neri. He valued, he wrote, the domestic religious ambiance of a house of fellowship with restricted numbers, enough 'for a fireside'. He wrote, 'whether or not I can do any thing at all in St Philip's way, at least I can do nothing in any other'.[6] These habits and outlooks remained with him, and deepened, as he entered old age. Philip, he believed, was a modern funnel for the 'three great masters of Christian teaching',[7] St Benedict, St Dominic, St Ignatius. St Philip learned, as Newman put it in a sermon, 'from Benedict what to be, and from Dominic what to do, so ... from Ignatius he learned how he was to do it'.[8] Ignatius and Philip were, for him, exemplars of how to carry religious practice into the world:

An earnest enforcement of interior religion, a jealousy of formal ceremonies, an insisting on obedience rather than sacrifice, on mental discipline rather than fasting or hairshirt, a mortification of the reason, that illumination and freedom of spirit which comes of love ... these are the peculiarities of a special school in the Church, and St Ignatius and St Philip are Masters in it.[9]

Among the many religious virtues Newman studied and sought to emulate, the greatest, he declared, was that of detachment, which he declares in his *Historical Sketches* that he has learnt from Philip.

To be detached is to be loosened from every tie which binds the soul to the earth, to be dependent on nothing sublunary, to lean on nothing temporal; it is to care simply nothing what other men choose to think or say of us, or do to us; to go about our own work, because it is our duty, as soldiers go to battle, without care for the consequences; to account credit, honour, name, easy circumstances, comfort, human affections, just nothing at all, when any religious obligation involves the sacrifice of them.[10]

'Work' now centred on the Mass, the liturgical round, and his prayer life. He was said to be punctual at every duty, arriving before the bell rang. One

Oratorian Father has recorded his impression of Newman saying Mass before he was made Cardinal:

Ready vested before the clock struck, punctual to the minute, he would come out of the sacristy, and as often as not, before 1879, go to the St Joseph's Altar or the Bona Mors Chapel beyond. The opening *Judica me Deus* psalm and *Gloria* were said swiftly, with a swaying to and fro in many directions; the words of consecration were in an audible whisper, with lingering emphasis and a tone of awe at *mysterium fidei*. The *Pater Noster* was given as expressively as ever, and had speaking pauses without much sense of broken continuity. *Panem nostrum quotidianum* and *ne nos inducas* were tenderly expressed. He would blow out the candles after the last Gospel. [11]

After he became a Cardinal a partition was erected in his room, and his sleeping area was replaced by an altar where he said Mass; his bed was removed to a neighbouring room. On the partition were pasted passages from the Psalms: 'I was dumb, and was humbled … thou has made me a reproach to the fool. I was dumb, and I opened not my mouth…. Commit thy way to the Lord and trust in him…. And he will bring forth thy justice as the light, and thy judgment as the noon day.' [12]

On the wall overlooking the Epistle or right-hand side of the altar Newman had hung pictures and pinned memorial cards of his departed friends – including Ambrose St John, Joseph Gordon, Edward Caswall. Corresponding to these images of past intimates, he had a notebook with a cloth needle-pointed binding made by Mrs Pusey during her last illness. It contained the names of all his friends who would be remembered immediately after the consecration on the dates of the anniversaries of their deaths, but, for special friends, on a daily basis. He said his last Mass at his private altar on Christmas Day, 1889, telling a member of the community later that day: 'Never again, never again.'

He had learned by heart a Requiem Mass and a Votive Mass, and would repeat one or the other daily, in part or in whole, in the hope that he might manage the service one more time if his health improved. As he sat repeating the words of these Masses his face would light up. Father Neville, who had taken the place of Ambrose St John, left this manuscript note:

On these occasions the brightness of his face, the speaking intelligence of his eyes, the suppleness of limb and joint and neck in his expressive little gestures, the vigour too with which his whole body seemed to be filled, were somehow wonderful to see – this is how memory pictures him at such times. So solemn was it to witness this, that it would bring a momentary feeling of both expectation and disappointment combined, as one then called to mind, what Gallonio and Bacci have described of St Philip. [13]

When he could no longer recite the Breviary he substituted the saying of the Rosary with Bishop Ullathorne's permission. His beads were always in his hands.

215

He claimed that its routine made up for the loss of the Divine Office. In time he gave up the Rosary when he could no longer feel the beads.

Bishop Ullathorne, himself an octogenarian, records a late encounter:

I have been visiting Cardinal Newman to-day. He is very much wasted, but very cheerful. Yesterday he went to London to see the oculist. When he tries to read, black specks are before his eyes. But his oculist tells him there is nothing wrong but old age. We had a long and cheery talk, but as I was rising to leave, an action of his caused a scene I shall never forget, for its sublime lesson to myself. He said in low and humble accents 'My dear Lord, will you do me a great favour?' 'What is it?' I asked. He glided down on his knees, bent down his venerable head and said 'Give me your blessing'. What could I do with him before me in such a posture? I could not refuse without giving him great embarrassment. So I laid my hand on his head and said: 'My dear Lord Cardinal, notwithstanding all laws to the contrary, I pray God to bless you, and that His Holy Spirit may be full in your heart.' As I walked to the door, refusing to put on his biretta as he went with me, he said: 'I have been indoors all my life, whilst you have battled for the Church in the world.' I felt annihilated in his presence: there is a Saint in that man! [14]

One last glimpse of Newman at prayer is recorded in Ward's biography. It was Good Friday, 1890, his last. He was kneeling in St Philip's Chapel, where, according to the rite of the day, the Blessed Sacrament was kept in 'repose'. He was observed 'with his face in his hands, or with his hands clasped against the back of his head'. [15]

DEATH

That summer Cardinal Newman was 89 and barely clinging to life. He had suffered several falls earlier in the year and was mainly confined to his room, capable of little more than shuffling a few yards; arthritic, toothless, with failing eyesight and faulty memory. Bishop Herbert Vaughan reported that he was now hardly recognizable from his former self: 'doubled up like a shrimp and walking with a stick longer than his doubled body ... his mind very much impaired.' [16] Another wrote that he 'looked like a corpse'.

Then, on Saturday, 9 August 1890, Father William Neville was surprised by approaching footsteps, 'firm and elastic'. Newman entered the room, 'unbent, erect to the full height of his best days in the fifties; he was without support of any kind'. His carriage, according to Father William, was 'soldier-like, and so dignified':

his countenance was most attractive to look at; even great age seemed to have gone from his face, and with it all careworn signs; his very look conveyed the cheerfulness and gratitude of his mind ... his voice was quite fresh and strong: his whole appearance was that of power combined with complete calm. [17]

Such is the stuff, one might think, of retrospective hagiography. But why would William Neville, who acted as the Oratorian infirmarian and was used to factual reporting, have exaggerated? Neville retired later that evening to the bedroom next to Newman's, believing that 'the Father', as he was known at the Oratory, had gained a new lease of life. After midnight Newman called out, complaining of hunger. Father William gave him something to eat. An hour later Newman called out again, saying that he felt 'very bad'. Doctors were summoned and pneumonia in one lung diagnosed. All day Sunday and into Monday he lay mostly unconscious, save for an hour on Sunday morning, when he asked Father William to read the Divine Office with him. Monday morning he received the last rites. His final words were: 'William, William ...' Around his neck was tied an old silk scarf given to him thirty years earlier during a bad period in his life. He liked to wear it as a comforter when troubled. Newman had once reflected that one passed, each year, without knowing, over the date of one's death, 'as if walking over one's own grave'. It was a quarter to nine in the evening, Monday, 11 August.

His body, mitred and vested, was placed within an open coffin on a catafalque in the Oratory church. The people of Birmingham came in their hundreds through the week. The *Catholic Times* reported: 'The effect of the pallid face with its clear cut features and aquiline nose, protruding chin and drawn lips, contrasting with the sable drapery of the church is startling in the extreme.' [18] A child who had strayed into the church declared to her mother that she had seen 'Mr Punch'.

The day after he died *The Times* newspaper confirmed his reputation for holiness: 'Of one thing we may be sure, that the memory of his pure and noble life, untouched by worldliness, unsoured by any trace of fanaticism, will endure, and that whether Rome canonises him or not he will be canonised in the thoughts of pious people of many creeds in England.' [19]

His Requiem Mass was celebrated in Birmingham on Monday, 18 August. In London, at the Brompton Oratory, there was a Mass at which his Eminence Cardinal Archbishop Henry Manning, Newman's chronic old antagonist, now aged 82, preached the eulogy. It was said of Manning during the winter of his life that 'the love of domination emanates from every pore of his body'. He appeared, according to the German historian Ferdinand Gregorovius, as a 'grey man looking as if encompassed with cobwebs'.

In his eulogy Manning emphasised not Newman's powerful and prophetic influence within the Catholic Church, but his past contributions to the Church of England which he had left forty five years earlier. He finished with this prayer: 'May our end be painless and peaceful like his.' [20] Two years later Manning himself would be dead.

If Manning's peroration was tepid, most others were fervid. Newman's friend

R. H. Hutton wrote to the bereaved Oratorian Fathers, that 'to the world that really knew him' his death left the impression of 'a white star extinguished, of a sign vanished, of an age impoverished, of a grace withdrawn'.[21]

Reflections on Newman's contribution to the Anglican and Catholic Churches were summed up by the lead article in *Guardian*:

Cardinal Newman is dead, and we lose in him not only one of the very greatest masters of English style, not only a man of singular purity and beauty of character, not only an eminent example of personal sanctity, but the founder, we may almost say, of the Church of England as we see it. What the Church of England would have become without the Tractarian Movement we can faintly guess, and of the Tractarian Movement Newman was the living soul and the inspiring genius. Great as his services have been to the communion in which he died, they are as nothing by the side of those he rendered to the communion in which the most eventful years of his life were spent.[22]

During the week of his death, the *Spectator* delivered perhaps the most thoughtful of all the eulogies in the secular press:

There was nothing in him of the spiritual pride and grandiosity of detachment from the world. He was detached from it in the simplest and most sensitively natural manner, as one who was all compact of the tenderest fibres of human feeling, even tho' he did not permit himself to plunge into its passions and its fascinations. Yet how delicately, how truly he read human nature – its smallness as well as its greatness; its eagerness about trifles; its love of the finest gossamer threads which connect it with its kind; ... all this Newman represented to himself and to his hearers with a vivacity which made his own detachment from the world all the more impressive, his own passionate absorption in the spiritual interests of life all the more unique and emphatic.[23]

The coffin was carried on a carriage to the graveyard in the Lickey Hills, a quiet spot among tall trees and rhododendrons, close to the Oratorian summer house. The *Birmingham Post* of 20 August 1890 takes up the story:

When the rites had been achieved, the crowd without the gates was suffered to enter by batches and see the grave; and then the coffin was covered with mould of a softer texture than the marly stratum in which the grave is cut. This was done in studious and affectionate fulfilment of a desire of Dr Newman's which some may deem fanciful, but which sprang from his reverence for the letter of the Divine Word; which, as he conceived, enjoins us to facilitate rather than impede the operation of the law 'Dust thou art, and unto dust shalt thou return'.

For some, in retrospect, that hope for rapid bodily corruption signified his acceptance of physical annihilation, in certain hope of the resurrection.

In a note in Father William Neville's keeping, following instructions on the funeral, Newman had written: 'If a tablet is put up in the cloister, such as the three there already, I should like the following, if good Latinity, and if there is no other objection – eg. it must not be, if persons to whom I should defer thought it sceptical.'[24] The inscription on the tablet is as follows:

JOANNES HENRICUS NEWMAN
EX UMBRIS ET IMAGINIBUS
IN VERITATEM
DIE – A.S.18
Requiescat in pace

It is interesting that Newman should think that the inscription might be taken amiss as 'sceptical'. Given the brevity of the epitaph, the scepticism Newman had in mind might have speculated on a Platonic view of life – the Cave, perhaps, where human beings are depicted as prisoners in an illusory world of images, which only dimly and inaccurately represent the truth.

CHAPTER 19

Connubium in death

'He came to me as Ruth to Naomi ...'

J. H. NEWMAN LETTER TO LADY KERR, 1875

The wish to be buried with Ambrose St John was first recorded on 23 July 1876, a year after St John's death, in the notebook carefully kept by William Neville for more than twenty-six years. 'I wish with all my heart, to be buried in Fr Ambrose St John's grave – and I give this as my last, my imperative will.'[1]

In February of 1881, Newman had added to the above instruction 'This I confirm and insist on', to which he had added 'and command'. He could not have been plainer: *confirm, insist, command ... wish with all my heart.*

Yet this is not the whole story of his instructions for burial. There is a small pencilled plan, close to these notebook burial instructions, made up of lines and initials. There is a sketch of what is clearly St John's grave, marked by '*asj*'; and on either side two other pencilled plots: one marked '*e*', the other marked '*joseph*'. The significance becomes clear to any visitor to the Oratorian graveyard at Rednal, which I first visited on that rainy day as a student at Oscott. The grave Newman shares with St John is flanked by those of Edward Caswall and Joseph Gordon, who had died in 1853 and 1878. It was Gordon who had died shortly after his exertions in Italy while attempting to find evidence to defend Newman in the Achilli libel trial. Caswall had in many respects taken on the heavy duties of St John, after his death in 1875. After Caswall's death, Newman had written a letter:

Though I want to do many things before I die, it seems unnatural that those who are so much younger than I am, should be called away and that I should remain. Three great and loyal friends of mine, Frs Joseph Gordon, Ambrose St John and Edward Caswall now lie side by side at Rednal, and I put them there.[2]

Did he mean that he had merely 'put them' side by side, or that he had actually 'put them', sent them, as a result of the burdens he put upon them, into early graves? From all that we know of Newman's remorse at their early deaths, he almost certainly meant both. While St John had a special place in his heart, confirmed by his insistence on their joint burial, he also saw himself in a loving relationship beyond death with his two other friends and helpmates. What is more, the companionship he envisages in death pointed forwards, while New-man was still alive, and backwards, in his imagination, to the communion of friends whose pictures looked down upon the altar in his room, drawing all of them into the fellowship in life and beyond death of the Eucharist – locating their immortal love in the Body of Christ – the very centre and ground of his spiritual life.

When the attempted exhumation of Newman's remains took place in October 2008, it was an occasion to ponder these circumstances and their significance. The popular media took over the story, obscuring to a large extent the nuanced, spiritual meaning of Newman's burial instructions. The Oratorian Fathers had announced the need to remove Newman's remains to a more accessible place for public veneration. But it was widely suggested that the Vatican had been anxious lest Newman's union in death with his friend in life should be interpreted as evidence of a gay relationship.

My memory of Newman and St John's grave had no context for me until I came across two more such joint, religious same-sex friendship unions in death. The discoveries occurred a quarter of a century apart, and raised questions about Newman and St John. In 1964 I arrived at Christ's College, Cambridge, as a graduate student. On the first day of term the Master, the famous chemist, Lord Todd, lectured new arrivals in the college chapel. It was an outlandish pep-talk on the importance of using condoms; there were three young Catholic monks from the Abbey of Downside seated opposite me, whose faces grew redder by the minute. But equally distracting, on the wall above the Communion table, was a magnificent monument. It was dedicated to two seventeenth century former members of the college, Sir John Finch and Sir Thomas Baines, whose remains were buried together in the chapel. The monument depicts two plinths, joined by a knotted sheet, surmounted by portraits in stone of the two men. Above is a single lighted vessel, as if to signify that two flames burn brighter than one. Surrounding and unifying the effigies is a sculpted garland of roses, tended by two cherubs, more suited for a nuptial than a funereal celebration. Finch and Baines, both unmarried, had been students together, forming a last-ing intimacy. The imagery of their monument is confirmed in the words of their epitaph: 'So that they who while living had mingled their interests, fortunes, counsels nay rather souls, might in the same manner, in death, at last mingle their sacred ashes.'

I was to remember that monument, twenty-five years on, when staying at the Venerable English College, the seminary for England and Wales in Rome. On the wall of the college chapel, again close to the altar, was a memorial to 'the Reverend Nicholas Morton, priest, Englishman and celebrated doctor of sacred theology'. The inscription proclaims that it was 'his wish to be buried in the same tomb with the Reverend John Seton with whom he fled from England for the same cause, that of religion, and who came to Rome at the same time'. I later learned that the two priests died twenty years apart, but Morton's love and determination on joint burial had survived the interval.

It was not until I read the late Alan Bray's remarkable book, *The Friend* (Chicago, 2003), that I came to appreciate the potential significance of these three joint same-sex burials of friends. Bray not only cited the three examples known to me, but a wide circuit of similar tombs and graves involving religious people, both men and women, from England to the Middle East, spread across the entire second millennium. They included a joint tomb at Gonville and Caius College, Cambridge, and another in the chapel of Merton College, Oxford. Quoting the inscription on the Christ's College monument, Bray argued that the text echoed Jeremy Taylor's seventeenth-century *Discourse on Friendship*, in which he speaks of friendships' 'marriages of the soul, and of fortunes and interests, and counsels'.[3] Bray saw the Christ's College burial, in the light of the monument's inscription, as a form of 'connubium', or marriage in death. He produced evidence that such public commitments to special friendship were common in pre-modern times, and he rejected the contemporary tendency to project homoerotic desires where none may have existed.[4]

In the final chapter of *The Friend*, published five years ahead of the attempted exhumation of Newman, Bray proposes that Newman's wish to be buried with St John connected with traditions of joint same-sex burial that had been eroded and finally lost in the Enlightenment:

My argument has been that Newman's burial with St John cannot be detached from Newman's understanding of the place of friendship in Christian belief or its long history … The Enlightenment put aside this traditional ethic with contempt and put in its place a Fraternity that it claimed would be 'universal', 'rational', even 'scientific'; but as the nineteenth century drew to its end, that experiment was terrifyingly failing and Europe was moving toward a war that would engulf the whole world, in fire and blood.[5]

Newman and St John lived and worked closely together for thirty years, but betrayed very little of the nature of their regard for each other save by unobtrusive public example. It was only following the death of St John, aged 60 in 1875, that Newman, then aged 74, recorded on 23 July 1876 his desire for joint burial. As he wrote, again and again, during this period of bereavement: 'he loved me with an intensity of love, which was unaccountable.'

RUTH AND NAOMI

Among his many letters after St John's death, Newman wrote to Lady Louisa Kerr, a convert to Catholicism, in thanks for her commiserations. The letter confirms a self-sacrificial devotion on St John's part, familiar in relationships where one partner supports an individual burdened with heavy responsibilities or demanding artistic toil. Newman accepted the support and service of St John as if it came from God. There is no indication that Newman returned the compliment of a supporting role in kind. He appears to have understood, in retrospect, however, that St John's self-sacrificing partnership allowed him freedom and energy to achieve his great literary, polemical and missionary goals.

At the same time, the letter indicates another, more intriguing and complex dimension of same-sex friendship, permeating their lives together. His letter to Lady Kerr begins:

I praise God for having given me for 32 years not merely an affectionate friend, but a help and stay such as a guardian from above might be, as making my path easy to me in difficulties, and cheering me by his sunny presence, as Raphael took the weight upon him of Tobias. I cannot think how I could have done anything without him, and, as knowing how timorous and unready I am, therefore doubtless God gave him to me. Just when all friends Protestant and Converts were removed from me, and I had to stand alone, he came to me as Ruth to Naomi.[6]

The drift of the letter is an admission that he was the passive recipient of St John's initiating love and practical service. The parallels from Scripture are of contrasting interest: first, the Angel Raphael in the Book of Tobit comes down from Heaven to assist Tobias, including salvation from live burial, and returns when his work is done. As Newman, and indeed others would recollect, when Newman and St John arrived in Rome to prepare for Catholic Holy Orders after their conversions, Ambrose was known among the Roman clergy as Newman's 'Angel Guardian', as much for his youthful face and golden hair as his role as faithful servant:

How I should ever in 1846 have gone to Oscott and then to Rome … how I should have journeyed to and fro, without him, I do not know and cannot fancy. At that time being young and fair he was even called by the Romans my Angel Guardian – and so on.[7]

As we shall see, St John would not long retain his angelic looks. He put on weight early, lost those golden locks, smoked cigars, and tended to speak loudly and ebulliently. His support of Newman, however, was unremitting, and he used his forceful, practical personality to ensure that Newman's every wish was fulfilled.

The second Biblical parallel, however, invokes the story of Ruth and Naomi. Naomi is an Israelite woman living in exile among heathens. She has lost her husband and two married sons, leaving her with two heathen daughters-in-law – Ruth and Oprah. Naomi tells her widowed daughters-in-law to return to their families in order to save themselves from want and danger. Oprah, after protestations of regretful sorrow, leaves, but Ruth refuses to abandon her Naomi.

Newman was to invoke this same story when preaching his final sermon before converting to Catholicism. It was known, as we have seen, as 'The Parting of Friends', preached before his Anglican congregation at Littlemore in 1844, the year before his conversion to Catholicism. That sermon, delivered in circumstances of high emotion, signalled his departure from the Anglican priesthood. Newman saw himself as the exiled Naomi, while Oprah represented friends who would remain within the Church of England. Ruth represented those who would stay with him on his sojourn into the Catholic Church, including St John.

In the letter to Lady Kerr, Newman evidently saw the parallel more in relation to their particular personal friendship over the years. To understand the significance of the Ruth-Naomi relationship, and how Newman might have viewed it, we need do no more than go to the words of Newman's 'Parting of Friends' sermon: 'Ruth clave unto her', preached Newman in the King James translation. 'And [Naomi] said, Behold, thy sister-in-law is gone back unto her people and unto her gods; return thou after thy sister-in-law. And Ruth said, Entreat me not to leave thee, or to return from following after thee: for whither thou goest, I will go; and where thou lodgest, I will lodge: thy people shall be my people, and thy God my God. Where thou diest, will I die, and there will I be buried; the Lord do so to me, and more also, if aught but death part thee and me.'[8] Newman now comments that the tears of the less loyal Oprah, the departing sister-in-law, were 'the dregs of affection'. He goes on, 'she clasped her mother-in-law once for all, that she might not cleave to her'. So, following the King James translation, Newman twice employs the verb 'to cleave', which means in this context to stick firmly to; although the connotation of the original Hebrew verb 'dabaq' extends to sexual and marital union, familiar in the second book of Genesis, where God ordains that Adam and Eve shall 'cleave' to each other. The 'cleave' verb is also used in the marriage service of the Book of Common Prayer.

It is hard to imagine that Newman, a master of subtle, multi-layered language, would not have appreciated the inferences to be drawn from Ruth's vow. Yet while there is a contemporary tendency to see a Lesbian or homosexual relationship in Ruth's devotion (the text of the vow is often used today in same-sex union ceremonies, as well as in marriages), this is only one reading of the story and the vow. The important feature of Newman's letter to Lady Kerr is his admission that he had acquiesced in a loving relationship, with nuptial undertones, not only until death, but beyond it. If Ruth is St John, as Newman claims, then the plea for joint burial, as Newman might have understood it, may well have come from St John.

The final section of the Lady Kerr letter, a summary of Newman's perception of the friendship, leaves no room to doubt the depths of St John's serviceable devotion and Newman's profound, almost addictive dependence on that devotion.

Never would he let me undertake any work without doing his part to save me the burden or the pain of it, as when he insisted on coming to Town with me on the day of your dear Brother's Requiem Mass. And so to the last, while his senses remained to him, his last thoughts were on a plan for my comfort; and, when he had lost them, he still knew me and flung his arms about my neck, and except one day when his fever was at its height, he obeyed whatever I ordered him and on the last day, when his senses were restored to him though he could not speak, again flung his arms over my neck and drew me tightly to him, he knowing he was near death, though we were exulting in the prospect of his recovery. [9]

Newman's bereavement was remarkable – he repeatedly told correspondents, as we have seen, that it exceeded the loss of a spouse:

I have ever thought no bereavement was equal to that of a husband's or a wife's, but I feel it difficult to believe that any can be greater, or any one's sorrow greater, than mine. [10]

That Newman's love for St John was essentially passive appears to be evinced by his statement, with echoes of the Book of Revelation: 'I was *his* first and last' [my italics]. In fact, with the exception of Hurrell Froude, Newman was all too conscious throughout his life of his essentially passive role in most of his deep friendships. 'It was not I who sought friends, but friends who sought me. Never man had kinder or more indulgent friends than I have had … Speaking of my blessings, I said, "Blessings of friends, which to my door *unasked, unhoped,* have come".' [11] Newman from the very beginning of his Catholic life declined, as we have seen, to follow the ordinance to avoid special or particular friendships – a principle of clerical ascetical practice established in the aftermath of the Counter-Reformation. His special friendship with St John, however, did not exclude affectionate relationships with others, both serially and simultaneously, including women. Not least of his women friends was Maria Giberne, an old friend of the family, who had painted Newman and St John sitting together at a table in the Propaganda College, Rome, in 1847. That painting is hung to this day, where it was during Newman's life, immediately outside his room. One of Giberne's descendents, Lance Sieveking, would describe her and her relationship with Newman, as it was passed down in the family, as follows:

She was a very beautiful woman with a wild, passionate nature … Many men fell in love with her, and so did women. She seems to have responded with embarrassing violence, irrespective of their sex, and with an entirely naïve innocence. The passionate friendship with John Henry Newman lasted all her life.

Sieveking also states laconically of her conversion to Roman Catholicism: 'She had fallen in love with John Henry Newman (later Cardinal), and this led to her conversion.'[12] She was not the only woman attracted to Newman by a combination of romantic and religious sentiment. Newman, however, while responsive in terms of the affectionate professions between friends of the time, including his wide circle of women, was always guarded, especially when sentimental demands were put upon him by women.

In 1844, Mary Holmes, a frequent correspondent who had evidently become infatuated with him in the period before they both became Catholics, scolded him for his failure to write to her with feeling: 'You are made of marble', she complained. And again: 'Cruel, hard-hearted Mr Newman, you would not even deign to tell me how you are … You keep me in the Church by a spell I cannot comprehend or break.'[13] A draft letter of rebuke from Newman, dated 4 February 1845, survives, in which he writes: 'What is my great offence but this, that I have ever regarded you in a religious point of view, not in an earthly? that I have ever thought how I might profit you in spiritual things, and, when I could do this no more, have felt my work as done.'[14]

Newman, however, was nevertheless capable of friendship with women that went well beyond purely spiritual profit. After the death of St John, Newman wrote to Maria Giberne, who had for many years been living as a nun in an enclosed convent in France under the religious name of Sister Maria Pia. The letter reveals a depth of sympathy that allows us to glimpse, albeit briefly, into Newman's own emotional vulnerability. First he commiserates with her for her own loss of St John, remarking that 'you have no partner nor confidant in your sorrow, and have no relief as having an outlet of it'. He adds a reflection about the oppressive 'feeling of solitariness' she must feel, before going on to describe the peculiarly receptive nature of his love for St John, and for her:

Since his death, I have been reproaching myself for not expressing to *him* how much I felt *his* love [Newman's emphasis] – and I write this lest I should feel the same about you, should it be God's will that I should outlive you.[15]

He goes on to mention how she had helped him when he was involved in the Achilli libel trial in 1852, this being 'only one specimen of the devotion, which by word and deed and prayer, you have been continually showing towards me most unworthy'. It seems to illustrate what the Abbé Brémond described as Newman's *autocentrisme*, a benignly self-referential, egoistic view of his life in relation to others. Was this *autocentrisme* unrelieved? Writing to a woman friend on 3 June 1875 he refers to Ambrose's death as a means of providential preparation for his own death, 'whenever that may be, to follow and to regain one who was my earthly light'.[16] '*My* earthly light.' It is the closest expression I have found in the vast evidence of Newman's writing of his own, outward-going, feelings for St John; and it is all the more powerful for its rarity.

NEWMAN, LOVE, AND THE CATHOLIC PRIESTHOOD

On the final page of the *Apologia*, Newman expressed gratitude to seven of his 'dearest brothers of this House, the Priests of the Birmingham Oratory'. For his friend St John, however, he reserved a special note of affection:

And to you especially, dear AMBROSE ST. JOHN; whom God gave me, when He took every one else away; who are the link between my old life and my new; who have now for twenty-one years been so devoted to me, so patient, so zealous, so tender; who have let me lean so hard upon you; who have watched me so narrowly; who have never thought of yourself, if I was in question. [17]

Reading that dedication George Eliot would write to a friend:

Pray mark that beautiful passage in which he thanks his friend Ambrose St. John. I know hardly anything that delights me more than such evidences of sweet brotherly love being a reality in the world. [18]

Newman thanks St John in the *Apologia* as the embodiment of all those 'affectionate companions and counsellors' who had been his 'daily solace and relief' in the early Oxford days, who showed 'true attachment' and who had 'never been disloyal to me by thought or deed'. [19] Other confreres are mentioned including Edward Caswall. Ever generous with tokens of gratitude, Newman had already dedicated the *The Dream of Gerontius* (published in 1865) to Joseph Gordon.

In contrast to the devotion and loyalty of the many friends cited in the *Apologia*, especially those he had known and loved in the Anglican days, Newman had for some years experienced the disloyalty of four Catholic priests who had nevertheless made professions of friendship. While Joseph Gordon was travelling fruitlessly around Italy during the Achilli trial days, Cardinal Wiseman, who possessed crucial trial evidence, could not be bothered to search for the necessary documents to relieve Newman's predicament. Wiseman even sent Gordon and Caswall on a futile journey to Naples to the wrong contacts. The same was true of Monsignor George Talbot, the Pope's 'Chamberlain', who for no cogent reason, save for apparent meanness of spirit, failed to provide another set of important trial papers in his keeping. As for Father Faber, during much of the period of the Achilli trial he was holidaying in Italy, consolidating yet another lengthy convalescence after one of his many hypochondriacal illnesses. He corresponded with Newman on several occasions, to report on his travels, diet, and health, but never a word of interest, much less commiseration, for Newman's trial; an omission Newman noted ruefully in a letter to St John. Meanwhile, Manning, as we saw in the matter of the *Rambler* article, was acting against him while offering bland tokens of friendship.

The relationship between Newman and Manning is of considerable interest since their scandalous quarrel resonates to our own day. Was Manning a cold, scheming autocrat who strove to undermine Newman as a result of their differences over papal authority and temporal power? Or is it possible that Newman himself was at least partly to blame for the antagonism between them? Was he, as Manning once alleged, 'a great hater'?

The historian, Professor Sheridan Gilley, has analysed with subtlety and breadth of understanding the gulf that opened up between these two crucially important religious leaders of the Victorian Age, arguing that their antagonisms were the result of 'different habits of mind'. Gilley claims that 'Manning saw no reason why intellectual and practical differences should cloud a personal friendship, even though in pursuit of a policy he would use a friendship to his own end'. Gilley is surely right to add that 'Newman gave unflinching loyalty to those who returned it, and where there had been a violation of that loyalty, no future friendship was possible'.[20] Gilley sees Manning's essential difference as his gift for politics in contrast to Newman's unpolitical nature. Yet there had been a time when Manning and Newman had shared a friendship based on mutual suffering.

When Newman and Manning were in their thirties, they had corresponded over the mortal illness of Manning's young wife of seven years. Newman wrote a characteristic letter of tenderness and consolation demonstrating not only his affection for Manning, but the profound nature of his understanding of love for those 'nearest to us when in the flesh'. It is a remarkable, paradoxical, reflection on the spiritual dimension of companionship in and beyond death:

If in His great wisdom and love He take away the desire of your eyes, it will only be to bring her really nearer to you. For those we love are not nearest to us when in the flesh, but they come into our very hearts as being spiritual beings, when they are removed from us. Alas! It is hard to persuade oneself of this, when we have the presence and are without the experience of the absence of those we love; yet the absence is often more than the presence.[21]

The conviction of this passage, as well as the compassion, reveals that Newman himself experienced such love, and very likely had in mind at that time the loss of his sister Mary and of Hurrell Froude. As he wrote in his 'David and Jonathan' poem: 'He bides with us who dies, he is but lost who lives.'[22]

After his wife's death, Manning would sit by her grave writing his sermons. Had he remained an Anglican priest he would hardly have continued this practice for a life time. But on becoming a Catholic and a priest he appears to have cauterised his feelings and instantaneously and deliberately, as if she had never existed. He destroyed all her letters and never spoke of her again. When he was informed that her grave had fallen into neglect, he remarked: 'It is best so, let it be. Time effaces all things.'[23] On becoming a Catholic priest this purging of sentiment may well have energised his political capacities. The impression, reinforced by Lytton Strachey's caricature, was that iron had entered his soul. And yet, this was not entirely so. As Manning lay dying he drew from under his pillow a book which he handed to Herbert Vaughan, his successor to be: 'Into this little book my dearest Wife wrote her prayers and meditations', he said. 'Not a day has passed since her death on which I have not prayed and meditated from this book. All the good I may have done, all the good I may have been, I owe to her. Take precious care of it.'[24] And yet, in common with the majority of conforming Catholic clergy Manning had not allowed another, or others, to take her place.

In 1848 we find Newman emphatically rejecting the isolation and inner reserve that went with the culture of Catholic clericalism. When he and Faber were together at St Wilfrid's, Cotton, Faber had reproved him for his evident 'special friendship' with St John. Faber, albeit superficially extravagant and sanctimonious in his endearments and professions of affection, was endorsing the Tridentine ascetical discipline that characterized close companionship with an occasion of sin. Newman, as we have seen, responded: 'I can do nothing to undo it, unless I actually did cease to love him as well as I do.'

It was perhaps unrealistic of Newman to think that he might have conducted a friendship with Manning such as he had experienced with Pusey, Keble, and others of his Anglican days. Experience had taught him that Manning, in common with those other English leaders of the ultramontane group, were capable of bland and smooth surface professions (as extolled by Cardinal Barnabò) concealing a quite different behaviour. Hence it was not only an act of disloyalty that stood between Newman and Manning, it was Newman's routine sense of not knowing where he stood with him. In August of 1867, four years on from the *Rambler* affair, Manning wrote to Newman suggesting a reconciliation: 'it would give me a great consolation to know from you anything, in which you have thought me to be wanting towards you.' Newman says it all in his reply:

I say frankly, then, and as a duty to friendship, that it is a distressing mistrust, which now for four years past I have been unable in prudence to dismiss from my mind, and which is but my own share of a general feeling (though men are slow to express it, especially to your immediate friends) that you are difficult to understand. I wish I could get myself to believe that the fault was my own, and that your words, your bearing, and your implications, ought, though they have not served, to prepare me for your acts.[25]

Newman added: 'I should rejoice indeed, if it were so easy to set matters right. It is only as time goes on, that new deeds can reverse the old. There is no short cut to a restoration of confidence, when confidence has been seriously damaged.'

The moving tributes to St John and others at the end of the *Apologia*, acknowledge friendship as the link of greatest value 'between my old life and my new'. St John embodied Newman's connection with the affectionate companionship, the 'daily solace and relief' of 'true attachment', learnt and treasured among his peer group as a young man in Oxford and carried into his life as a Catholic priest. Newman's greatest gift to the daily lives of Roman Catholic priests may yet be a lesson in the scope for mature, intimate friendship within a life of priestly celibacy.

CHAPTER 20

Newman's legacy

'The religious history of each individual', he once said, 'is as
solitary and complete as the history of the world.'

J. H. NEWMAN SERMON, 'STEADFASTNESS IN OLD PATHS', 1830

A friend of the Oxford days, Mark Pattison, wrote to Newman in their latter
years: 'However remote my intellectual standpoint may now be from that which
I may presume to be your own, I can still truly say that I have learnt more from
you than from any one else with whom I have ever been in contact.'[1] Newman,
as I suggested at the outset of this narrative, was, and is, for his time, and for
subsequent generations, one of those rare individuals who answers a variety of
needs in the souls of many – however remote his own standpoint from theirs,
or theirs from his. It is an appropriate juncture, then, to ask how Newman speaks
today to all manner of Christians, peoples of different Faiths, and indeed no Faith
at all.

Newman's broadest lesson is contained in the narrative of his life, and points
to a powerful basis for religious freedom and respect for all religions. Each, he
believed, will find God in the act of searching. Life is a pilgrimage, every personal
history unique. 'The religious history of each individual', he once said, 'is as solitary and complete as the history of the world.'[2] Writing in 1850 of the 'process
by which a soul is led from falsehood to truth', he asks:

Is *every* one born in a true system? is it not undeniable that, if there *be* a truth, the
majority of men *have* to change? *Can* they change without doubt and inquiry? Do you
think that those who have become Catholics, have done so to their own *gratification*?
Was truth forced on them, or a change passionately and greedily sought for?[3]

Having travelled through early scepticism, to Evangelicalism, to High Anglicanism, to Tractarianism, before finally coming to rest in the Catholic Church,
Newman of all people recognised the responsibility of each individual to be a
seeker after the truth: wherever it might lead. As he wrote in his poem 'The Pilgrim', of himself, he 'kept safe his pledge, prizing his pilgrim-lot'.[4] And this is a
pilgrim who not only finds himself, early in the journey, wandering by night
across rough terrain without roads, without maps, but climbing mountains.

We make progress, Newman wrote, 'not unlike a clamberer on a steep cliff,
who, by quick eye, prompt hand, and firm foot, ascends how he knows not

himself, by personal endowments and by practice, rather than by rule'.[5] He warns against blind leaps of faith, or acquiescence in unquestioned authority. The 'pledged pilgrim' accepts nevertheless without question the universal reality of individual conscience, and freedom of the will. None is spared, he is saying, the promptings of the voice of conscience; we are moral agents with the capacity and the obligation to make moral choices. While he encountered from his youth intimations of a personal Moral Judge within the voice of conscience, he was nevertheless seeking a religious truth that had a reality beyond himself. He was utterly opposed to the modern tendency to relegate religion to the realms of the private, the purely subjective. From the Early Fathers he adopted the notion that 'seeds of the Word' were spread throughout the great religions of the world, with salvic potential for those who had not been exposed to Christianity; the same idea would surface in the Second Vatican Council.[6]

The search for truth, he insisted, engages the whole person: 'The heart is commonly reached not through the reason, but through the imagination …' And the power of imagination was for Newman dialectical, playing on polarities that were familiar in the poetry of the preceding generation. Coleridge had anticipated Newman's dialectical 'saying and unsaying' in a vivid metaphor in the *Biographia Literaria*: like an insect caught in the eddies of a stream: '… the little animal *wins* its way up against the stream, by alternate pulses of active and passive motion, now resisting the current, and now yielding to it in order to gather strength and a momentary *fulcrum* for a further propulsion. This is no unapt emblem of the mind's self-experience in the act of thinking.'[7] Again, in the *Dejection Ode*, Coleridge employs the metaphor of the polarities of a magnet to suggest the 'polar forces', opposites that are neither mutually exclusive, nor self-contradictory. This dynamic in the expression of thoughts and images of God and religion is described more prosaically, yet no less powerfully, by Newman:

We can only remedy their insufficiency by confessing it. We can do no more than put ourselves on the guard as to our own proceeding, and protest against it, while we do adhere to it. We can only set right one error of expression by another. By this method of antagonism we steady our minds, not so as to reach their object, but to point them in the right direction … approximating little by little, by saying and unsaying, to a positive result.[8]

Following Bishop Joseph Butler, he counseled that 'doubt is the condition of our nature, and that the merit of faith consists in making ventures'.[9]

For the 'pledged pilgrim' there are moments of awakening, enlightenment. In the *Pillar of the Cloud*, the turning point is that moment of surrender to the light – 'Lead kindly light' – after the long, stagnant sterility of 'pride ruled my will'. Yet how is one to justify the ways of a good and all-powerful God?

Newman's 'saying and unsaying to a positive result' urges a remarkable mode of meditation based on evidence of the human condition and the possibility of God. It points to the obligation to journey, intellectually and imaginatively, back through the history of the writings, beliefs and rituals within our traditions; to explore the current claims and counter-claims of belief and unbelief in the light of our knowledge of good and evil through direct experience, and through our reading. As Newman puts it in a footnote to his translation of St Athanasius: 'Here one image corrects another; and the accumulation of images is not, as is often thought, the restless and fruitless effect of the mind to *enter into the Mystery*, but is a *safeguard* against any one image, nay, any collection of images, being supposed *sufficient*.' [10]

Newman's vision, I believe, goes to the heart of the problem of our own time: how do we foster spirituality and the common good in a complex, pluralist contemporary society, largely literate, enjoying the advantages of science and technology, and composed of people of different ethnic backgrounds and cultures, languages, religions, and indeed those who do not profess a religion at all? And the diversity includes not only religion, but education, art, literature, and indeed the vehicle of diversity in a modern developed society: publishing and the media.

Do we create the good society by allowing individuals and groups of individuals to search and choose their own values and beliefs, obviously within the constraints of civil law and under the protection of a more or less secular government? Or do we believe that our values and beliefs are best imposed, and accepted unquestioningly, top down? The options illustrate the difference between pluralism and fundamentalism: Newman, for all his animosity towards liberalism in religion, clearly would have defended religious pluralism today, and opposed fundamentalism. Taking his life as an exemplar, Newman insists that we must be free to seek our values and beliefs, free to refuse uncritical acquiescence to impositions from family, class, education, and established religion. At the same time, the conviction that each individual encounters the divine presence in the voice of conscience, leads to a powerful theological basis for universal respect. And if this is no less than the grounding of Christian *agape* – unconditional universal love based on human exaltation – it acknowledges the context in which such love must be struggled and worked for: 'Quarry the granite rock …': the deep stain in our nature. He was convinced that our evident exaltation and fallenness fits entirely with the truth of Christianity. That same acknowledgment, moreover, matched by an individual's right and duty to seek after truth, while respecting the life journeys of others, offers a resilient and robust condition for a flourishing pluralist society.

SCIENCE AND RELIGION

In Newman's day, as in ours today, science was seen as a formidable challenge to religious faith. The 1860s and 1870s, the years of the writing of the *Apologia* and the *Grammar of Assent*, were marked by a heated and noisy science-religion battle that reverberates to this day. While he attempted to distinguish between scientific and religious ways of knowing, he never saw them as inimical to each other. He thought deeply about science, respected scientific research, and attempted to keep abreast of the latest theories, while reflecting on the connections and distinctions between empirical method and faith. In the original fifth discourse of the *Idea of a University* he argues that there is nothing 'singular' or 'special' about theology which is not 'partaken by other sciences in their measure':

On the contrary, Theology is one branch of knowledge, and Secular Sciences are other branches. Theology is the highest indeed, and widest, but it does not interfere with the real freedom of any secular science in its own particular department.[11]

Newman believed that science and revelation must coexist, for both came from the same author. Science and religion, however, occupy different areas of discourse, and just as science should not interfere outside its province, so the Church should not interfere with the conduct of science. Science, in other words, needs elbow room. On the creation debate, which, again, was as vexed in the second half of the nineteenth century as it is today, Newman believed that the precise details of the Biblical account, six days and so forth, have never 'engaged the formal attention of the Church'; this being the case, 'it is not at all probable that any discoveries ever should be made by physical inquiries incompatible at the same time with one and all of the senses which the letter admits, and which are still open'.[12] Which seems a deliberately prolix way of suggesting, without frightening the orthodoxy watchdogs, that expression of cosmological facts in Scripture should remain forever open to interpretation. In a letter to J. M. Capes, editor of the *Rambler*, on 14 November, 1850, he wrote a remarkably insightful single line on the 'allowableness', and the 'advisableness' of exploiting new scientific theories, or discoveries, to bolster religion. 'We ought not to theorize the teaching of Moses, till philosophers have demonstrated their theories of physics. If "the Spirit of God" is gas in 1850, it may be electro-magnetism in 1860.'[13] The same might well be said, for example, of the version of the Anthropic Principle which finds God in the gap suggested by the accumulation of numerical accidents discovered within the laws of physics and chemistry that underpin a Universe hospitable to life.

On the question of the origin of species, Newman proved to be far less alarmed than his clerical peers. As early as 1840 he had commented on a familiar pre-

Darwinian version of evolution, which suggested the emergence of 'man's being originally of some brute nature, some vast mis-shapen lizard of the primeval period, which at length by the force of nature, from whatever secret causes, was exalted into a rational being, and gradually shaped its proportions and refined its properties by the influence of the rational principle which got possession of it'.[14] He went on to remark that 'such a theory is of course irreconcilable with the letter of the sacred text, to say no more', thus displaying an admirable if laconic openness to the notion that evolution might be true.

A year on from the publication of Darwin's *On the Origin of Species* we find Newman scoffing at Keble for suggesting that God had placed the fossils in the rocks so as create the impression of evolution. 'There is as much want of simplicity in the idea of the creation of distinct species', he wrote in a notebook in 1863, 'as in that of the creation of trees in full growth, or of rocks with fossils in them. I mean that it is as strange that monkeys should be so like men, with no *historical* connection between them, as that there should be no course of facts by which fossil bones got into rocks.' He went on to observe: 'I will either go whole hog with Darwin, or, dispensing with time and history altogether, hold, not only the theory of distinct species but that also of the creation of fossil-bearing rocks.'[15] Newman was not one to dispense with time and history.

Newman's most remarkable commentary on the *Origin*, however, is to be found in a letter to a Canon John Walker of Scarborough in 1868, ten years on from Darwin's publication of the theory. The Canon had sent Newman for inspection a critical review of Darwin's theory by a 'Graduate of the University of Cambridge'. Newman responded in the politest terms that the anonymous writer's critique was muddled – that it lacked certain points 'to be made good before it can cohere'. But then, to the point: 'I do not fear the theory so much as he seems to do – and it seems to me that he is hard upon Darwin sometimes.' There follows Newman's own reading of the theory:

It does not seem to me to follow that creation is denied because the Creator, millions of years ago, gave laws to matter. He first created matter and then he created laws for it – laws which should *construct* it into its present wonderful beauty, and accurate adjustment and harmony of parts *gradually*. We do not deny or circumscribe the Creator, because we hold he has created the self acting originating human mind, which has almost a creative gift; much less then do we deny or circumscribe His power, if we hold that He gave matter such laws as by their blind instrumentality moulded and constructed through innumerable ages the world as we see it.[16]

God's gift of human creativity – the 'originating human mind' – does not limit the Creator; so why should we limit the Creator's mode of creation? There is no necessary collision, he goes on, between such a theory of evolution, or as Newman puts it, 'principle' of development, 'or', he goes on, 'what I have called construction', and 'revealed truth'.[17] There follows a meditation on God's under-pinning authorship of design in the world, without appealing to a worked out proposal for Intelligent Design familiar in evolutionary debates today:

As to the Divine *Design*, is it not an instance of incomprehensibly and infinitely mar-vellous Wisdom and Design to have given certain laws to matter millions of ages ago, which have surely and precisely worked out, in the long course of those ages, those effects which He from the first proposed.[18]

The thought does not provide for an intervening, continuing, active process of 'Intelligent Design' on the part of God. He concludes with the reflection, 'I do not see that "the *accidental* evolution of organic beings" is inconsistent with divine design – It is accidental to *us*, not to *God*.' It would become a familiar refrain of Newman's down the years. To his friend St George Mivart, the Catholic zoologist, he would write, 'You must not suppose I have personally any great dislike or dread of his theory'. And to another: 'I see nothing in the theory of evolution inconsistent with an Almighty God and protector.'[19]

NEWMAN AND CHRISTIANITY TODAY

Newman's historic articulation of the fullness of Christianity is revealed in the entire story of his life. He and his fellow Tractarians had an enduring effect on the Church of England. After his death, some wrote that his influence over Anglicanism was greater than over his adopted Church. None then could have imagined his profound contribution to the renewal of the Catholic Church into the twenty-first century.

His influence begins with his manner of writing. His theological style, as we have seen, was literary, with a preference for the essay form, reacting to the promptings of occasions and circumstances, rather than an attempt at a system-atic opus. His beautifully crafted sermons, replete with fresh theological insights, followed the Church's year and its cycle of scriptural readings. He liked to describe himself as a 'controversialist' rather than a theologian. His literary imagination was alive with creative connections, his prose ever musical and elegant. His mode of writing was concrete, dialectical, interrogative: treading carefully, tentatively, towards a conclusion. By comparison, the Catholic theo-logical treatises of his time, many of them surviving down the generations into the twentieth century, were unrelievedly deductive, dogmatic, abstract, ahis-torical. He brought freshness, readability, clear thinking, accessibility, to the discipline of theology.

The sources of his theology, a legacy from Anglicanism, were in Holy Scripture; but then he became a master of the writings of the Early Fathers and the history of the early Church; he believed that tradition and Scripture were inseparable. He encouraged a historical approach to theology; he thought in terms of processes, development, as opposed to the timeless abstractions of neo-scholasticism. He employed the principle of development to rebut charges that Roman Catholicism had nurtured corruptions; the same notion would be invoked by future Catholic theologians to defend doctrines such as religious freedom. One can see the continuation of his influence in the works of the great French theologians of the mid-twentieth century – Henri de Lubac, Yves Congar, M. D. Chenu – who turned to the early Fathers and to history, exerting a powerful influence on the renewals and *resourcement* of the Second Vatican Council.

Newman's regard for the Virgin Mary was sober and constrained. Following the teaching of Ephesus, he accepted that Mary was the Mother of God, 'The Second Eve'. He enthusiastically accepted Mary's birth without original sin (the dogma of the Immaculate Conception, defined by Pius IX in 1854). When Pius XII was preparing to define the dogma of the Assumption, supporting commentaries, citing Newman, were written by the theologian Dr Henry Francis Davis of Oscott College who was the first promoter of Newman's cause for canonization. Newman, however, could not accept that Mary was the Mediatrix of All Graces, or a Co-Redemptrix, or that she was corporeally present in the Blessed Sacrament.

As we have seen, Newman insisted, often vehemently, that the role of the laity should be recognized, honoured, celebrated; that the laity was an indispensible part of the Church's 'faithful' ('the Church would look foolish without them'); the faithful gave back that crucial echo of authentic doctrine: the consensus. In his famous essay *On Consulting the Faithful in Matters of Doctrine*, he accused the bishops of the fourth century of having failed in their duty to defend the Church's orthodoxy: it was the faithful, embracing the laity, that saved the Church from error.

Newman criticized excessive clericalism, Roman centralization (ultramontanism), creeping infallibility, and the denial of the laity's right to make a contribution to the intellectual life of the Church. While defending the Church's teaching, and the necessity of nurturing an informed conscience, he nevertheless spoke boldly of the primacy of conscience over papal authority ('I shall drink to the Pope if you please – still, to conscience first and to the Pope afterwards …'). He saw the Church as a communion, and he urged that Catholics, and all Christians, should work for unity.

All these features – historicity, patristics, development, ecumenism, conscience, moderate Marianism, the role of the laity, local discretion over Roman centralization – underpinned the renewals of the Second Vatican Council leading to Paul VI's verdict that it was 'Newman's Council'. But the Council had its dissenters, resisters, at the very heart of the Curia. Cardinal Giuseppe Pizzardo, one of those who represented the continuity of the Curia of Pius XII at the Council, commented that these 'new ideas and tendencies' were 'not only exaggerated but even erroneous'.[20] That resistance to the renewals of the Council, and hence to Newman's influence, was never entirely broken, and it is arguable that the tide has been turning in recent decades with the promotion of the view that nothing of importance had been altered, or renewed, by Vatican II.

Will the beatification, and probable canonization of Newman, break this resistance? Will this honouring of Newman prove, as theologian Nicholas Lash hopes, 'a powerful signal that the Church has not abdicated its dedication to the movement of renewal and reform that the Council so wholeheartedly initiated'?[21] Those who share Lash's perspective have urged that Newman should be named a Doctor of the Church in confirmation of the acceptance of his theology.

There is, of course, another possibility: that Newman's elevation to the altar might signal the taming and enfeebling of his legacy by the resisters of Vatican II and of the fullness of his teaching. Newman's habit of 'saying and unsaying' towards a conclusion makes him vulnerable to distortion (obviously by those on both sides of the Catholic divide). One can only hope that his unforgotten voice will continue to find its way home and into the hearts of all pilgrims of conscience for the benefit of the fullness of Christianity.

Epilogue

Newman was aware that people thought him saintly, and he suspected that the Church might attempt to make him an official saint. In the time-honoured tradition of most figures who make it to sainthood, Newman assured his contemporaries, and posterity, that he was no saint; his reason: that he was a 'literary' man. It is likely that the request that his grave be filled with compost was to ensure that there would be no relics left to venerate. As it happens, Newman's beatification was sanctioned with some difficulties and after half a century, despite an inflation in saint-making during the long reign of Pope John Paul II.

While cults of sainthood developed around the relics of thousands of holy people from Christian antiquity to the end of the Middle Ages, the saint-making process, as it is practised in the Catholic Church today, is relatively recent, dating from the seventeenth century. Saints or Blesseds are traditionally deemed to have led exemplary lives. They provide the faithful with examples of how God wishes us to behave: not always an obvious notion since some behaved very oddly indeed by contemporary standards of holiness. Saint Simeon Stylites sat naked for thirty years on top of a pillar sixty feet high; the aerodynamic Joseph of Cupertino (patron saint of pilots, along with Our Lady of Loretto) used to fly up to the church rafters and scream when in ecstasy; Saint Margaret Mary Alacoque would routinely eat cheese, to which she was allergic, to bring on a vomiting fit. Benedict XVI recently promoted the life of Saint Jean Vianney, the Curé d'Ars, as an exemplar for today's priests, although it is known that he beat himself with a metal scourge at night, and slept on the floor with a log for a pillow.

John Paul II canonized and beatified a great many individuals, more apparently than all the previous popes put together from the time that the formal processes began in the reign of Pope Urban VIII (1623–1644). The choices were invariably associated with his many trips around the world. He was criticized by Spanish socialists for proclaiming the holiness of large numbers of priests and nuns killed in the Spanish Civil War. Many non-Catholics also died at the hands of Franco and his army. John Paul angered liberal Catholics, moreover, for canonizing the founder of the traditionalist Spanish group, Opus Dei. Sensitivity to the political fall-out attendant on the proposed beatification of the wartime Pope, Pius XII, has prompted controversy.

John Paul's enthusiasm for saint-making in Southern Europe, Africa, and South America, contrasts with a marked lack of new Blesseds and Saints in the Northern hemisphere during the same period. A senior Vatican official I spoke with during the millennium year informed me that, according to John Paul II, 'North European Catholics don't believe in sainthood or miracles in the way they used to. So they don't pray to candidates for sainthood to produce miracles essential for making more saints.' Normally one approved miracle is required for beatification (the recognition of a local cult), and a second for canonisation (recognition of a universal cult). An example of this lack of Northern miracles, I was assured, was Cardinal Newman. My informant said that John Paul frequently grumbled: 'I would like to beatify Cardinal Newman, but he won't do a miracle.' And the reason he would not, so John Paul believed, was that Catholics in England had not prayed for one.[1]

NEWMAN ON MIRACLES

The Church of England in Newman's day was not inclined to endorse miracle claims beyond the death of the last Apostle. So, even before becoming a Catholic, Newman felt obliged to explore and defend Catholic belief in miracles, as a feature of authentic Anglo-Catholicism against the Protestant wing of the Church of England.

When he was a don at Oriel and Vicar of St Mary's, he appears to have held not so much a sceptical view of miracles outside of Scripture as doubts about the very point of them. 'In matter of fact, then', he preached, 'whatever be the reason, nothing is gained by miracles, nothing comes of miracles, as regards our religious views, principles and habits. Hard as it is to believe, miracles certainly do not make men better; the history of Israel proves it.'[2] Without denying that miracles have ever taken place after the death of the last apostle, he asserts that since everyday life is full of miracles, what need have we of miracles beyond the evident works of God?

Now what truth would a miracle convey to you which you do not learn from the works of God around you? What would it teach you concerning God which you do not already believe without having seen it?[3]

A summation of Newman's views on miracles is to be found in the notes to the *Apologia* (see the Ian Ker Penguin edition),[4] where Newman explains his position in consequence of Charles Kingsley's criticisms. Kingsley had accused Newman of 'irrationality' for believing that the oil flowing from the bones of Saint Walburga, venerated in Anglo-Saxon times, had performed miracles of healing.

Newman makes a distinction between miracles performed in Apostolic times, and 'Ecclesiastical Miracles' performed down the ages by 'holy' people. He defends the authenticity of these, later Ecclesiastical miracles according to the logic of analogy: if God over-ruled the laws of nature during Apostolic times, there is surely no reason why He could not, or would not, do so in subsequent times. He makes a distinction between the two, however, which he had clarified in 1851, writing to Samuel Hinds, Bishop of Norwich:

The scripture miracles are credible – i.e. provable, on a ground peculiar to themselves, on the authority of God's word. Observe my expressions: I think it '*impossible to withstand the evidence* which is brought for the liquefaction of the blood of St Januarius'. Should I thus speak of the resurrection of Lazarus? – should I say, 'I think it impossible to *withstand the evidence* for his resurrection?' ... a Catholic would say, 'I believe it with a certainty beyond all other certainty, *for* God has spoken'.... On the other hand, ecclesiastical miracles may be believed, one more than another, and more or less by different persons.[5]

As for the incidence of ecclesiastical miracles, Newman's views coincide precisely with John Paul's on the reasons for geographical or cultural unevenness – for example, the absence of miracles in the Protestant North:

Since, generally, they are granted to faith and prayer, therefore in a country in which faith and prayer abound, they will be more likely to occur, than where and when faith and prayer are not; so that their occurrence is irregular.[6]

But how could and should one discern a miraculous event? Newman declares: 'Persons ... will of necessity, the necessity of good logic, be led to say, first, "It *may* be", and secondly, "But I must have *good evidence* in order to believe it".' He goes on, 'It *may* be, because miracles take place in all ages; it must be clearly *proved*, because perhaps after all it may be only a providential mercy, or an exaggeration, or a mistake, or an imposture'.

What does Newman mean by proof?

(1) That the event occurred as stated, and is not a false report or an exaggeration. (2) That it is clearly miraculous, and not a mere providence or answer to prayer within the order of nature.

Newman then proceeds to raise the question of science and miracles. 'I frankly confess that the present advance of science tends to make it probable that various facts take place, and have taken place, in the order of nature, which hitherto have been considered by Catholics as simply supernatural.' Does this not subvert the capacity to judge a great many alleged miracles as outside 'the order of nature'? He steps, however, beyond the official Vatican criteria for saint and beatus making miracles by insisting that God might well use the laws of nature to perform a miracle by merely interfering with the sequences of cause and effect:

An event which is possible in the way of nature, is certainly possible too to Divine Power without the sequence of natural cause and effect at all. A conflagration, to take a parallel, may be the work of an incendiary [arsonist], or the result of a flash of lightning; nor would a jury think it safe to find a man guilty of arson, if a dangerous thunderstorm was raging at the very time when the fire broke out … That the Lawgiver always acts through His own laws, is an assumption, of which I never saw a proof. In a given case, then, the possibility of assigning a human cause for an event does not *ipso facto* prove that it is not miraculous.[7]

Newman goes on to write of the supernatural nature of what he terms 'providences' or *grazie*, in other words extraordinary events that may have been the answer to prayer, or God's mercy or providence, without being clearly against the laws of nature.

Providences or *grazie*, though they do not rise to the order of miracles, yet, if they occur again and again in connexion with the same persons, institutions, or doctrines, may supply a cumulative evidence of the fact of a supernatural presence in the quarter in which they are found.[8]

For a growing number of Catholics, the criterion of inexplicability under-pinning a miracle is unsatisfactory for the reasons already cited by Newman – the shifting nature of explanation in science. A sea change in Catholic attitudes, following Newman's view, as above, may well be set to challenge the official 'scientific' scrutinies in Rome. But an alteration in the rules is unlikely without a battle.

An example of a more inclusive appeal of the miraculous is to be seen in the case of the Blessed Rupert Mayer, a Jesuit persecuted by the Nazis, who died in 1945. For many years in the post-war era there were as many as 8,000 visitors to Mayer's tomb in Munich on a single day. The Vatican apparently received up to 30,000 letters a year from the faithful with reports of remarkable changes in their lives after visiting his shrine: the jobless finding work, the depressed and suicidal returning to psychological health, broken marriages reconciled, alcoholics cured. But not one of these blessings could be taken as evidence for his beatification process. John Paul did not want to lose the idea that God intervenes directly, tangibly, and subject to 'proof', in answer to prayer.

JACK SULLIVAN'S MIRACLE

One wonders against this background what Newman would have made of the miracle in support of his own beatification. On 29 May 2008 five members of the 70-strong Consulta Medica, the body of medical experts available to the Congregation for Saints, announced that Mr Jack Sullivan, a 70-year-old Catholic deacon in Boston, Mass., was, in their view, healed in a manner that defied natural explanation. Mr Sullivan had been suffering from a serious back condition that threatened eventual paralysis, and caused him debilitating pain. He was obliged to walk virtually doubled-up. On two separate occasions, following two separate episodes of insupportable pain, Jack Sullivan prayed to Newman, and the pain disappeared. In the first instance the alleviation was for several weeks; in the second it was permanent, although this followed an operation that was intended to cure the underlying condition and bring long term relief.

The medical scrutineers do not speak of miracles, they state merely that the healing event was 'immediate, complete, lasting, and inexplicable'. A recommendation on the miraculous nature of the event is then made by a panel of theologians at the Congregation for the Causes of Saints before being passed up to the Pope for his decision. The following account is taken from the '*positio*' on Sullivan's miracle, the official investigation conducted by the Congregation at the Vatican. The succeeding citations in this chapter are drawn from that document, published by the Holy See in 2008.[9]

John Sullivan was born on 19 October 1938 and lives at Marshfield, Massachusetts, in the United States. On 6 June 2000 he began to suffer serious and debilitating pain in the back and both legs. He was taken to Jordan Hospital in Plymouth, Massachusetts, and the physician in the Emergency Room ordered a CAT scan. The scan revealed a serious succession of deformities to vertebrae in the lumbar area from L2–L5. His spine was badly 'herniated' causing severe 'stenosis' (the compression or choking of nerves in the lower back) resulting in pain and weakness in both legs.

There had been no evidence of previous trauma or history of chronic spinal deformity to warrant the condition. The doctor explained to him that the vertebrae and discs were depressed inward so as to intrude upon the spinal canal, squeezing his spinal cord and femoral nerves. He was advised to seek treatment immediately from specialists in Boston.

Sullivan was following a course of instruction in preparation for ordination as a deacon. Without relief from the pain he would be obliged to drop out of the course. On 26 June, he happened to be watching a TV program on Mother Angelica's EWTN channel on the life of Cardinal Newman. The viewers were asked to contact the Postulator of Newman's cause for beatification if they had received any 'divine favours or extraordinary experiences' resulting from their prayers for Newman's intercession. The address was posted on the screen. Sullivan says: 'In my anxiety over the prospect of losing my vocation [to the diaconate], I then felt a strong compulsion to pray to Cardinal Newman with all my heart.' Sullivan says that he made the following prayer: 'Please help me to some-how get back to classes and be ordained.'[10] He adds that he did not pray par-ticularly for healing but for greater persistence and courage that was evident in Newman's life. 'Immediately after my prayer', he reports, 'I suddenly experienced a new and uplifting sense of trust and confidence. I knew something would hap-pen as a result of my supplications.'

The next morning he got out of bed virtually pain free and began to walk without difficulty, whereas the day before he had been hunched over, having to place his right hand on his right knee to support himself when attempting to walk. 'The joy of that first moment filled my heart with gratitude for Cardinal Newman's intercession with God.'

Sullivan was examined on 6 July by a back specialist, Dr Stephen Parazin of Newton, Massachusetts. The doctor said that all Sullivan's lower functions could suddenly shut down at any time. 'Paradoxically', says Sullivan, '… I had normal strength in both legs and walked upright without major difficulty.' The doctor said that surgery seemed unnecessary, as the pain was almost gone. He then stated that he thought Sullivan could carry on with his diaconate classes, but if the pain returned or if he had any difficulties with his lower functions, he should immediately seek hospitalization.

On 15 July he went to see the neurologist Dr Brick. He took a scan and said that the vertebrae and the discs at L2–L5 were completely compressed on the spinal chord threatening the nerves associated with legs. He said that even if the pain had gone, he needed an operation. Perplexed by these two opinions he consulted a third specialist, Dr Cueni, who referred him to a Dr Banco, said to be the best neurologist in Boston. Banco said that the operation was very delicate, and since he had no pain it would be better for him to 'wait and see'.

In May of 2001 the pain came back again and his condition began to deteri-orate once more. He could only walk with difficulty. He went to see Dr Banco who was amazed that Sullivan had lasted for so long, but said that an operation was now inevitable. Sullivan says that he continued to pray to Cardinal Newman during this period. The operation was performed on 9 August and lasted for about six hours. Afterwards Dr Banco explained that the procedure was com-plicated. The lower spine was badly ruptured and there was significant tearing of the *dura mater* (the membrane surrounding the spinal cord housing protec-tive fluids). The fluids leak out causing the protruding bony areas to rub against the spinal cord. Dr Banco apparently said that it was a 'miracle' that Sullivan had survived throughout the summer. He said at one of the post-op meetings: 'I have absolutely no medical explanation to give you as to why your pain stopped. The MRI and subsequent surgery bear out the severity of your condi-tion. With the tear in your *dura mater* your condition should have been much worse. I have no medical or scientific answer for you. If you want an answer, ask God.'

After the operation Sullivan was in great pain and unable to walk, as was expected. On 15 August, sitting on his bed, he 'silently but fervently' prayed to Cardinal Newman: 'Please Cardinal Newman, help me to walk, so that I am able to get back to my classes.' Suddenly, he reports, 'I felt a very warm sensation all over my body and a sense of real peace and joy came over me. I immediately began to shudder and felt a very strong tingling sensation, which gripped my entire body. It lasted for what seemed a very long time, and was very strong. Then I felt a surge of strength and confidence that I could finally walk. I was suddenly free of my crippling pain even without the Demerol. My healing in this one moment became remarkably accelerated – two to three months in one moment of time. I then smiled, refused the walker and said: "I will walk with the cane." For the first time in several months I was walking upright, normally, and with real strength in both legs.' [11]

Sullivan went from strength to strength and as of September 2009, he has been free of pain and capable of walking normally. His doctors have expressed in writing their surprise at both instances of alleviation of pain and return of normal function. Dr Banco has testified that Sullivan's recovery after the operation was 'unbelievable, 100 per cent, totally remarkable! … I have never seen a healing process occur so quickly and completely.'

Dr Banco put in writing the following statement to Sullivan: 'Your recovery was extremely rapid and is clearly very much a rare exception rather than the rule for recovery after this type of surgery. I have been in practice for 15 years and have seen many cases similar to your case. I have treated probably over 1,500 patients with spinal stenosis. Your lack of pain preoperatively for that time period as well as your post operative recovery were truly miraculous, in my opinion.' [12]

What is one to make of this series of events? What is clear from the various accounts is that Jack Sullivan's underlying physical condition was neither altered nor cured by his prayers. In fact, it seems likely that his ability to continue walking on being relieved of the pain in June 2000 did further damage to his spine. The inexplicable nature of his condition relates to the relief of his pain on both occasions, and his consequent confidence to walk in June, and again, after his operation in August of the following year. According to the rules of the Congregation for Causes of the Saints the 'miracle' should be long-lasting; but the first relief was only temporary; the pain and debilitation returned the following summer. The rules further stipulate that improvement should not be the result of intervention, such as an operation; yet it is clear that the long-term healing of Sullivan's condition has been a result of his operation in 2001. The remarkable factor, therefore, relates to pain and swifter healing than was normal for such a condition. As Dr Banco wrote: Sullivan's recovery 'was extremely rapid and is clearly very much a rare exception rather than the rule for recovery after this type of surgery'. This seems to leave the door open to natural explanation: rare exception is hardly an admission of inexplicability as to the laws of nature.

Is it possible that Sullivan's 'miracle' was purely a matter of relief of pain and therefore explicable by placebo effect? The conclusions of the scientific board of five lay medical experts in the Vatican was that Sullivan's condition, on both occasions, would have made it impossible for him to walk normally, and that it was not simply a matter of relief of pain, but of an inexplicable underlying 'mechanical' physiology. In consequence the chair of the board, Professor Massimo Gandolfini, could state that the events were 'not completely explicable in scientific terms'.[13] By any criterion the events are unusual. It might be argued, however, that the relief of pain was a placebo effect and that the underlying problem was cured by surgery. Even so, the relief of pain fits at least with Newman's view of 'an event which is possible in the way of nature ...' performed by 'Divine Power without the sequence of natural cause and effect at all'.

Acknowledgements

For hospitality I thank Fathers Paul Chavasse and Gregory Winterton, former Provosts of the Birmingham Oratory, Dr Mark Harris of Oriel College, Oxford, and Sir Ivor Roberts, President of Trinity College, Oxford. For conversation and advice I thank Father Robert Byrne (Provost of the Oxford Oratory), Father Philip Cleeveley (of the Birmingham Oratory), Dr Padraig Conway (of Newman House, Dublin) and Dr David McLoughlin (of Newman University College, Birmingham); also Dr Tim Jenkins, Dr Ian Ker, Dr Kate Kirkpatrick, Dr Michael McGhee, Dr Rod Mengham, Professor Véronique Mottier, Professor John Milbank, Ashley Peatfield, Professor Stephen Prickett, Dr Roderick Strange. My friend and fellow 'Academician' Patrick O'Connor, who died suddenly in February 2010, presented me with a rare early recording of Elgar's 'Dream of Gerontius'. I benefited from the services of the Cambridge University Library, the British Library, and the London Library. I am grateful to Judith Champ, archivist at Oscott College, and Gerard Boylan, Oscott's librarian, for assistance with materials in his keeping, and the Fathers of the Birmingham Oratory for permission to quote from the 32 volumes of published Letters and Diaries of Newman. I am especially grateful to Professor Stephen Heath, Professor Nicholas Lash and John Wilkins for generously reading and commenting on the manuscript. Any remaining errors and misapprehensions are entirely my own.

    I thank James Bowman, Tony Lansbury, Jeff Scott, and Robin Baird-Smith. I owe a debt of gratitude to the Master and Fellows of Jesus College, Cambridge, for providing an ideal circumstance for research and writing. I thank Crispin Rope, as ever, for encouragement and support. Finally I thank my friend and agent Clare Alexander.

Notes to the chapters

Abbreviations used in the Notes:

A	J. H. Newman, *Apologia Pro Vita Sua* (Penguin, London, 2000) Ian Ker (ed.).
AW	Henry Tristram (Ed.), *John Henry Newman Autobiographical Writings* (New York, 1956).
Bouyer	*Newman: His Life and Spirituality* (London, 1958).
Culler	A. Dwight Culler, *The Imperial Intellect* (Yale, 1955).
Dessain	Charles Stephen Dessain, *John Henry Newman* (London, 1966).
Dev	J. H. Newman, *An Essay on the Development of Christian Doctrine* (Foreword by Ian Ker) (South Bend, Indiana, 1989).
G	J. H. Newman, *An Essay In aid of A Grammar of Assent* (London, 1891).
Gilley	Sheridan Gilley, *Newman and his Age* (London paperback edition, 2003).
Idea	J. H. Newman, *Idea of a University* (London, 1891).
Ker	*John Henry Newman* (Oxford, 1988).
LD	*The Letters and Diaries of John Henry Newman* (Ed. Charles Stephen Dessain, *et al.*), 32 vols (Oxford and London, 1961–2008).
PN	Edward Sillem, Ed., *The Philosophical Notebook of John Henry Newman*, 2 vols (Louvain, 1969–1970).
PPS	*Plain and Parochial Sermons*, 8 Vols (London, 1875).
Trevor i, ii	Meriol Trevor i, *Newman: The Pillar of the Cloud*; ii, *Newman: Light in Winter* (London, 1962).
Tristram	Henry Tristram, *Newman Centenary Essays* (London, 1945).
US	*Oxford University Sermons* (London, 1890).
Ward i, ii	Wilfrid Ward, *The Life of John Henry Cardinal Newman*, 2 vols (London, 1912).

The Notes

PREFACE

1. LD xx 443.

PROLOGUE

1. J. H. Newman, *Discourses to Mixed Congregations* (Leominster, 2002), 371–372.
2. *Ibid.* 373.

CHAPTER 1

1. A 15.
2. Trevor ii 338.
3. See G. Egner, *Apologia Pro Kingsley* (London, 1969), 4.
4. Quoted *ibid.*
5. L. B. C. Butler, *Life Ullathorne* (1926), 159.
6. James Joyce, *A Portrait of the Artist as a Young Man* (Ed. Seamus Deane) (Penguin; London, 2000), 190.
7. Quoted Samuel Hall, *A Short History of the Oxford Movement* (London, 1906). 51.
8. A 226.
9. Ward ii 361.
10. LD xx 169.

11. *Ibid.* vi 193.
12. Idea 284, 285.
13. I am indebted for this reflection to the late Geoffrey Tillotson's excellent introduction to the None-such edition of Newman, alas out of print.
14. J. H. Newman, *Discourses Addressed to Mixed Congregations,* 90.
15. Ward i 229.
16. A 213.
17. *The Theological Papers of John Henry Newman on Faith and Certainty* (Ed. J. Derek Holmes) (Oxford, 1976), 102.
18. A 219.
19. LD xxiv 77.
20. Idea 126.
21. J. H. Newman, *Office and Work of Universities* (London, 1856), 24–25.

CHAPTER 2

1. Ward i 64.
2. LD ix 457.
3. Quoted J. E. Adams, *Dandies and Desert Saints* (Ithaca, 1995), 81.
4. *Ibid.*
5. *Correspondence of John Henry Newman with John Keble and Others, 1839–1845* (London, 1917), 390.
6. J. A. Froude, *Short Studies on Great Subjects* (London, 1868), 286.
7. T. Arnold Jr., *Passages in a Wandering Life* (London, 1900), 57.
8. A 272; see also for comment Oliver S. Buckton, *Secret Selves* (North Carolina, 1998), 46.
9. Quoted Culler 54.
10. LD xxx 410.
11. Quoted Tristram 128.
12. J. H. Newman, *Loss and Gain* (London, 1881), 206–207.
13. AW 194.
14. Matthew Arnold, *Discourses in America* (London, 1885), 139–140.
15. David J. DeLaura, 'O unforgotten voice', in *Renascence* 43 (1990–1991), 81–104, here 97.
16. Gilley 176.
17. Aubrey de Vere, quoted Ward i 66.
18. Ward ii 348.
19. *Ibid.* 349.
20. LD x 337.
21. A 358.
22. Charles Kingsley, *His Letters and Memories of his Life* (London, 1882), i 201.
23. Idea 210.
24. AW 254–255.
25. Unnamed observer, quoted Tristram, *Newman and His Friends*, 164.
26. Edward White Benson, quoted Ker 337.
27. Arthur Christopher Benson, *The Life of Edward White Benson*, i 63.
28. Aubrey de Vere, *Recollections* (New York, 1897), 275.
29. Quoted Trevor ii 194.
30. Quoted Ward ii 369–370.
31. LD xxii 9.
32. LD xxxii n365.
33. LD ii 260.
34. Quoted Dessain 163.
35. Tristram 111.
36. LD xiii 32.
37. Francis William Newman, *Contributions Chiefly to the Early History of the Late Cardinal Newman* (London, 2008), 51.
38. Rosemary Hill, *God's Architect; Pugin and the Building of Romantic Britain* (London, 2007), 459–460.
39. Geoffrey Faber, *Oxford Apostles* (London, paperback, 1974), 346.

CHAPTER 3

1. A 23.
2. Lytton Strachey, *Eminent Victorians* (London, Penguin, 1986), 36.
3. S. T. Coleridge, *The Friend* (Princeton, 1969), i 148.
4. A 23.
5. *Ibid.* 25.
6. A 28.
7. PPS vi 98.
8. LD xix 415.
9. LD x 303.
10. LD i 126.
11. Quoted from *Family Adventures*, H. E. Newman (Mrs Thomas Mozley) in Tristram, 101–102.
12. A 25.
13. David Hume, *An Enquiry Concerning Human Understanding*, section X, Part 1, sections 90–91.
14. A 25.
15. *Ibid.*
16. A 26
17. A 25.
18. *Ibid.*
19. Bouyer 24.
20. A 27.
21. AW 166.
22. A 28.
23. AW 49–50.
24. Matthew Arnold, *Lectures and Essays in Criticism* (Ed. R. H. Super) (Michigan, 1962), 290.
25. LD i 82.
26. AW 37.
27. LD i 46.
28. LD i 35.
29. LD i 40.
30. *Ibid.*
31. *Ibid.* 36.
32. AW 157.
33. *Ibid.*
34. LD i 40.
35. LD i 43.
36. *Ibid.* 68.
37. AW 166–167.
38. LD i 70.
39. *Ibid.* 160–161.
40. LD i 63–64.
41. *Ibid.* 72.
42. *Ibid.* 173.
43. LD i 66.
44. LD i 30.
45. AW 160.
46. Idea 276.
47. LD i 84.
48. LD i 84, 85.
49. AW 47.
50. LD i 94
51. *Ibid.* 95.
52. *Ibid.* 123.
53. *Ibid.* 109.
54. *Ibid.* 139.

CHAPTER 4

1. Quoted Ian Ker (Ed.) in J. H. Newman, *Idea of a University* (South Bend, 1976), 611.
2. Culler 27.
3. *Ibid.* 33.
4. *Ibid.* 38.
5. LD i 131.
6. Quoted Culler 38.
7. LD i 307.
8. Quoted Brian Martin, *John Henry Newman* (London, 1982), 28.
9. AW 66.
10. AW 75.
11. *Ibid.* 70.
12. *Ibid.* 76.
13. *Ibid.* 200.
14. A 29.
15. See Ker 22.
16. For a critique of Joseph Butler and Newman's conscience as natural theology see Alasdair MacIntyre, *God, Philosophy, Universities: A History of the Catholic Philosophical Tradition* (London, 2009), 141.
17. US 18–19.
18. AW 206.
19. Quoted Ker 23.
20. AW 193–194.
21. For the correspondence between Charles and John Henry, see LD i 212–215.
22. LD i n224.
23. LD i 182.
24. LD i 219–220.
25. *Ibid.*
26. US 284.
27. Quoted Trevor i 78.
28. Louise Imogen Guiney, *Hurrell Froude: Memoranda and Comments* (London, 1904), 254.
29. A 41.
30. *Ibid.*
31. *Ibid.*
32. *Remains of the Reverend Richard Hurrell Froude* (Ed. Newman, Keble, Mozley) (London, 1838), i 15, 454.
33. *Ibid.* 170.
34. *Ibid.* 137.
35. *Ibid.* 62.
36. *Ibid.* 92.
37. *Ibid.* 94.
38. *Ibid.* 95.
39. LD i 240.
40. *The Month*, Vol. 8 (1868), 209.
41. AW 212.
42. Quoted Culler 60.
43. LD ii 61.
44. LD ii 69.
45. LD ii 70.
46. LD ii n47.
47. LD i 142.
48. LD ii 66.
49. Culler 55
50. Quoted Adams 78.
51. Culler 54.
52. Culler 52.
53. *Ibid.*

54. Quoted Ker 49.
55. J. H. Newman, *Arians of the Fourth Century* (Leominster, 2001), 393.

CHAPTER 5

1. LD xxxii, Appendix 4, 539.
2. Idea 409.
3. Quoted Dessain 16.
4. PPS i 252.
5. PPS i 41.
6. PPS ii 55.
7. PPS i 167–168.
8. James Anthony Froude, *Nemesis of Faith* (London, 1849), 144.
9. US 157.
10. A 46.
11. LD viii 153.
12. LD iii 130–131.
13. *Ibid.* 213.
14. *Ibid.* 224.
15. LD iii 233–234.
16. *Ibid.* 277.
17. *Ibid.*
18. LD iii 303.
19. A 50.
20. *Lyra Apostolica*, 230.
21. Ker 80.
22. Quoted Tristram 105.
23. *Ibid.*
24. LD iii 133.
25. A 50.

CHAPTER 6

1. Quoted Martin 56.
2. John Keble, *Sermons Academical and Occasional* (London, 1848), 146.
3. LD iv 290.
4. LD v 249.
5. A 82.
6. LD v 299.
7. Henry Parry Liddon, *Life of Edward Bouverie Pusey* (London, 1893), i 406.
8. LD vi 164.
9. Quoted Adams, *Dandies and Desert Saints*, 75.
10. Quoted Adams 76.
11. *Ibid.*
12. Froude, *Nemesis*, 152.
13. Ward i 60.
14. J. A. Froude, *Short Studies on Great Subjects* (London, 1907), 246.
15. Quoted Ward i 61–63.
16. LD vi 18.
17. LD v 175.
18. LD iv 169–170.
19. LD iv 170.
20. Quoted Trevor i 234.
21. J. B. Mozley, *Letters* (London, 1885), 102.
22. A 441.
23. *Ibid.*
24. AW 137.
25. *Lyra Apostolica*, 36.

26. *Ibid.* 20.
27. *Ibid.* 20–21.
28. *Ibid.* 32.
29. Gregory Woods, *A History of Gay Literature* (London, paperback edn, 1999), 171.
30. Ronald Chapman, *Father Faber* (London, 1961), 48.
31. George Sydney Smythe, *Historic Fancies* (London, 1844), 102.
32. Chapman 48.
33. J. M. J., *The Holy Family Hymns* (London, 1860), 16.
34. Gerard Manley Hopkins, *Poems and Prose* (London, 1985), 29.
35. LD ii 95.
36. Quoted Geoffrey Tillotson, 'Newman's Essay on Poetry' in Tristram 189.
37. Quoted Ker 322.
38. LD xii 311.

CHAPTER 7

1. LG 248.
2. A 114.
3. LD vii 154.
4. A 116.
5. A 141.
6. LD viii 555.
7. LD viii 555–556.
8. *Ibid.* 556.
9. AW 217.
10. *Ibid.* 218.
11. *Ibid.*
12. *Ibid.* 217.
13. A 85.
14. A 134.
15. LD viii 299.
16. A 140.
17. AW 220.
18. Trevor i 271.
19. LD viii 410.
20. A 158–159.
21. LG 371.
22. A 468.
23. J. H. Newman, *Two Essays on Biblical and on Ecclesiastical Miracles* (London, Longmans, 1890), 64–65.
24. Strachey, *Eminent Victorians*, n259.
25. LD ix xvii.
26. US 313–314.
27. US 338.
28. *Ibid.* 345.
29. *Ibid.* 347–348.
30. *Ibid.* 346–347.
31. A 161.
32. LD ix 279.
33. A 190.
34. LD ix 489–490.
35. Quoted Gilley 227.
36. *Ibid.*
37. Quoted Gilley 227.
38. Quoted *ibid.* 232.
39. LD v 346.

CHAPTER 8

1. Quoted Gilley 232.
2. 'Cardinal Manning' in Lytton Strachey, *Eminent Victorians* (London, Penguin, 1986), p. 38.
3. See Frank M. Turner, *John Henry Newman: the Challenge to Evangelical Religion* (Newhaven, 2002), 533.
4. Dev 357–358.
5. Dev xxv.
6. Avery Dulles, *John Henry Newman* (London, 2002), 74.
7. Dev 195.
8. *Ibid.* 196.
9. *Ibid.* 199–200.
10. *Ibid.* 204.
11. *Ibid.* 442.
12. *Ibid.* 426.
13. Stephen Prickett, *Romanticism and Religion* (Cambridge, 1976), 164.
14. Dev 36.
15. Owen Chadwick, *From Bossuet to Newman* (Cambridge, 1957), Chap. 1.
16. Dev 56.
17. Quoted Stephen Prickett, *Modernity and the Reinvention of Tradition* (Cambridge, 2009), 44.
18. Dev 39–40.
19. Quoted Prickett, *Romanticism and Religion* (Cambridge, 1976), 165–166.
20. Anthony Kenny, *A Path from Rome* (Oxford paperback, 1986), 165.
21. LD x 697.

CHAPTER 9

1. A 211.
2. Trevor i 358–359.
3. LD xi 141.
4. A 213.
5. John Morley, *Life of Gladstone* (London, 1968), i 317.
6. Quoted Robert Lindsay Schuettinger, *Lord Acton: Historian of Liberty* (LaSalle, IL, 1976), 22.
7. Quoted Ker 319–320.
8. LD xi 129.
9. LD xi 131.
10. AW 255.
11. LD xiv 248.
12. AW 255.
13. LD xi 283.
14. *Ibid.* xi 263.
15. LD xi 252–253.
16. LD xi 254.
17. *Ibid.* 253.
18. *Ibid.* 259
19. LD xii 24.
20. *Ibid.* 24.
21. LD xi 285.
22. Trevor i 400.
23. Quoted Bouyer 355.
24. Quoted Trevor i 401.
25. LD xiii 333–334.
26. LD xii 40.
27. For the full text, see AW 246–247.
28. AW 245.
29. Quoted Tristram 111.
30. AW 245.
31. AW 246.

32. AW 248.
33. *Ibid.*
34. AW 245.
35. AW 245–246.
36. AW 246.
37. AW 247.
38. LD xii 97.
39. LD xii 121–122.
40. LD xii 153–154.
41. LG 19.
42. LG 24.
43. LG 2.
44. LG 3.
45. LD xi 69.
46. Quoted in Nicholas Lash, 'How Do We Know Where We Are', in *Theology on the Way to Emmaus* (London, 1986), 62.
47. LG 17.
48. LG 294.
49. LG 379.
50. LG 203.
51. Dairmaid MacCulloch, *A History of Christianity* (London, 2009), 842.
52. Quoted in G. Trevelyan, *Garibaldi's Defence of the Roman Republic* (London, 1928), 228.
53. Diff (London, 1850), 148–149 (only one volume in this edition).
54. LD xxv 169.
55. *Ibid.* 230–231.
56. *Ibid.* 231.

CHAPTER 10

1. LD xiii 77.
2. *Ibid.* xiv 183.
3. Ronald Chapman, *Father Faber* (London, 1961), 180–181.
4. LD xiii 29.
5. *Ibid.* 30–31.
6. *Discourses Addressed to Mixed Congregations*, 70.
7. LD xiii 166.
8. LD xiii 145.
9. Quoted LD xiii 211.
10. LD xiii 41.
11. *Ibid.* xiv 143.
12. LD xiii 129–131.
13. *Ibid.* 177 n1.
14. LD xiii 55–56.
15. LD xiii 336.
16. *Ibid.* 62.
17. Idea 493.
18. Diff xi.
19. Diff 6–7.
20. *Ibid.* 137–138.
21. *Ibid.* 199.
22. LD xiv 110.
23. LD xiv 283.
24. J. H. N., *Lectures on Catholicism in England* (Birmingham, 1851), 43.
25. Prepos 230, 240.
26. *Ibid.* 43.
27. LD xiv Appendix 3, 501.
28. *Ibid.* 442.

29. Quoted Henry Tristram, *Newman and His Friends* (London, 1933), 115–116.
30. LD xv 183.
31. *Ibid.* 253.
32. *Ibid.* 256–257.
33. Extract form the Diary of Sir John Taylor Coleridge in *This for Remembrance*, Bernard Lord Coleridge (London, 1925), quoted in LD xv n284.
34. LD xv 280.
35. LD xv 363.

CHAPTER 11

1. LD xiv 375.
2. Quoted Ker 376.
3. Quoted *ibid.* 377.
4. LD xv n425.
5. LD xvi 31.
6. LD xvi 550.
7. LD xvi n551.
8. LD xv 71.
9. Idea 121; for discussion of this passage see Joseph S. O'Leary, 'Newman on Education and Original Sin', in *English Literature and Language 31* (1994), 11–45.
10. LD xiv 261.
11. Idea 103–113.
12. *Ibid.* 113.
13. *Ibid.* 139.
14. Hastings, *The Shaping Prophecy* (London, 1995), 46.
15. Idea 164, 177.
16. *Ibid.* 165–166.
17. *Ibid.* 125–126.
18. J. H. N., *The Office and Work of Universities* (London, 1856), 157.
19. Edward Said, *Reflections on Exile* (London, 2001), 401.
20. *Ibid.*
21. Idea 137.
22. *Reflections* 403.
23. Idea 180.
24. *Ibid.* 208–209.
25. *Ibid.* 194.
26. *Ibid.* 195–196.
27. *Ibid.* 184.
28. *Ibid.* 126.
29. *Lectures on Certain Difficulties Felt by Anglicans in Submitting to the Catholic Church* (2nd ed.) (London, 1850).
30. Idea 234–235.
31. LD xvii 303.
32. James Joyce, *Portrait of the Artist as a Young Man* (Ed. Seamus Deane) (London, Penguin paperback, 2000), 178–179; Idea 14.
33. Portrait 186.
34. Quoted Jill Muller, 'Newman and the education of Stephen Dedalus', JJQ vol. 33, 4, 1996, to whom I am indebted for the insights that follow.
35. Portrait 200.
36. *Ibid.* 201.
37. Idea 109.
38. See Jill Muller, *op. cit.*
39. A 107, 437.
40. Portrait 203.
41. *Stephen Hero* 156; and see contrast between chapters 5 and 6 in *Grammar of Assent.*
42. Portrait 164.

43. A 163.
44. Idea 276.
45. Allan Bloom, *The Closing of the American Mind* (New York, 1987), 16.
46. Saul Bellow, *Humboldt's Gift* (London, Penguin, 1977), 118.
47. Bellow in Allan Bloom, *The Closing of the American Mind* (New York, 1987), 17.
48. Ward i 398.
49. Idea 187.

CHAPTER 12

1. J. H. Newman, *Sermons Preached On Various Occasions* (London, 1858), 238.
2. *Ibid.* 226, 229.
3. *Ibid.* 234.
4. Ibid. 179.
5. Ker 463; and see Mary Heimann, *Catholic Devotion in Victorian England* (Oxford, 1995).
6. LD xvii 39.
7. *Ibid.*
8. Newman account of the journey in *ibid.* 116–118.
9. LD xvii 118.
10. LD xvii 119.
11. LD xvii 135–136.
12. LD xvii 138.
13. LD xvii 361.
14. Quoted Brian Martin, *John Henry Newman* (London, 1982), 106.
15. LD xvii 362.
16. 'There was hardly an issue or an institution in the Irish church that MacHale did not use to confront or contest Cullen's power and influence.' Memet Larkin, 'Cullen, Paul (1803–1878)', in *Oxford Dictionary of National Biography*.
17. LD xvii 426.
18. Chapman, *Father Faber*, 282.
19. LD xvii 235–236.
20. Chapman 283–284.
21. Quoted Dessain 120.
22. Quoted *ibid.* 112.
23. Quoted *ibid.* 112.
24. LD xix 89.
25. Quoted Dessain 113.
26. LD xix 141.
27. LD xix 151.
28. Quoted Ward i 499–500.
29. See Ian Ker, 'John Henry Newman and the Aftermath of Vatican II', in *The Venerabile Magazine* (Rome, 2009); and Ian Ker, 'Newman on the Consensus Fidelium as "the voice of the Infallible Church"', in *Newman and the Word* (Ed. Terence Mirrigan and Ian T. Ker) (Louvain, 2000), 68–69.
30. J. H. Newman, *On Consulting the Faithful in Matters of Doctrine* (Ed. John Coulson) (London, 1962), 63.
31. *Ibid.* 113–114.
32. *Ibid.* 25.
33. Ward ii 146–147.
34. Robert Gray, *Cardinal Manning* (1985), 236–237.
35. AW 272.
36. LD xx 30.
37. LD xix 331.
38. AW 249, 151.
39. LD xix 311.
40. AW 251.
41. Quoted Trevor ii 238.
42. LD xx 30.

43. *Ibid.* 31.
44. AW 252.
45. Dessain 118.
46. A full account of Newman and the Oratory School is contained in Paul Shrimpton, *A Catholic Eton: Newman's Oratory School* (Leominster, 2005).
47. LD xx 138–139.
48. LD xxviii 421.
49. *Ibid.* xx 17.
50. *Ibid.* 17.
51. LD xx 75.
52. *Ibid.* 82.
53. *Ibid.* 139.
54. *Ibid.* 139–140.
55. Quoted Trevor ii 366.
56. *Ibid.*
57. LD xx 208–209.
58. *Ibid.* 209.
59. *Ibid.* 209–210.
60. *Ibid.* 215–216.
61. *Ibid.* 254.
62. LD xx 445.
63. *Ibid.* 447.

CHAPTER 13

1. Quoted A 358.
2. *Ibid.* 359–360.
3. LD xxii 12.
4. Quoted *Macmillan's Magazine*, George John Worth, p. 36.
5. A 366.
6. A 372–373.
7. A 365.
8. LD xxi 61 n2.
9. *Ibid.* 120.
10. *Ibid.* 90–91.
11. LD xx 444.
12. LD xxi 97.
13. LD xxxii 366.
14. LD xxi 126.
15. A xviii.
16. LD xxi 131.
17. A 25.
18. LD viii 556.
19. A 96.
20. A 158.
21. J. H. Newman, *Historical Sketches* (London, 1886), ii 227.
22. A 196.
23. *Ibid.* 183.
24. A 96.
25. LD xxx 133.
26. A 225–226.
27. *Ibid.* 116.
28. *Ibid.* 185.
29. *Ibid.* 187.
30. *Ibid.* 187.
31. *Ibid.* 114.
32. *Ibid.* 116.

33. *Ibid.* 216.
34. Quoted in Michael Jacobs, *D. W. Winnicott* (London, 1995), 51.
35. A 216.
36. *Ibid.* 217.
37. *Ibid.*
38. *Ibid.* 218.
39. *Ibid.* 217.
40. *Ibid.* 217–218.
41. *Ibid.* 218–220.
42. *Ibid.* 225.
43. *Quarterly Review*, 115-6 (1864), 274.
44. R. W. Church, *Occasional Powers*, II, 383–385.
45. *The George Eliot Letters* (Ed. Gordon S. Haight), Vol. IV (New Haven 1954), 159.
46. LD xxix 388.
47. Quoted in Margot Asquith, *An Autobiography* (New York, 1920), ii 113.
48. G. Egner, *Apologia Pro Charles Kingsley* (London, 1969), xii–xiii.
49. John George Snead-Cox, *The Life of Cardinal Vaughan* (London, 1910), i 215.
50. LD xxi 166.
51. *Ibid.* n166, 167.
52. LD xxi 308.
53. *Ibid.* 327.
54. *Ibid.* 383.
55. *Ibid.* 475.
56. *Ibid.* 466.
57. *Ibid.* 477.
58. Quoted Ward ii 105.
59. Edmund Sheridan Purcell, *Life of Cardinal Manning Archbishop of Westminster*, 2 vols (London, 1896), ii 323.
60. *Ibid.* 322–323.
61. *Ibid.* 300.
62. LD xxii 314–315.
63. LD xiii 129.
64. *Ibid.* 10.
65. *Ibid.* 91.
66. LD xxiii 130.
67. *Ibid.* 139.
68. Purcell ii 316.
69. *Ibid.* 318.
70. LD xxiii 190
71. LD xxii 109.
72. LD xxiv 94.

CHAPTER 14

1. LD xxii 72.
2. J. H. N., *Philosophical Notebook* (Louvain, 1970), ii 154.
3. PPS iv 83.
4. *The Prelude* (1805 ed. de Selincourt), Book v.
5. PPS iv 211.
6. LD xxix 11.
7. Henry Augustin Beers, *A History of English Romanticism in the Nineteenth Century* (London, 1901), 358.
8. J. H. Newman, *Second Spring* (London, 1852), 10.
9. A 226.
10. Quoted Culler 206.
11. J. H. Newman, *Essays Critical and Historical*, ii 442.
12. I am grateful to Stephen Prickett for this insight. See his *Romanticism and Religion* (Cambridge,

1976), 176ff.
13. Diff 8.
14. *Ibid.* 6–7.
15. G 502.
16. *Ibid.*
17. Evelyn Underhill, *Mystics of the Church* (London, 1925), 26–27.

CHAPTER 15

1. A 218.
2. *Ibid.*
3. Dessain 148.
4. LD xix 294.
5. LD xxv 35.
6. *Ibid.* 29.
7. LD xix 284.
8. G 330.
9. *Ibid.* 126.
10. J. H. Newman, *Callista: A Sketch of the Third Century* (New York, 1856), 224.
11. G 116.
12. MD 496 (1893 ed.).
13. G 288.
14. *Ibid.* 132–133.
15. *Ibid.*
16. G 140.
17. *Ibid.* 220.
18. *Ibid.* 238.
19. A 37.
20. US 256.
21. LD xxi 146 n1.
22. *Ibid.*
23. *Ibid.*
24. LD xix 460.
25. G 316.
26. A. Kenny, *A Brief History of Western Philosophy* (Oxford, 1998), 312–313.
27. G 196.
28. J. H. Newman, *Essays Critical and Historical* (London, 1901), ii 514.

CHAPTER 16

1. See Pius IX encyclical, *Nullis Certis*, 19 January 1860.
2. See, *passim*, D. Kertzer, *The Kidnapping of Edgardo Mortara* (London, 1997).
3. H. Daniel-Rops, *The Church in an Age of Revolution 1789–1870* (London, 1965), 276.
4. Gray, *Cardinal Manning* (London, 1987), 227.
5. *Ibid.* 229.
6. Ward ii 332.
7. LD xiv 366–367.
8. LD xxv 18–19.
9. Denzinger-Schönmetzer, *Enchyridion symbolorum definitionum declarationum* (Rome, 1976), 508.
10. LD xxxii 364.
11. J. H. Newman, *A Letter Addressed to His Grace the Duke of Norfolk: On Occasion of Mr Gladstone's Recent Expostulation* (London, 1875), 56–57.
12. *Ibid.* 60.
13. *Ibid.* 94.
14. *Ibid.* 83, 66.
15. Quoted Gilley 391.

261

CHAPTER 17

1. Newman's account of St John's death, LD xxvii 415.
2. *Ibid.*
3. *Ibid.*
4. *Ibid.* 417.
5. *Ibid.* 418.
6. *Ibid.* 419.
7. *Ibid.* 420.
8. LD xxvii 421.
9. Ward i 22.
10. Ker 694.
11. Trevor ii 527.
12. LD xxvii 305–312.
13. *Ibid.* 322.
14. LD xxv 3.
15. AW 258.
16. LD xxviii 279.
17. *Ibid.* 279.
18. LD xxviii 324.
19. Purcell, *Manning*, ii 576.
20. Quoted J. D. Holmes, *The Triumph of the Holy See* (London, 1962), 160.
21. Quoted Trevor ii 552.
22. *Ibid.* 556.
23. LD xxix 121
24. *Ibid.* 58.
25. Ward ii 463.
26. *Ibid.* 460.
27. *Ibid.* 461.
28. *Ibid.*
29. Ward ii 461–462.
30. *Ibid.* 462.
31. Ker 715.

CHAPTER 18

1. LD xxxii n365.
2. David J. DeLaura, *Hebrew and Hellene* (Austin, 1969), 5–6.
3. Robert H. Ellison, *The Victorian Pulpit* (London, 1998), 155.
4. Tristram 112.
5. MD 597–599.
6. Idea 238.
7. Tristram 119.
8. *Ibid.*
9. *Ibid.*
10. Tristram 120.
11. *Ibid.* 124–125.
12. *Ibid.* 123.
13. *Ibid.* 126.
14. C. Butler, *Life of Ullathorne*, ii 283–284.
15. Ward ii 359.
16. Trevor ii 639.
17. *Ibid.* 537.
18. Trevor ii 646.
19. Quoted Philip Boyce, 'Newman as Seen by His Contemporaries at the Time of His Death', in *John Henry Newman: Lover of Truth* (Ed. Strolz and Binder) (Rome, 1991), 113.
20. Gray, *Manning*, 316.
21. LD xxxii 628.

22. *Guardian*, 13 August 1990 (LD xxxii 601).
23. Quoted Tristram 54, and given in LD xxxii 629–630.
24. LD xxviii 89.

CHAPTER 19

1. Ms notebook in the keeping of the Birmingham Oratory, cited in Alan Bray, *The Friend* (Chicago, 2003).
2. LD xxviii 303.
3. Bray 143.
4. Bray to some extent undermines his own argument, however, by reminding the reader that the joint burial at the Venerable English College would have been interpreted by England's Protestants as the brazen gesture of 'defiant and outspoken sodomites'. Quoting Ephraim Pagitt's popular *Heresiography*, Bray shows how the Protestants portrayed the Jesuits as practising defenders of sodomy:
    'These take upon them to justifie all the Errours and abominations of Antichrist; yea, their Idol-atries, and Sodomiticall uncleannesse they will defend and maintain' [Bray 180–181].
5. Bray 304.
6. LD xxvii 321.
7. *Ibid.*
8. Ruth I.14-17: quoted by Newman in *Parting of Friends*, Appendix 7, LD ix 736–737.
9. LD xxvii 321–322.
10. *Ibid.* 322.
11. A 34.
12. See Joyce Sugg, *Ever Yours Affly: John Henry Newman and His Female Circle* (London, 1996).
13. Quoted Gilley 233.
14. LD x 521.
15. *Ibid.* xxvii 311.
16. *Ibid.* 310.
17. A 250.
18. *The George Eliot Letters*, Vol. IV, 160.
19. A 250.
20. Gilley 362–363.
21. LD vi 95.
22. *Lyra Apostolica* 21.
23. Purcell i 124.
24. Quoted in Gray, *Manning*, 320.
25. LD xxiii 290.

CHAPTER 20

1. Trevor ii 620.
2. PPS vii 248.
3. LD xiv 45.
4. J. H. Newman, *Verses on Various Occasions* (London, 1868), 48.
5. J. H. Newman, *Philosophical Notebooks* (Louvain, 1969), i 85.
6. *Cf.* Vatican II decrees *Ad gentes, Lumen gentium Gaudium et spes, Nostra aetate, Redemptoris missio.*
7. S. T. Coleridge, *Biographia Literaria* (London, 1852), 242.
8. J. H. Newman, *The Theological Papers of John Henry Newman. On Faith and Certainty* (Oxford 1976), 107.
9. LD xi 61.
10. J. H. Newman, *Select Treatises of St. Athanasius in Controversy with the Arians* (Oxford, 1844), 44.
11. Quoted Culler 264.
12. Quoted Culler 266.
13. LD xiv 127.
14. J. H. Newman, *Essays Critical and Historical*, 193–194.
15. Quoted Culler 267.
16. LD xxiv 77.

263

17. *Ibid.* 77.
18. *Ibid.*
19. Quoted Culler 267.
20. Thomas O'Meara, 'Raid on the Dominicans', *America*, 5 February 1994.
21. Nicholas Lash, 'Waiting for Doctor Newman', *America*, 1 February 2010.

EPILOGUE

1. John Cornwell, *Breaking Faith* (London, 2001), 227–228.
2. PPS viii 77.
3. *Ibid.* 81.
4. A 263ff.
5. LD xiv 386.
6. A 465.
7. *Ibid.* 266–267.
8. *Ibid.* 267.
9. *Positio Super Miro* (Holy See, Vatican City, 2008).
10. Positio 130.
11. *Ibid.* 220.
12. *Ibid.* 77.
13. 'Judicium Medicum Legale' 7: appendix to the *Positio.*

Index